ADVANCED SOCIOLOGY

P. L. Selfe

M
MACMILLAN

First published 1987 by Pan Books Ltd
Reprinted five times
This edition published 1992 by
THE MACMILLAN PRESS LTD
Houndmills, Basingstoke, Hampshire RG21 2XS
and London
Companies and representatives
throughout the world

ISBN 0-333-58594-1

Text design by Peter Ward
Text illustrations by ML Design

Printed in Spain by Mateu Cromo, S.A.
Madrid

10   9   8   7   6   5   4   3   2   1
01 00 99 98 97 96 95 94 93 92

To Jessica

CONTENTS

Contents

ACKNOWLEDGEMENTS

I am grateful to the examination boards for permission to reproduce questions from past papers.

INTRODUCTION

The aim of this book is to provide a comprehensive revision aid which covers the areas examined by the six boards. The past papers from recent years have been used as the basis of the revision material presented in it. Representative examples have been taken from each topic area to illustrate how the student could approach particular types of question.

It is important to remember that there are no 'correct' answers to questions: of course, you may be incorrect in your reference to an authority, your use of statistical detail or your definitions of terms, but assuming this is not the case, it would be possible for two students using similar accurate data to reach different conclusions. In sociology, you are being asked to discuss or debate an issue. This means that you must be able to approach the question from different perspectives and to decide whether one produces a more valid conclusion than another.

Each of the chapters in the book contains a section in which the theoretical perspectives are considered. However, you should be aware that there is always a danger in categorising material in a way that oversimplifies its complexities. Although it is useful from the point of view of revision to examine issues from the functionalist, Marxist and interactionist perspectives you must remember that in the course of research a variety of methods and approaches may be adopted.

You should also be aware that examination questions often ask you to produce an answer by drawing on material from a range of topic areas; for example the family and religion or the mass media and politics. You must, therefore, learn to become flexible in your thinking when revising for exams.

To assist you in your revision programme, each of the chapters in this book begins by noting the question areas which appear to be tested most frequently in the exam, so that you can decide which specific issue you intend to work on. Generally, however, you are advised to look at a range of issues within the topic to see how they interrelate.

The book is oriented around typical examination questions, but there are no 'model answers' provided. This is because examiners are looking for your ability to debate an issue and not for some 'correct' explanation. The student must be active in revision and use the relevant material presented to tackle alternative questions.

All the boards assess the ability of the candidate to write a structured essay. Some also include questions based on stimulus response passages to test the ability to draw conclusions from data and to present a critical analysis of issues raised.

It is most important to be very familiar with the structure of the examination paper you are going to face and to be aware of the precise requirements specified in the rubric of the paper.

PREPARING FOR THE EXAMINATION

There are six boards which examine A level sociology.

You should become familiar with the syllabus that you are studying, since there are some variations between boards.

You should also be familiar with the structure of the examination paper. Past papers are available at a small cost from the boards.

Board	Number of papers	Time allowed	Any optional studies	Number of questions to answer	Choice	Number of compulsory stimulus response	Number of full essays to write
Ox	2	3 hours	No	4	14	None	4
			No	4	14	None	4
AEB	2	3	No	4	15	1	3
			No	4	12	None	4
JMB	2	3	Yes	5	12	3	2
			Yes	6	10	4	2
Cam	2	3	No	4	14	None	4
			No	4	23	None	4
Wel	2	3	No	4	14	1	3
			Yes	4	24	None	4
Lon	2	3	No	4	12	None	4
			No	3	12	2	1

It is important to remember that success normally comes to those who prepare carefully for the exam and who work consistently throughout the course of study. You are therefore advised to keep an orderly file; read widely around the subject matter; debate the issues you are studying from time to time with someone; start revision programmes early and ask questions when in doubt.

THE EXAMINATION BOARDS

The addresses below are those from which copies of syllabuses and past examination papers may be ordered. The abbreviations (AEB etc.) are those used in the text to identify actual questions.

Associated Examining Board (AEB), Stag Hill House, Guildford, Surrey GU2 5WX

University of Cambridge Local Examinations Syndicate (CAM), Syndicate Buildings, 1 Hills Road, Cambridge CB1 2EU

Joint Matriculation Board (JMB), Manchester MI5 6EU

University of London School Examinations Department (LOND), 52 Gordon Square, London WC1H 0PJ

Oxford Delegacy of Local Examinations (OX), Ewert Place, Summertown, Oxford OX2 7BZ

Welsh Joint Education Committee (WEL), 245 Western Avenue, Cardiff CF5 2YX

WRITING AN ESSAY IN SOCIOLOGY

1   Read the questions carefully.
To test your understanding re-write the question in your own words.
Example: Do the mass media have an influence on the attitudes of the audience?
Meaning:

Do you agree that the media (TV, radio, press) cause people to modify, change or reinforce their beliefs and behaviour?

---

2   Do you know a possible answer to the question?

'Yes, I do agree'; 'No, I do not agree'; 'Perhaps, in special circumstances.'

---

3   Decide on the answer you intend to pursue. This is important since it will determine the shape your essay will take and the conclusion you will reach. If you do not know an answer at the start, you would be unwise to embark on the question.

4   Organise your material according to a simple plan:
Introduction, discussion, development and conclusion.
(*a*)   Start by explaining what the question is asking and indicate how you will answer it. For example:

There is much debate among the sociologists of the media as to whether or not they do cause poeple to modify, change or reinforce their attitudes and patterns of behaviour. Some have argued that they do have a direct effect, citing evidence that indicates that aggression, racial hostility etc. are shaped by media messages. Others argue that this is not necessarily the case and they point to other influences such as the family, school etc. A third view is that in some cases they may shape attitudes, although this is unusual, and depends on particular circumstances in which the information is received . . .

Notice how an opening such as this sets up a structure for your essay. It should go on to take up these three positions. If you can only think of two main arguments then these will form the two halves of the essay.

5   The conclusion is very important. You have been asked a question and you must endeavour to answer it. Do not merely summarise your essay, but try to show how your arguments and evidence lead to a justifiable conclusion. This may be 'we do not know whether or not the mass media affect attitudes because there is so much conflicting evidence arising from research studies'. This is an acceptable point on which to end providing it follows from the main body of your answer.

6   A moderator for the AEB Board has made it clear that the first ten marks in the exam are easy to get. It is possible to pass the exam on the first page of each of your answers. The mistake that many candidates make is to try to get the last five marks before they have the first ten.

   To get ten marks:
   (a)   Explain what the question is asking.
   (b)   Explain why it is a problem worth considering.
   (c)   Specify some authorities who have thrown light on the question.
   (e)   Specify some answers to the questions.

   To obtain the next ten marks go on to elaborate and debate the points made in the introduction in finer detail. Argue logically, step by step, using references, statistics and other supporting evidence. It is possible for an outstanding answer to get twenty-five marks.

7   You are advised to write simply. Use sociological language which you understand. Use your own language but not slang or ambiguous terms. Don't try to memorise or quote large sections of text books.

8   Avoid using value judgements (I think that the functionalist perspective is a bad one because all it does is support the status quo . . .')

9   The better answers will contain perceptive criticisms of studies, articles or books (where relevant to a question). Students are not expected to introduce any original theories in their answers. Criticisms must be based on ideas worked out before entering the exam room. Don't attempt criticisms of studies if you haven't first studied them to ensure your points are justified.

10   It is useful to be able to quote studies and examples to illustrate points; knowledge of particular authors and their work may also help the student to recall detail. However, it is possible to write adequate answers with few references. Do not be afraid to use well-known examples if necessary so long as they are relevant and provide weight to the answer.

11 It is also wise to raise what may seem to be simple and obvious points in an answer. For example, when discussing methods of sociological research explain why a particular method was used in preference to another; explain how a particular method arises from a perspective or theory; explain the problems and constraints that face researchers.

12 Although examiners may try to ignore spelling mistakes, errors of punctuation and poor handwriting, where there is a combination of these, the answer is unlikely to impress. Some boards (e.g., JMB) clearly state that 'careless work and untidy work will be penalised'.

INTERPRETING QUESTIONS

You must read the wording of the question carefully and answer it in the terms specified:

1 *Discuss* Present a thorough analysis of the question by examining all sides of the arguments.

2 *Compare* Present the similarities and the differences between the features mentioned.

3 *Evaluate* Present a judgement as to the relative value of the features mentioned.

4 *To what extent* Weigh up the arguments and state the relative importance of the feature mentioned.

5 *Interpret* Present an explanation of the facts.

6 *Critically examine* State clearly the pros and cons of the issue raised. Your final decision must be supported by evidence and the reasons why you have rejected alternatives explained.

7 *Distinguish between* Draw clear distinctions between the features mentioned.

8 *Assess* Establish the strengths and weaknesses of the feature mentioned.

Remember that examiners are looking for an answer to their questions which follows logical arguments. Relevant facts, statistics, and other authorities to support your line of analysis are always useful, but reference to authors and their books may not be essential to your success. It is crucial to show an understanding of the question and a possible answer to it, using sociological ideas.

STIMULUS RESPONSE QUESTIONS

Several boards (especially AEB, JMB, Lon) include questions of this type. To do well in answering them you must read the passage carefully and note how many marks are available for each section. You should try to write as fully as possible on each section and consider that you will gain marks for each point you make; it would therefore be unwise to write too expansively on a single issue when there may be several different points to make. Remember, too, that you may be able to spend as many as forty minutes on the question; a thorough discussion is therefore expected, especially on those parts of the question which may carry eight to ten marks.

For example, consider the following question and the suggested marking scheme:

Sociologists use a variety of methods in their research. Much use is made of questionnaires and interviews. There are some examples of small-scale experiments, usually conducted in the field to discover more about behaviour in its social context. But important information has been obtained by correlating statistical details obtained from court records, divorce proceedings etc. and the social background of those involved. Some researchers have used only observational techniques to great effect, especially in the understanding of group behaviour. In some cases sociologists have had to make use of secondary sources, such as diaries, letters and biographical details in order to add depth to their knowledge. The reliability of such results has been questioned by some critics; the question has been raised as to whether it is only by traditional scientific methods that valid results can be obained.

(a) Which is the most reliable method of obtaining data and why? (8)
(b) Discuss the advantages of recorded statistics over diaries and letters. (8)
(c) Why would a researcher choose one method at the expense of another? (9)

MARKING SCHEME
Possible marks

Remember: there is no 'correct' answer.

Part (a) Which is the most reliable method: why?

2 Discuss problems of 'reliability'.
2 Choose ONE method – show why/how it is reliable.
2 Show the source of its reliability.
2 Explain how EVERY method has limitations and success levels.

e.g. Whether or not a method is reliable depends to a great extent on the care and skill of the researcher. The collection of statistics may not be reliable if the researcher is careless (expand briefly/illustrate).

A social survey, using structured interviews, in which a large random sample has been carefully selected according to the principles of selection, ought to be reliable in its results. (Explain *random; sampling frame; representative sample*.)

The source of the reliability is in the scientific procedures which are followed (briefly expand).

However, it must be said that every method has its limitations, as well as its chances of success.

Observational techniques may be criticised for the element of subjectivity which enters the account. But, if well trained, the researcher may produce extremely reliable results.

Part (b) Advantages of statistics and records over diaries as secondary sources

2 1 Explain secondary sources (and primary sources).
   2 State a range of advantages of statistics and records.

6   List the disadvantages of diaries and letters:

Advantages	Disadvantages

3   Can you suggest an example of a study in which it was an advantage to use recorded statistics rather than other secondary sources? (e.g. *The World We Have Lost*.)

Part (c) Reasons for choosing a particular method

6   1   Suggest a wide selection of factors which affect the decision to use a particular research method. (Think of about six.)

3   2   Try to relate these suggestions to particular theories or perspectives: i.e. a positivist chooses a method in terms of the perspective from which s/he starts; as does an interactionist.

25

Remember that this represents a marking scheme: You must always write a coherent answer in normal 'essay' style – and not as a series of points; but it is worth making the points first and then linking them into a series of paragraphs.

STUDY SKILLS

1   When revising, establish a set of goals. Make sure that you achieve them. For example, analyse one question; read five pages of a text book during a specific revision period.

2   Make a time-table which specifies the time available for revision and the tasks to be achieved. Keep to it.

3   Work in comfortable silent conditions.

4   Establish your concentration span and work within it. Take a break before continuing. There is no point in revising when very tired.

5   Before each period of revision spend ten minutes recalling the material on which you have been previously working. It is important to recall recently learned material frequently.

6   Use a range of revision and learning techniques: for example, write detailed notes; make notes of notes; make skeleton essay plans for lengthy essays, from which it would be possible to rebuild the essay to its original length; write timed essays; analyse questions; establish their meanings and possible answers to them; debate and discuss ideas with someone so that you verbalise the arguments. This will help later recall.

8   If problems arise in your understanding of questions or issues, be sure to make a note of them and ask for clarification as soon as possible, or seek the answer in a text book.

9   Use coloured pens for making notes, each colour representing a

different aspect of a question; use coloured highlighting pens for marking articles, cuttings etc. (so long as they belong to you!). Make additional notes from these to supplement or update your own existing information.

10 There are many useful books on the market which may assist you in your study techniques:

Maddox	*How to Study*	Pan
Buzan	*Use Your Head*	BBC Publications
Open University	*Preparing to Study*	
Freeman	*Mastering Study Skills*	MacMillan
Rowntree	*Learning How to Study*	MacDonald
Salimbene	*Strengthening Your Study Skills*	Newby House

THEORIES
AND METHODS
IN SOCIOLOGY

CONTENTS

All the exam boards include numerous questions to test your knowledge and understanding of these areas. Questions are wide-ranging. Some boards provide stimulus-response questions and others have compulsory sections on either or both areas. It is important therefore to be familiar with the following:

1 The origins of sociology.
2 Positivism and phenomenology.
3 Factors affecting choice of method in research.
4 Methods of data collection:
   (a)   Social surveys.
   (b)   Sampling techniques.
   (c)   Interviewing.
5 The reliability of data.
6 Secondary sources of data.
7 Sociology and ideology: can sociology be value free?
8 Theories in sociology.
9 The relationship between theory and method:
   (a)   Types of studies and relevant methods.
10 The sociological perspectives:
   (a)   Functionalism.
   (b)   Marxism.
   (c)   Phenomenology.
   (d)   Ethnomethodology.
11 Observational methods.
12 Sociology, art or science?
13 The comparative and the experimental methods.
14 Social problems and social policy.

THE ORIGINS OF SOCIOLOGY

To what extent is it correct to suggest that sociology emerged out of the aftermath of the industrial and political revolutions of the eighteenth and nineteenth centuries and is still obsessed with their consequences?

In this period there developed a greater awareness of the need to understand the causes and consequences of changes in society following the major upheavals in social life.

Political revolutions
1789 The French Revolution; 1832 The Great Reform Bill; 1848 Revolutionary movements throughout Europe (publication of the Communist Manifesto); 1848 The Chartist demands in Britain.

Industrial revolution
This began in the eighteenth century in Britain. It helped develop the factory system and greater division of labour. There was also the growth of *urbanisation*, with the movement of population from rural to urban areas and the development of *secularisation*, the decline in the significance of religious values, especially following the publication of Darwin's *Origin of Species* (1857).

The Enlightenment
This was a philosophical movement which encouraged a more scientific analysis of the social world and opposed the more traditional metaphysical speculations based on religious principles. Beliefs in individual liberty and equality were promoted. New disciplines emerged, including sociology, psychology, economics and anthropology.

THE DEVELOPMENT OF SOCIOLOGY

1   The word was first used by Comte (1834). He wished to establish a science of society which would help to reveal the social laws which he believed controlled development and change.
2   The application of scientific rationalism to an analysis of society was an attempt to find the source of order in a time of rapid change.
3   The origin of sociology is within a strong conservative tradition. The aim was to conserve the best of the past and to find ways of controlling the dangerous forces of change.
4   As the discipline became more established new perspectives emerged:

Functionalism maintained an interest in order and stability.

Marxism focussed on areas of conflict and disorder.

Interactionism provided an analysis of how people's behaviour is shaped by their interactions in social situations.

Ethnomethodology has more recently returned to the problem of how people establish and maintain order and meaning in their everyday lives.

It is convenient (although an oversimplification) to divide sociological theories under two main descriptive perspectives. These are Positivism (the traditional scientific approach) and Phenomenology, which can be described as 'less scientific' in that some researchers reject the idea of building theories by the application of the scientific method, preferring to use more interpretive methods.

Questions appear on all the examination boards to test your knowledge of these approaches. It is important to know the fundamental differences between them and also to know some details from the theories they subsume.

You will notice from an examination of the questions that the underlying issue is generally 'Is sociology a science?' You should notice, too, that some are phrased to imply that it is:

Examine the claim that it is possible to apply the methods of natural science to the study of man. (AEB)

Sociological data, like the data examined by physicists, must be examined objectively. Discuss. (Ox)

Other questions imply that it is not:

The logic and method of science are inappropriate for sociology. Discuss. (AEB)

It is not possible to make use of the experimental method in the study of the social world. Do you agree? What are the implications of your conclusions for the conduct of sociological research? (Cam)

These questions imply that more interpretive methods should be adopted by sociologists. Although you may recognise the central area of debate, you must approach the question according to its phraseology. Do not prepare a general answer to a hoped-for question in the exam; you must use your material to answer the question set and not the one you hoped would be asked!

PERSPECTIVES IN SOCIOLOGY

Within the Positivist school of sociology there are two dominant theoretical perspectives. These include functionalism and Marxism. Both tend to produce their findings from scientific techniques. Interactionists belong to the Phenomenological school, although they may also use some scientific observational methods.

Questions may be asked specifically about Marxism, functionalism or interactionism, or about the underlying philosophies which direct the methods of positivism and phenomenology which are associated with them.

Frequently questions can be answered from either point of view.

FUNCTIONALISM

Using a range of examples, explain and illustrate the main features of functional analysis. What are the main strengths and weaknesses of this form of analysis?   (JMB)

Functionalism provides a perspective from which to base an analysis of a society. The central concern is with the source of order and stability in society. The focus is on:

A   The way social institutions help maintain order in social life.
B   The way structural arrangements in society influence behaviour.
Main concept used by functionalists:

Social system An organised structure made up of interrelated parts: social culture, family, school etc.

Social Structure The interrelated parts of a society which form a framework for social organisation.

Institutions Approved customs or organisations which help establish relevant behaviour (family, religion).

Culture The values and beliefs which are transmitted from one generation to the next.

Socialisation The process by which values and beliefs are transmitted and absorbed by people through such agencies as family, school, work place.

Value consensus Values and beliefs shared by members of a group or in society as a whole, which promote order.

*Manifest functions Those which are clearly intended.

*Latent functions Those functions which are less obvious or hidden below the surface (a latent function of education may be to promote punctuality and obedience).

*Dysfunction This explains those features of a social system which are not functional in a positive way (the imposition of new school rules may be dysfunctional if they result in more conflict and hostility).
*(NB: these concepts were introduced by Merton in 1949).

▶ Example of functional analysis

1 Shils and Young *The Meaning of the Coronation* (1953)

They note how particular ceremonies and rituals serve a positive function to promote social integration. The series of rituals involving monarch, church leaders, government leaders etc., involves public promises. As a result the monarch 'symbolically proclaims her community with her subjects . . .'

2 Functionalists argue that the continued existence of the family as a social institution can be accounted for in terms of the functions it performs for society and the individual. Parsons argues that industrial society requires a stable family system to maintain the balanced personalities of those subject to its demands. It also functions to promote the successful socialisation of the young into the values of industrial society.

Some criticisms of functionalism	Some strengths of functionalism
1. Functionalist views emphasise the significance of the social structure of behaviour. They do not take account of the individual's motives in acting. 2. It is difficult to know what all the functions of a social institution are and which are the most essential. 3. It cannot be assumed that something functional for one group is functional for everyone else. 4. It may be difficult to see how all institutions are related: e.g. marriage and political system.	1. It is a perspective that is concerned with order and directs attention to agencies which help to promote it. 2. It is preoccupied with discovering the positive functions of institutions which will benefit the smooth running of society. 3. The argument that certain arrangements in society are functional and beneficial leads to arguments against radical change. It focuses on institutions which need protection when under threat (e.g. marriage, family etc.).

MARXISM

Marxists who operate with a conflict perspective would interpret the same events in a different way. For example, the Coronation, seen by functionalists as a source of social integration, would be seen as a means of deluding the public by a Marxist. The conflict structuralist would explain such events as evidence of the power of the ruling class to exploit and dupe people and to reinforce their domination. The failure to realise this is an indication of the power of the ruling élite to control thought and consciousness.

Criticisms of Marxism	Some possible strengths
1. Marxism sees a conspiracy at every level of organisation in a capitalist society so that exploitation can continue. 2. It is hard to prove that people are necessarily duped in the process of watching the Coronation. 3. Excessive reference to ideology may make arguments presented less acceptable and encourage a belief in the bias of the researchers.	1. It forces us to look critically at structures and institutions which may otherwise be taken for granted. 2. It is a perspective that concentrates on sources of conflict and may encourage social change to remedy major inequalities. 3. It provides an alternative view to the functionalist justification for the 'status quo'.

SOME KEY DIFFERENCES BETWEEN THE TWO PERSPECTIVES

Positivism

The traditional method of sociology. It is based on the attempt to emulate the methods of natural science:
a. Identification of a problem.
b. Collection of data.
c. Explanatory hypothesis.
d. Method to test hypothesis.
e. Analysis of results.
f. Re-test if necessary.
g. Interpreting results: report.

Implications:

1. There is an objective world which is capable of being understood in objective, scientific terms.

2. The whole of society is subject to investigation to see how behaviour is influenced by the structure and function of institutions.

3. Scientific analysis using interviews, surveys, statistical data etc. shows the extent to which people are shaped and controlled by agencies of socialisation.
4. Behaviour is fairly predictable since the actors are 'trained' to keep to their 'scripts'. Order is thereby maintained and conflict managed.

Major theories include:

a. Functionalism (structural/organic).
b. Marxism: conflict structuralism.

Phenomenology

This provides a different way of viewing social phenomena. Less emphasis is placed on the need to develop objective methods of study and more on the value of seeing the world through the eyes of those being studied.

Implications:

1. There is not necessarily a social world capable of objective study. More interpretive methods are required.
2. If people constantly construe their reality in every situation of interaction then methods of interview, questionnaire etc. are generally inappropriate. People may not know or be able to explain their actions.
3. People act according to the meanings they derive from situations of interaction, not just as a result of environmental pressures.

4. Behaviour is less predictable because the actors can 'improvise' as situations and knowledge change.

Major theories include:

a. Action theory.
b. Symbolic interactionism.

Method	Underlying philosophy	Perspective
1. Comparative	This stresses the need to use historical and cross-cultural data to understand social structures and institutions.	Positivism and phenomenology.
2. Survey/statistical	These stress the need for neutrality and objectivity in research.	Positivism.
3. Ethnography observational	These stress the need to understand the subjective interpretations of actors.	Phenomenology.

CHOICE OF RESEARCH METHOD

Different methods of sociological research are appropriate for different types of research problem. Discuss with reference to examples from empirical sociological studies with which you are familiar. (Ox)

Ackroyd and Hughes (*Data Collection in Context*) say that 'to put it very simply, social science is concerned with the explanation of human behaviour. Data of some kind will play an important role in such explanations, and to this end social scientists have devised methods for the systematic collection of data.'

Empirical evidence That which derives from scientific analysis. Knowledge is obtained from experiences of the world. There is some debate as to whether this is strictly the province of the positivist who adopts 'scientific' methods in research, since the phenomenologist accepts subjective, interpretive data as part of his or her explanations. However, if science is taken to mean a method rather than a body of knowledge then so long as this is rational, logical and methodical and produces insights about the social world and why people behave as they do, then both perspectives may be said to produce empirical evidence.

Data Ackroyd and Hughes also make the point that what counts as data will be determined by the theory involved in the formulation of the research project. They say 'the world only exists as data through the interpretations that are placed upon it.' Marxists and functionalists, adopting a scientific perspective, may agree on the evidence but reach different conclusions about its significance.

Types of research problems A sociologist undertakes research to achieve an answer to a question. The research may:
(a)   add to the knowledge we have of the world and society.
(b)   explain a phenomenon which has been observed.
(c)   examine social problems.
(d)   justify a social policy.
(e)   explain both normal and abnormal behaviour.
(f)   monitor the effects of a particular policy.

The choice of topic This may arise out of the specific interests of the researcher or following a directive from a university department; a company; a government department; a charity etc.

METHODS OF DATA COLLECTION

There are frequently questions which ask you to discuss, evaluate or examine critically particular methods of data collection.

What are the limitations of the social survey as a method in sociology?

Outline a method of gaining sociological data and discuss the advantages and disadvantages associated with it.

▶   General points:
1   Data are collected by a method (or methods) related to the research design.

2   Problems should be revealed in a pilot study, when a small sample is taken and the method is tested on them. Revisions can be made if it is necessary.

3   The collected data must be analysed, tabulated and processed with great care.

4   Conclusions must be drawn on the basis of the interpretations arising from the analysis. The original hypothesis may be accepted or rejected according to the findings.

SOCIAL SURVEYS

Gardner (*Social Surveys for Social Planners*) says that the purpose of a survey is to provide information. The more accurate and comprehensive the information the better can be the planning. The hopes of the community can then be achieved more fully.

▶   The classification of surveys:

1   Descriptive: to describe what exists and to identify need.

2   Explanatory: to identify changes and their causes.

3   Predictive: to predict future changes and possible effects of new policies.

4   Evaluative: to evaluate the results of past policies.

▶   Preparing the survey:

1   It must be clear what the objectives are. A careful plan must be made.

2   The researchers must remain unbiased. They must be familiar with the problem area.

3   A pilot study must be undertaken to test the methods to be used.

4   The researchers must decide whether to use a random or quota sample. This may depend on whether or not they have an adequate sampling frame from which to draw a random sample, and whether statistical tests are to be used.

5   Interviewers must be obtained and trained.

SAMPLING

Researchers normally obtain a sample of the large population in whom they are interested. It is not necessary to ask everyone so long as the sample drawn is representative of the whole. The quality of the data is more important than the quantity.

Random (probability) sampling Each unit in the population has an equal chance of being included. This is the only way of obtaining a sample which is representative.

Non-random sampling (Quota samples) These are easy to obtain but whilst they may be representative in some known respects (e.g. age, sex, class), they are not in terms of others. There may be interviewer bias, preference for particular faces, the more articulate etc.

Sampling frame The lists, registers or records from which the random sample is drawn must be accurate, contain the relevant information, be up to date and be easily accessible.

Sample size Accuracy is increased by obtaining a large sample, but it is possible to obtain accuracy by using a sampling ratio of as low as eleven out of every 100,000 voters. Gardner suggests that samples of less than thirty or forty from a relatively large population are usually inadequate for statistical analysis.

Non-response The efforts of the researcher will be wasted if response rates are very low. Respondents selected at random may have to be visited several times. This may increase the costs of the survey but it is necessary. This can be a major problem with a postal survey.

The questionnaire This must be carefully prepared and tested to check its value. Words and phrases must be familiar and simple; questions must not be ambiguous; it should demand short and easy-to-analyse answers; it should be value free and it should provide the data from which the hypothesis can be tested.

The researchers must decide whether to use it in a face-to-face interview or to send it through the post.

INTERVIEWS

1   The structured, formal interview follows a set pattern. All the questions are decided beforehand and the exact wording remains the same in each one. It is standardised and controlled.
2   The informal, unstructured interview allows the respondent to expand and develop answers. A tape recorder is essential. The interviewer must be skilled and able to direct the respondent in order to obtain information relevant to the study.

Gardner describes the continuum:

Informal ◄──	────────	────────	────────	──► Formal
Unsystematic questioning	Casual conversation	Unguided, non-directive	Gently guided	Firmly guided, systematic

The choice of the interview method depends on the aim of the study, the time and funds available and the skill of the researcher. The more standardised answers may help to provide a more specific picture of attitudes and opinions since comparisons can be made between answers. The more open-ended answers help to provide a more detailed picture which is particularly useful in a case study.

3

The advantages of interviews	The disadvantages of interviews
a. They are more personal than questionnaires. b. The interviewer can clarify problems of meaning. c. Answers can be probed if necessary. d. The respondent may be better motivated to reply. e. There is a better chance of a full response. f. The interviewer has better control over the situation in which responses are made. (Consultations can be prevented.) g. Problems can be more easily located and remedied.	a. The interviewer may cause antagonism in the respondent. b. The interviewer may be biased in selecting respondents. c. Errors may be made in recording answers. d. It may add greatly to the cost to obtain and train interviewers. e. Failure to train the interviewer may result in incomplete answers, mistakes etc.

Conclusions

1   It may be argued that one limitation of the survey is that it makes use of fixed-choice questions. These are selected by the researcher and imposed on the respondent. It is assumed that they have the same understanding of terms and concepts as the researcher.

2   Marxists might argue that opinion surveys reveal nothing more than the false ideologies of the ruling class which have been absorbed by working-class respondents.

3   Ethnomethodologists might argue that the only valid means of understanding people's behaviour is to observe it in naturalistic settings. Formal interviewing is an inadequate method.

4   Phenomenologists might argue that structured questionnaires do not allow people to define their own meanings and interpretations, so that answers to such questionnaires are largely valueless.

5   Other critics may argue that social surveys can help create attitudes which previously did not exist. This is sometimes used to explain the failure of polls to predict accurately election results.

6   It may also be argued that the limitations of the social survey are similar to the limitations of any method of data collection. They are all subject to the problems of reliability, validity and representativeness. Where these can be controlled the social survey should be a useful tool of research; if not its value is seriously limited.

Consider the following more specific question.

THE RELIABILITY OF DATA

A major problem of sociological research concerns the validity and reliability of data. Discuss with reference to questionnaires and interviews.   (Cam)

▶   Main points:
McNeill (*Research Methods*) emphasises three key concepts:

Reliability This means that it ought to be possible to repeat interviews at a later time with the same respondents and the same interviewers and achieve the same results; it ought to be possible, too, for others to repeat the study under similar conditions and confirm the results.

Validity This means that the researcher should be confident that the picture that has emerged is one that really describes what is being studied and is not contaminated by bias, mistakes, or any kind of deliberate deception on the part of the respondents.

Representativeness This means that those questioned must be typical of everyone in the population affected by the event (e.g. the election) with which the survey is concerned. If they are not then the results will be misleading. (In the 1930s a researcher obtained a large sample from a telephone directory and failed to predict the result of a presidential election because of an unrepresentative sample.)

Social surveys are used to obtain data quickly from a large number of people using questionnaires and interviews. Their use is advocated particularly in positivist research projects. This approach is based on the following principles:

1   It should be possible to establish a hypothesis which can be tested.
2   It must be possible to obtain a sample which is representative and of sufficient size to test the hypothesis.
    (*a*)   Random sample: each person in the population from which the sample is drawn has an equal chance of selection. Everyone who can be sampled is listed and every Nth name is drawn until the sample is filled. This allows complicated statistical tests to be undertaken on results.
    (*b*)   Stratified samples may be drawn if the study requires division by age, sex, class etc; multi-phased samples allow detailed comparisons of results from a smaller sub-sample.
    (*c*)   Quota samples may be used where results are required more quickly and with less statistical precision (e.g. street-corner sampling; 150 people in the quota: 75 men and 75 women all aged 30–50).
3   A schedule of questions must be drawn up. Concepts may have to be operationalised (defined for research purposes; e.g. leisure will mean 'free from the constraints of paid work'). These should be tested in a provisional pilot study to clarify difficulties.
4   If the study is on a large scale interviewers may have to be trained.
5   The results must be carefully analysed and written up in a final report. This must be done in a thorough and honest way. All material must be open to inspection so that others may criticise or repeat the study and compare results.

Researchers may fail to produce valid and reliable results if:
(*a*)   They have not followed the rules of the scientific method (as above).
(*b*)   In the course of interviewing they have antagonised respondents and received dubious answers.
(*c*)   There has been low response rate making it impossible to draw conclusions or apply statistical tests.

(*d*)   There have been careless mistakes in coding and analysing results.

(*e*)   There has been deliberate bias in the interpretation of results.

(*f*)   Results are inadvertently drawn which are not supported by the evidence.

SOURCES OF DATA

Discuss the advantages and disadvantages for the sociologist of using secondary sources of data in research.

Sociologists make use of both primary and secondary data in research. Primary is that which they collect themselves by means of interviews, questionnaires, observation etc. directly from respondents.

Secondary data is that which they collect from other sources and which has already been recorded (although not necessarily for public consumption) for other purposes.

It is important to remember that much research makes use of both types.

Secondary data can be considered in terms of level of reliability.

Low reliability (expressive documents)

(a) Biography (b) Autobiography (c) Letters (d) Diaries (e) Novels.

▶ Advantages:

(*a*)   Useful where the sociologist is conducting a case study or community study and wishes to gain a rich picture of the social life of a period or particular people and their perceptions.

(*b*)   Novelists etc. may have particular skills in portraying the life and culture of a period and reveal the impact of social change.

(e.g. Sillitoe: *Saturday Night and Sunday Morning* for alienation;

Camus: *The Outsider* for anomie).

▶ Disadvantages:

(*a*)   Such sources have a high level of subjective interpretation on the part of the authors.

(*b*)   Such documents were not necessarily produced for publication (e.g. diaries) and may not be reliable.

(*c*)   They must be handled with care to be sure they are dealt with in a systematic way – from most reliable to least.

Greater reliability

(a) Journals (b) Quality newspapers (c) Radio broadcasts (d) TV programmes.

▶ ADVANTAGES;

(*a*)   Media reports, especially in specialist sections, are likely to be accurate and well researched.

(*b*)   They may be presented and compiled by people trained in the field. They can be subjected to content analysis.

(*c*)   The data obtained may be useful in supporting evidence obtained from primary sources.

▶ Disadvantages:

(*a*)   Reports in the popular press may distort issues and extract elements of sensation at the expense of accuracy.

(*b*)   There is the danger of bias in the construction of press reports to suit the political position of the publication.

High reliability

(a) Census data from the office of the Registrar General. (b) Records from business firms. (c) Registration data: births, deaths etc. (d) Court records; social service departments etc. (e) Government records, relating to economy etc. (f) Data from charities; pressure groups etc.

▶ Advantages:

(*a*)   The data are likely to be carefully recorded.

(*b*)   They are published frequently and easily obtained.

▶ Disadvantages:

The key question for critics of such data is always: who has collected them? For what purpose? What are the interpretations produced by those who make use of them? (E.g. is more policing of an area justified by reference to an 'increasing crime rate' based on statistics which the police themselves have collected?)

AREAS OF DEBATE IN SOCIOLOGY

Is sociology inevitably ideological?	(Ox)
Examine the view that sociology should be value free.	(AEB)

Arguments for the view that it is not inevitably ideological and can be value free.

1. Positivism is based on the principles of scientific objectivity.
2. To be objective means to study some social feature without allowing one's own values, moral beliefs or ideological preferences to influence the work in any way.
3. All conclusions reached will be true facts. The sociologist may disapprove of them but if so this is evidence of lack of bias in the study. Therefore, it is quite possible for the entire project, from choice of subject to final conclusions, to be value free.
4. The interactionist, although using interpretive methods, could argue that seeing the world through the eyes of those studied avoids the danger of introducing one's own values. Behaviour is understood in terms of the interpretations of the other person. This kind of study also remains value free.

Arguments for the view that it is inevitably ideological and that it cannot be value free.

1. An ideology is a set of beliefs and values which provide a person with a way of interpreting the world. Sociologists must have theirs like anyone else. This is bound to influence them.
2. Their own values will influence:
a. choice of subject for research
b. ways of interpreting data.
3. Marxists start from a radical and utopian view of society. They see a constant conspiracy by the ruling class. Functionalists hold a more conservative ideology which justifies the *status quo*, including major inequalities in a society since they are functionally necessary.
    Interactionists introduce value into their studies by defining a situation as 'a problem' worthy of investigation. Becker says 'it is impossible to conduct research uncontaminated by personal sympathies. . .'
4. Sociologists cannot escape their own past experiences or their intellectual analysis of 'problems' and their causes and consequences. Therefore, values and ideology enter at every point.

You should now consider a conclusion to the question; e.g. Although sociologists must have values and their own ideological preferences, it would be possible to imagine a situation in which a study was conducted by a functionalist, Marxist and Weberian using agreed methods, which uncovered inequality in the distribution of housing in a city. They may all agree on the data, but each would interpret the material in a different way according to their values.

THEORIES IN SOCIOLOGY

To what extent and why should sociologists concentrate on developing theory?

(Ox)

'No real observation of any kind of phenomena is possible, except in so far as it is first directed and then finally interpreted by some theory' (Comte). Discuss.

Whatever school of sociology the researchers work in, the aim is to make clear sense of some aspect of social behaviour or social organisation.

In making their analysis they may make use of the following:

Concept	An idea of the attributes of the thing being analysed: its main characteristics.
Model	An abstract construction in which various features to be analysed are organised into their related parts: e.g. a functionalist model of society shows the relationships between parts of society.
Hypotheses	Assumptions or guesses about particular events to try to establish their causes. A very early stage in the research process.
Theories	A network of ideas which state the existence of a relationship between a number of features which normally vary. The linked ideas help to explain the observed events. A theory explains by showing the relations between a number of variables.

Types of theory
Cohen (*Sociological Theory*) describes four main types:

Analytic	Like those of mathematics which are true by definition but which state nothing about the social world.
Normative	Specify ethical values.
Metaphysical	Not testable in a scientific way.
Scientific	Open to scientific test.

►   Main points:

1   Sociologists are concerned with the scientific type. Positivists in particular make propositions which at their simplest level link two or more variables. They state that whenever A occurs then B follows. Such statements must be open to empirical test: it must be possible to observe results and see whether they confirm or refute the hypothesis.

2   A theory that linked social class, parental occupation, attitude towards school and academic success of the child should enable the sociologist to make predictions about the conditions under which particular patterns of behaviour occur; e.g.: the social class background of a child (in terms of parental occupation) has a strong effect on the child's academic performance and attitude towards school. The higher the social class the more likely is the child to achieve high academic success.

3   Popper (a philosopher) says that it is never possible to prove any theory conclusively, because although the same results have been achieved a hundred times we cannot be sure that on the one hundred and first test they will not be different. This is true in both natural and social science.

You may be asked to assess or evaluate a theory. To answer such a question you must be able to explain what theories are and why they are used and then show why some theories are more useful than others.

A strong theory	A weak theory
1. It is a scientific theory which can be tested and re-tested. Each time it produces similar results. 2. There may be some competing theories but they are less effective as explanations. 3. It helps to focus on new areas for research and raises new questions.	1. It is not scientific. 2. It is difficult to re-test (too time consuming, costly). 3. It leaves much unexplained, e.g.: how are middle-class failures or deviants explained if the theory predicts that the key factor is low class membership? 4. The theory is too general or wide-ranging as an explanation.

THE RELATIONSHIP BETWEEN THEORY AND METHOD

Different types of research problem require different research methods.   (Ox)

'It is increasingly clear to sociologists that theoretical and methodological issues are well nigh inseparable' (Cuff and Payne). Examine this statement with reference to one perspective.   (AEB)

Every sociologist who conducts research sets out to find possible answers to a series of questions. To obtain these answers will require the use of an appropriate method or possibly a variety of methods.

To answer the question adequately you must be familiar with:

(*a*)   The main sociological perspectives: positivism and phenomenology.

(*b*)   The schools of thought associated with each (see page 24).

(*c*)   The methods associated with each (see page 24).

Research methods will be selected according to:

(*a*)   The school of thought in which the sociologist has been trained. The 'pure' positivist will tend to rely on methods which will result in quantifiable facts.

The 'pure' phenomenologist will tend to prefer interpretive methods which may rely much more on observation and recall.

(*b*)   The type of question being asked may make one method more suitable than another. It may not be possible to interview football fans on the rampage with a questionnaire in order to discover the factors that motivate their behaviour.

(*c*)   The sociologist's own preference for a particular technique may cause one method to be favoured at the expense of another.

▶ Example:

Question asked	Method used
How many divorces occur each year? Are some categories of people more likely to divorce than others? Do children from homes where there has been divorce do less well in school?	*Positivist:* would use recorded statistics. Use statistical techniques to establish correlations between occupation and frequency of divorce. *Phenomenologist:* might spend time observing children in social situations to see whether they had lower self-esteem than those from other homes.

Type of study	Brief details	Methods	Examples
1. Case study	Usually small scale; a single group of event is studied in great depth. May help to reveal details of the processes by which changes occur over time.	Observation; interviews; questionnaires; press reports; letters; diaries; participation.	Lane and Roberts (*Strike at Pilkington*) see page 340.
2. Comparative	Information is collected about the institution or structure being examined in different societies so that similarities and differences can be established (e.g. families; political organisation).	Use of statistics; interviews; observation.	Durkheim (*Suicide*)
3. Content analysis	A means of studying an event by examining the frequency with which it appears in the media; it is a means of supporting evidence obtained from other sources.	Books, papers, advertisements etc. may be examined for bias (gender; race; political etc.). Statistical data can be obtained.	Philo and Glasgow Media group (*Bad News; More Bad News*) see pages 149–50.

4. Experimental	Researcher conducts a small-scale study in which subjects can be manipulated, observed and tested in a controlled environment.	Laboratory conditions are required; frequently statistical data is obtained.	Daniel (*Racial Discrimination in England*) see page 308.
	Ethnomethodologists often make use of experiments when they seek to disrupt patterns of taken-for-granted behaviour (e.g. 'candid camera' type situations).	Statistical results are not considered important. Researchers break social rules to see what happens.	Garfinkel (*Studies in Ethnomethodology*)
5. Life history	An unusual method; the aim is to provide an account of what it was like to live in a specific area or time by studying an individual who is representative of it.	Use of letters; diaries; interviews.	Blythe (*Ackenfield*) Thomas and Znanieki (*The Polish Peasant in Europe and America*
6. Longitudinal	A study is conducted and the sample re-interviewed at different periods of time to see what changes have occurred in the group.	Questionnaires; interviews (observation less likely since sample is large).	Davie, Butler and Goldstein (*From Birth to Seven*) Douglas (*The Home and the School*) Newson (*Patterns of Infant Care*)
7. Observational Ethnographic	a. The researcher is involved in the lives of those being studied, either openly, or covertly.	Participant observation.	Whyte (*Street Corner Society*) Patrick (*A Glasgow Street Gang Observed*)
	b. The observer is in the group but detached from it emotionally. In both cases the aim is to see behaviour in the context in which it occurs.	Non-participant observation ('complete observer'); e.g. classroom observation.	Hargreaves (*Deviance in Classroom*)
8. Questionnaires	a. A researcher wishes to obtain data from a scattered population.	Questionnaires are sent by post.	The Census.
	b. A researcher wishes to obtain detailed answers to a complex questionnaire; respondents can give elaborate answers.	Face-to-face interview. *NB:* these may be used in addition to observation etc.	Opinion Polls. Willmott and Young (*Family and Kinship In East London*).
9. Statistical studies: a. Contemporary	The researcher wishes to correlate variables by reference to statistical data (e.g. class and rates of delinquency).	Statistics are collected from such sources as court records; doctors' files; school records etc.	West (*The Young Offender*) Willet (*Criminal on the Road*)
b. Demographic Historical	The researcher wishes to study the changes in population, family structure etc., over time.	Use of parish registers; historical records; novels.	Laslett (*The World We Have Lost*) Wrigley (*Population and History*)
10 Community Research	A large team of sociologists spend time in an area. Each member has a specific task. The aim is to provide a rich description of a place and its inhabitants and processes of development and change.	Observation; use of public records; press reports; attending meetings; informal visits; formal interviews; diaries; biographical data.	Stacey (*Tradition and Change*) and Frankenberg (*Village on the Border*) Lynd (*Middletown*) Gans (*The Urban Villagers*)

▶ Concluding points:

1 It must be remembered that Positivism and Phenomenology are not necessarily alternative perspectives. Some researchers make use of both and consequently adopt methods associated with each school of thought.

2 Some phenomenologists use forms of scientific procedures in their research. They adopt logical, methodical techniques, which may include forms of experimentation, in order to get at the meaning that people draw from events. In this sense scientific methods are not necessarily the monopoly of the positivist.

3 Generally, it is true that theories and methods are almost inseparable. Different schools of sociology have developed different types of theory. These require different methods of research.

THE PHENOMENOLOGICAL PERSPECTIVE

ACTION THEORY

Explain and assess the view that social life is nothing more than or less than face-to-face interaction; sociology is inadequate unless it proceeds from that premise.   (JMB)

The primary objective of social science is the understanding of social action. Discuss.
(OX)

Questions such as these require a full discussion of the phenomenological/action perspective, with reference to Weber and later writers.

Weber's Action Theory

1 He advocated an interpretive sociology which would show how an actor planned action by taking account of the behaviour of others.

2 He said actors have motives and goals which derive from the broader cultural structure of society (the desire people have to maximise their opportunities to obtain scarce resources will be related to their social status in the society).

3 He regarded explanations which stressed only the causes and consequences of the social structure on behaviour as inadequate. They take no account of people's conscious intentions.

4 He said the aim must be to show how the social world is constructed by people in their interactions.

Mead's Theory of Symbolic Interaction (1863–1931)

1 His work derives from Weber in that he also favoured the method of 'role-taking'; i.e. imagining oneself in the position of the person with whom there is an interaction. This helps to make sense of their responses and behaviour.

2 This ability is the origin of one's own 'self-concept'. We learn who we are through interacting with others. We develop concepts and thoughts and the ability to direct our own action in a way that has meaning and consequence.

ETHNOMETHODOLOGY

1 This is the most recent perspective in sociology. It arose from the work of Austrian philosopher and sociologist, Schutz (1934). It has more recently been developed by Garfinkel (1962).

2 It means the study of the methods used by people to make sense of their everyday lives.

3 People try to establish some rational patterns on events which occur in their lives. This is true even when the events are bizarre or weird. Studies on the TV programme *Candid Camera* illustrate this! People are able to impose some apparent order and sense even where there is chaos around them.

4 Ethnomethodologists wish to uncover the rules that people apply in such situations when there has been no socialisation or training in how to respond.

5 In their studies they devise ways of challenging securely held common-sense assumptions about the world so that interaction no longer makes 'obvious sense' to them.

6 Their studies show how when dissonance occurs (lack of harmony between expectations and facts) then people try to impose some rational explanation for the events to make them understandable.

7 The aim of ethnomethodology, therefore, is to reveal the general nature of social processes, not to try to change society.

▶ Examples of their studies:

(*a*) Students are asked to pretend to be boarders in their own homes. This forces them to consider the taken-for-granted rules of daily life. It caused much anger among parents who were mystified by such bizarre behaviour; many thought their children were ill.

(*b*) Students assumed they were being given genuine advice from an apparent 'expert' about social problems. They received random 'yes'/'no' answers, many of which were contradictory. Yet they were able to 'make sense' of the advice and see that it fitted a general helpful pattern.

Criticisms of ethnomethodology	Strengths of ethnomethodology
1. It is excessively individualistic and focusses only on small-scale interactions. 2. The researcher may often rely on the reports of people who are not trained observers. 3. It is difficult for the researcher to know when the principles on which a person is acting have been uncovered. 4. It may provide much description but not very much wide-ranging theoretical explanation.	1. It does focus on a small area and show the rule-making process in social situations. 2. The perspective does help to show how rules emerge and how they are applied to make the social world orderly where no other explanations are available. 3. It does help to provide insights which other methods do not; e.g. how people cope socially without instruction or previous experience in particular situations.

Consider how you might answer the following questions making use of a phenomenological perspective (in all its forms: Action theory, Symbolic interactionism and Ethnomethodology.) Remember, you must apply the ideas to the question you are answering. It is not enough simply to list facts.

Analyse in detail how social actors can be said to manage themselves and others in face-to-face interactions. What factors should be borne in mind when evaluating this particular sociological approach?   (JMB)

THE OBSERVATIONAL METHOD

Why is participant observation a central method of ethnographers?

Participant observation provides a licence for unverifiable subjectivity. It has no place in sociology. Is this assessment justified?   (Ox)

ETHNOGRAPHY

Mitchell (*A Dictionary of Sociology*) says it is usual to refer to the descriptive account of the way of life of a particular people as ethnography.

Herskovits (*Man and His Works*) defines it as 'the description of individual cultures'.

McNeill (*Research Methods*) says it can be taken to mean 'writing about a way of life'.

Ethnography derives from anthropological studies undertaken to observe the social and cultural behaviour of people in pre-literate societies and provides descriptions of them.

Participant observation

Becker and Greer (*Participant Observation and Interviewing in Qualitative Methodology*) state that it is that method in which the observer participates in the daily life of the people under study, either openly or covertly in some disguised role.

Kluckhohn (*American Journal of Sociology*: 1940) says that 'its purpose is to obtain data about behaviour through direct contact and in terms of specific situations in which the distortion that results from the investigator being an outside agent is reduced to the minimum. . .'

Types of observation

▶ Complete participation: the observer becomes a completely integrated member of the group observed: e.g. Whyte (*Street Corner Society*). He lived in an Italian slum district in the 1930s and observed the lifestyles and subcultural values of street gangs. He took on the role of secretary of the Italian Community Club.

▶ Overt observation as participator: the observer informs the___ they are being observed: e.g. Leibow (*Tally's Corner*). He s___ world of negro street-corner men. He said 'they knew I was them, yet they allowed me to participate in their activities ...u take part in their lives to a degree that continues to surprise me. . .'

▶ Non-participant observation: the observer stands apart from the group and observes in a detached way; e.g. Collins ('Researching Spoonbending', in *Social Researching*). He describes his unobtrusive observation of an experiment through a one-way screen.

Why participant observation is used

1 The researcher wishes to know the meaning of events for those involved.

2 The method seeks to produce an account of the lives, behaviour, values etc. of people in their normal environment.

3 Other methods may be unsuitable for certain investigations (e.g. why gang members behave in aggressive ways).

4 It may be necessary to 'be there' to understand the dynamics of the situation being observed (e.g. crowd violence).

5 The observer must look at the events with a fresh eye, uncontaminated by personal preference or experience.

6 The method may help reveal explanations for behaviour which the actors themselves could not explain.

7 Ethnomethodologists disrupt 'normal behaviour' to reveal the taken-for-granted rules about 'correct ways of behaving'.

Criticisms of the method

1. The presence of the observer may change the behaviour of the group.

2. It relies too heavily on the interpretations of the observer. It is too subjective.

3. The observer may become too involved with the group observed and fail to locate the meanings.

4. There can be no re-testing of results since the behaviour is not observed under controlled conditions.

5. The researcher can never be sure that the real motivations and interpretations have been uncovered to explain the behaviour.

6. The method lacks the scientific rigour of positivism which deals in quantifiable facts.

Advantages of the method

1. The observer can check to see whether the behaviour is affected by his presence.

2. The observer does not introduce subjective assumptions into the findings. The subjective element is located within the group observed. The observer must reveal these to show their influence.

3. The observer can seek to increase reliability and validity by conducting observations at different times and places.

4. The observer does not set out with established hypotheses; these may develop in the course of the study.

5. McNeill makes the point that the ethnographer's central concern is to provide a description that is faithful to the world-view of the participants in the social context being described . . . what makes the work scientific is the care taken to avoid error, to be thorough, exhaustive and to check and re-check all findings. . .'

SOCIOLOGY, ART OR SCIENCE?

Related to questions about major perspectives are some which ask quite specifically about the status of sociology as a discipline in terms of methods used.

It would be quite possible to tackle these using the material presented so far. However, another line of argument is possible. You should therefore consider the following.

Is sociology more of an art than a science?

To what extent is modern sociology an attempt to combine the methodological procedures and objectivity of physical sciences with the speculation, imagination and subjectivity of the arts?

The main difficulty with such questions would perhaps be dealing with the relationship between art and science.

1 Nisbett (*Sociology as an Art Form*) considers that sociology is closer to art than science. He argues:
(*a*)   The key ideas of Weber, Durkheim and Marx are related to the great art movement of the nineteenth century known as Romanticism: concepts like anomie, ideal types, alienation etc. are abstract and largely utopian.
(*b*)   Such terms are also non-scientific in that they are not easy to quantify or measure.
(*c*)   The sociologist, like the artist, can forever learn from re-reading earlier writers. There is a limit to what the physicist can learn from re-reading Newton.

2 Dr Bronowski (a scientist) says there is a likeness between the creative acts of mind in art and in science. 'The discoveries of science, like works of art are explosions of hidden likenesses.' He is claiming that science is not unlike art.

3 Kaplan (*The Conduct of Enquiry*) argues that in science valid discoveries can be made by non-scientific procedures. These include imagination, inspiration and intuition. He concludes that it is a mistake to draw too fine a line between what is considered to be 'science' and what is not. This leads to the view that practitioners in the social sciences should also use any methods that provide insights and discoveries about the behaviour they are studying.

4 Many phenomenologists would accept that sociology may not be scientific, but that it doesn't matter if it isn't.

THE COMPARATIVE METHOD

The comparative method is the equivalent in the social sciences of the experimental method in the natural sciences. Discuss.   (Ox)

Giner (*Sociology*) says that the analyses of social change in history are carried out with the help of several methods. One of the most favoured is the comparative method. This entails the study of different groups and institutions in order to examine similarities and differences. The feature under examination may occur in the same society, for example a comparison of rates of mobility between different classes. They may appear in different societies; for example rates of mobility may be compared between societies.

1   Fox and Miller (*Occupational Stratification and Mobility*) state that in making comparisons among nations, a leap of courage must be made. 'Many of the difficulties of individual studies are compounded in comparative perspective. Some national studies are of poor technical quality, but we have no choice of substitutes if we wish to include a particular nation in a comparison. Time periods differ in various studies; occupational titles and ratings are not fully comparable.' They conclude that it is important to remember that any comparisons 'are at best only approximations'.

2   Murdock (*Social Structure*) used cross-cultural research methods to examine the structure and function of the family. He sampled 250 societies, from simple to economically complex. He found that some form of family existed in every one. In particular he found evidence of the universality of the nuclear family 'either as the sole prevailing form of the family or as the basic unit from which more complex forms are compounded. . .'

3   Thompson (*Emile Durkheim*) says that Durkheim drew up classifications of behaviour (e.g. suicide rates) to make it possible to test hypotheses about the relationship between social phenomena. The typology could be used when making comparisons. This is 'the nearest thing to an experimental method in sociology. . .' Durkheim favoured the comparative-historical approach because sociologists could not carry out experiments and had to rely on the method of indirect experiment (the comparison of similar cases in a systematic way). Thompson comments that this was, for Durkheim, 'the core of sociological methodology'.

THE EXPERIMENTAL (LABORATORY) METHOD

The experiment is an operation in a controlled situation in which the researcher tries to discover the effects produced by introducing one new variable into an experimental group and not into an otherwise identical control group. If the behaviour of the experimental group changes and that of the control does not, then the change can be attributed to the introduction of the new variable. This is a method favoured in the natural sciences. Laboratory conditions enable the experimenter to control all the variables. However, there are examples in sociology of 'field experiments'. These take place in the 'real world' and not in a laboratory. Those whose behaviour is studied in response to 'actors' engaged by the researcher do not know that a study is being conducted. Some of these types of research studies have certain of the characteristics of the comparative method.

1   Daniel (*Racial Discrimination in England*) wished to discover the extent

of racial discrimination in Britain in 1965. He arranged for three applicants to seek jobs, accommodation and insurance cover. These were an Englishman, a West Indian and a Hungarian. Each was given 'identical qualifications'; they were of similar age and had good command of English. The findings showed that it was the Englishman who did best in every aspect of the test, followed by the Hungarian. The West Indian always had the least success.

2 Myerson ('Experiments Without Rats': in Meighan) asks 'have you ever walked into a café and noticed where people sit when they come in? Have you ever tried to see what happens when you try to share a table when there are other ones free? If so, then you have been carrying out an experiment of the sort that has recently become popular within a particular area of sociology. . .' She describes some studies which have been conducted to 'invade territory' in such public places and to 'violate expectations' of the unsuspecting public to uncover the rules of taken-for-granted life in libraries, cafés, etc.

▶ *Conclusions:*

1 Giner says that even if a research project is not specifically comparative, it is advisable that it should be put into perspective and its results contrasted with those of similar studies in other areas.

2 Although there are some examples of small-scale experimentation in sociology, the comparative method is the most frequently used means of explaining processes of change, especially on a large scale, and of drawing attention to particular cultural and structural features of a society in relation to others.

3 McNeill makes the point that 'any sociologist who is trying to identify the causes of social events and behaviour is going to be involved in making comparisons, whether by means of surveys among different groups or by conducting experiments'.

SOCIOLOGY, SOCIAL PROBLEMS AND SOCIAL POLICY

Examine the relationship between sociology and social policy. (AEB)

Has sociology exercised any influence on the development of social policy? Illustrate your answer with specific examples. (Ox)

Sociology and sociological problems

(*a*)   We live in a social world which has social and legal rules together with many institutions all of which go to form the structure of society.

(*b*)   Sociologists investigate these features of social life to understand how and why people behave as they do.

(*c*)   They adopt various perspectives and make use of many theoretical structures in their investigations.

(*d*)   Sociological problems are questions of investigation of the phenomena that exist around the sociologist, regardless of whether or not he approves of them. They exist and so can be studied, just as a physicist's 'problems' are those which relate to the physical world which he wishes to investigate.

Social problems

(a)   A social problem is something which has been labelled by some individual or group as being socially undesirable. It may then become the subject of wider concern so that pressures are brought to remedy it in some way.

(b)   Some may argue that the term 'problem' is attached by those who have a specific interest in the matter (usually powerful people who 'set' the social agenda).

(c)   Sociologists are sometimes accused of generating problems as a result of their investigations.

(d)   Although much sociological research is concerned with issues that have been designated 'problems' (poverty, race, crimes, strikes etc.) some is also interested in how issues become defined as problems and the processes by which they reach the public consciousness.

Examples of sociological problems, social problems and social policy

Sociological problems 1. Positivist method 2. Phenomenological	How to investigate the social factors associated with suicide. How does a death come to be defined as suicide?
Social problem	The increasing number of drug-related suicides.
Social policy	What agencies or organisations can be introduced to combat the number of drug-related suicides?

Social policy

The drawing up and implementation of social policies involves political decisions.

1   In drawing up a social policy a government bases its decisions on its philosophy of how a society ought to be run.

2   Social scientists are often called on to undertake a programme of research because they are trained in the technique required.

3   Examples of research which was commissioned by a government department and on which social policy was later based:

(a)   Kelsall (*Women and Teaching*) 1965. The study looked at the number of women teachers who had left the profession, their reasons for doing so and the chances of recalling them later if necessary.

(b)   Rose and Deakin (*Colour and Citizenship*) 1969. This was undertaken for the Institute of Race Relations. The aim was to uncover the problems faced by ethnic minorities in Britain and to suggest remedies.

(c)   Equal Opportunities Commission 1975. This body encourages research to see how well the package of Acts in 1975 to increase the equality of women in British society is working and to advise the government accordingly.

4 Shipman (*The Limitations of Social Research*) makes the point that commissions are set up to examine crucial issues without social scientists being represented. Yet it is rare for evidence from social science to be ignored in the final report.

5 One of the most important contributions the sociologist can make is to reveal the gap between the real situation and that assumed by the general public. How problems are remedied is not for the sociologist to decide but the agencies which implement social policy.

THE SOCIOLOGY OF KNOWLEDGE

CONTENTS

There are quite specific questions set every year by the AEB board. These will make use of the phrase 'sociology of knowledge' in the question. However, there may be an opportunity to make use of your understanding of this subject matter in answering questions from other boards which relate to such topic areas as education and religion.

The specific questions (AEB) relate primarily to the following areas:

1   The Marxist view which relates the sociology of knowledge to the social structure.
2   The phenomenological view which relates it to the process of interaction.
3   A more general question which asks you to show the contribution made by the sociology of knowledge to any one area of social life (e.g. education, religion).

It is preparation for this type of question which may enable you to answer a question on another board from this perspective.

---

e.g. 'It has been suggested that education is the most important means of activity maintaining capitalist relations of production.' What do you understand by this claim? How adequate is it as an explanation of the role of contemporary educational institutions?   (JMB)

To answer questions on this topic you must:
(*a*)   know a definition of the sociology of knowledge
(*b*)   be able to explain its significance and meaning
(*c*)   be able to refer to some examples of analysis undertaken using these ideas (especially from a Marxist and a phenomenological perspective)
(*d*)   be familiar with some of the strengths and weaknesses of the perspectives.

▶   *Overview*
Philosophers have asked 'how is knowing the world possible'? Sociologists have answered the question by stressing the social context in which people claim to know about society and the use to which their knowledge is put.

In his *New Introductory Reader*, O'Donnell makes the point that much sociology is, in a sense, the sociology of knowledge. 'This is because the sociology of knowledge is concerned with explaining how different groups and individuals perceive and understand the world in often radically different ways . . .'

Examine critically the contribution made by one sociologist or group of sociologists to the sociology of knowledge.   (AEB)

Explanations of the sociology of knowledge

(*a*)   Mannheim (*Ideology and Utopia*): 'The sociology of knowledge is the study of the relationship between knowledge and existence.'

(*b*)   Berger and Luckmann (*The Social Construction of Reality*): 'The sociology of knowledge must concern itself with everything that passes for knowledge.'

(*c*)   Coser and Rosenberg (*Sociological Theory*): 'The branch of sociology that concerns itself with relations between thoughts and society.'

(*e*)   Marx and Engels (*German Ideology*, ed. R. Pascal): 'The class that has the means of material production at its disposal has control at the same time of the means of mental production, so that thereby, generally speaking, the ideas of those who lack the means of mental production are subject to it . . .'

The implication of these definitions

1   Knowledge is seen to be social in its production.
2   There is a relationship between the social structure and knowledge.
3   Knowledge can be used in the interests of those who possess it.
4   To have knowledge is to have power. This point can be illustrated in the following example:

▶   In a society people make sense of everyday events in terms of the norms and values which they have absorbed as members of it. This is the source of their knowledge and understanding. Sudden and unexpected illness may be explained by the fact that someone has broken important social rules. If there are particular expectations about how to behave and these rules are not followed then severe consequences may be predicted. In pre-industrial societies such events may be explained by witchcraft. The wrong-doer is bewitched. Those who control the patterns of behaviour (witch doctors or shamen) can use their knowledge of social rules to their advantage. They may cure or explain the death of the bewitched person. This ability gives them and those they may serve power over others. Consider the following questions:

The sociology of knowledge attempts to relate knowledge to social structure. Offer a critical account of any one contribution to this branch of sociology.   (AEB)

Examine the similarities and differences between the major approaches to the sociology of knowledge.   (AEB)

THEORIES OF THE SOCIOLOGY OF KNOWLEDGE

MARXIST INTERPRETATION

▶ 'The ideas of the ruling class are in every epoch the ruling ideas . . .' By this he implies that all knowledge is ideological. It consists of and reflects all those ideas and beliefs which justify class division and ruling-class power.

▶ The economic infrastructures determine the way that people think and behave in a society.

▶ By controlling their social superstructure and the norms, values and beliefs that relate to it, the ruling class ensure that their dominance is maintained.

The following writers use a Marxist perspective based on the sociology of knowledge to analyse the educational system.

1 Althusser (*Ideology and Ideological State Apparatuses*).
(*a*) The education system is part of the superstructure.
(*b*) It operates to serve the interests of the ruling elite.
(*c*) The educational system will be used to reproduce the kind of labour force required: producing many low-skilled workers who can endure boredom and routine.
(*d*) Control is both by sanctions and punishments, but also through the imposition of ideological beliefs about the normality and inevitability of these everyday patterns.
(*e*) These ideological beliefs are imposed through such 'state apparatuses' as the mass media, religion, the family etc.

2 Bordieu (*Reproduction in Education, Society and Culture*)
(*a*) One of the major aims of the educational system is the transmission of the dominant values of the society. In effect this is the culture of the dominant ruling class.
(*d*) It becomes defined as the most valuable and worthy of all cultures.
(*c*) He refers to this as 'culture capital' because when shared it can lead to the accumulation of wealth and power.
(*d*) Those who fail to do so are those who fail in the education system. This justifies their low class position. They do not have knowledge and so a label of 'low IQ' is attached.

PHENOMENOLOGICAL PERSPECTIVE

The following sociologists adopt a phenomenological perspective to the sociology of knowledge.

▶ Their emphasis is on the way that knowledge is socially constructed by people in the process of interaction.

► Their aim is to show how people construct their reality and make common sense explanations of their perceptions clear.

1 Keddie (*Classroom Knowledge*)
She says that the important aim for sociologists is to:
(*a*)   Examine the meanings that lie beneath 'what counts as knowledge' in the classroom.
(*b*)   Discover the methods by which teachers evaluate a child's knowledge. (She notes that knowledge presented in an abstract form is considered superior to concrete forms, for example),
(*c*)   Discover how children are labelled in terms of their ability which is based on the teacher's 'knowledge' of them in the process of classroom evaluation.

2 Berger and Luckmann (*The Social Construction of Reality*).
They look at religion in terms of the sociology of knowledge to see what part it plays in helping people to make sense of and know their society through their social experience.

They start from the assumption that every society has a body of beliefs, knowledge and values which they refer to as 'universes of meaning.' Members absorb and learn these meanings in their everyday social relationships.
(*a*)   The universes of meaning help people make sense of their lives.
(*b*)   People must know how their beliefs can be justified as 'true' and worthwhile, otherwise life would be without meaning.
(*c*)   Religion is one of the important institutions which provides some evidence for the beliefs.
(*d*)   The religious beliefs are also rooted in the structures of society. These give them 'plausibility' (the presence of churches, clergy and church-related rituals.)
(*e*)   People can make sense of the mysteries of life by reference to the structures and the beliefs they engender and sustain.
(*f*)   By these means people come to know and understand their own society.

SUMMARY

The Marxist View	The phenomenological view
1. The use of a macro-perspective entails an analysis of how people know their society, its rules and values, by looking at the ways in which the ideology of the ruling class is sustained in every major social institution.	1. The use of a micro-perspective entails an analysis of how people know how to behave and respond in the processes of interaction. It also examines how people acquire knowledge of each other in their interpersonal relationships.
2. The superstructure of society is said to operate in the interest of this elite. Ideas about the class structure, differences in ability, the legitimacy of the social hierarchy etc. are all imposed and reinforced through such institutions as education, family, religion, mass media etc.	2. This leads, for example, to an analysis of how teachers know what to expect of particular pupils, and pupils of teachers; how labels become attached; how we know who the deviants are and how to develop knowledge of what causes their behaviour. ('He's been a trouble-maker from the day he walked into the school . . . what more can you expect?')

3. By accepting such knowledge people's lives are shaped and controlled.

3. It may help show how people justify and rationalise their knowledge by reference to wider institutions.

Some of the strengths and weaknesses of the views:

THE MARXIST VIEW

Strengths

1. It provides explanations of why the poor accept their low-status positions and do not press for major social change.
2. It illustrates how knowledge can be seen to be man-made to promote particular political ends.
3. It explains why some forms of knowledge are more highly regarded than others at particular times (because they fit more closely with prevailing elite ideology).
4. It explains the relationship between power and knowledge and why it is difficult for those from the lowest classes to obtain power.

Weaknesses

1. It is an explanation that is itself grounded in a particular ideology.
2. It tends to produce explanations about beliefs which cannot easily be tested or refuted. (Those who disagree with the argument can be accused of false class consciousness).
3. It suggests that there is a conspiracy to discourage people from seeking the knowledge which will enable them to achieve improved social position.
4. Weberians would argue that it may not be true to say that people are deliberately denied power. They claim it is available to all who seek it.

THE PHENOMENOLOGICAL VIEW

Strengths

1. Those who adopt it do not rely on the view that there is a dominant ideological view-point being imposed on people.
2. They look at people in the process of interaction to see how they extract meanings and assume 'knowledge' of events.
3. It corresponds more closely with 'common sense' views that people do make use of stereotypes in order to develop a knowledge of what someone is like (by looking at clothes, manners, speech).
4. It illustrates the dangers of such assumptions and the problems that can ensue (e.g. from using knowledge of behaviour to label a person).

Weaknesses

1. Where the wider social structure is not taken into account it could be argued that knowledge gained is limited and partial. Class factors, for example, may be important in explaining aspects of behaviour.
2. Phenomenologists generally rely on interpretive methods to see how people obtain the meanings which form their knowledge. Such techniques are open to the methodological criticisms which can be levelled at all such analyses (see page 39).
3. Whilst opposing the deterministic view of the Marxists, this perspective can lead to a relativistic view in which all beliefs and knowledge are equally valid.

Consider how you might introduce a discussion of the sociology of knowledge into the following questions:

Religion and the mass media constitute a major source of knowledge and belief for members of industrial societies. Examine the view in relation to either the mass media or religion.   (AEB)

Discuss the view that education in Britain is concerned with the creation and maintenance of an adequate and efficient labour force of men and women.   (Wel)

The major role of the educational system is to legitimise the inter-generational transmission of cultural capital. Explain and evaluate this view.   (Ox)

CHAPTER THREE

THE WELFARE STATE

CONTENTS

A variety of questions on this topic appears on exam papers set by all boards. Some relate specifically to the welfare state, others combine a discussion of poverty and the distribution of income and wealth.

The main topic areas in relation to the welfare state are:

1   The aims of welfare provision:
    (a)   To eliminate major social evils.
    (b)   To increase equality.
    (c)   To eliminate poverty.
    (d)   To provide for those who fall into hard times as a result of factors beyond their own control.
2   The welfare state: analysis of issues in terms of different perspectives and theories: functionalist, Marxist and Weberian.
3   The welfare state and the family.

THE AIMS OF THE WELFARE STATE

Why was the welfare state introduced in Britain? Have the main aims been achieved?

Assess the contribution of the welfare state in achieving equality in Britain.

To answer these types of question which test a general understanding of the aims, structure and consequences of the welfare state you need to know:

(a)   something of its origins
(b)   some of the organising legislation
(c)   some studies, statistics etc. in order to discuss the levels of success which have been achieved. (These details will be fundamental to almost any question on the topic since you will need to discuss changing numbers in poverty, statistics relating to distribution of wealth and income in many other related questions).

Definition: The acceptance of total responsibility by the state (central Government) for the welfare and well-being of all its members by the provision of appropriate social policies. The government provides minimum standards of livelihood as a right of citizenship. It includes the National Health Service, a free education system, and a range of benefits including pensions, unemployment and sickness benefits.

THE ORIGIN OF THE WELFARE STATE IN BRITAIN

Leslie Paul (*Where After Welfare*) says that its development was a response to the perception that welfare provision should be based on social needs rather than on the individual's moral failure. Marsh (*The Welfare State*) says that attempts to relieve poverty have been made for over three centuries, but it is only recently that the concept of the welfare state has been introduced.

1601 Poor Law denied help to the able-bodied poor and kept those who received assistance at a standard below that of the poorest independent worker. The pauper's parish was responsible for providing relief.

1834 Poor Law Amendment Act introduced workhouses for the destitute.

1905–9 The Poor Law Commission produced two reports:
(a)   The Majority Report supported the existing legislation.
(b)   The Minority Report said the emphasis should be removed from the individual's moral failure to that of the community and the state which failed to cope with such problems adequately.

1906–13 The Liberal government introduced the first limited benefits for the needy.

1909 Beveridge wrote *Unemployment: A Problem for Industry* in which he said there should be a move towards the redistribution of income to help abolish poverty. 'There should be bread for everyone before cake for anybody.'

The introduction of the modern welfare state

1942 The Beveridge Report was published: 'Social Insurance and Allied Services'. This produced a scheme to deal with the five giant evils of Want, Squalor, Disease, Ignorance and Idleness. His scheme was based on a system of contributions for insurance against hardship. The payment would be made by employers and employees so that all citizens would have a right to benefit if they fell on hard times. Assistance would be available from 'the cradle to the grave'.

1946 Bevan introduced the National Insurance Act which provided unemployment and sickness benefit; retirement pensions, widows' pensions and maternity grants.

1948 National Assistance Act which provided benefits for anyone whose income fell below a set level (replaced by Supplementary Benefit in 1966).

1946 National Health Service Act introduced a free health service with no prescription or other charges.

1942–8 This period marks the introduction of the modern welfare state. In addition to the reforms in social security there was also the major reform in the education system with the 1944 Education Act which introduced three stages of free education. There have been subsequently many developments and changes in the structure and organization of the system with a gradual move away from the original intentions of Beveridge as more benefits became subject to means tests.

In order to discuss the issues in the questions on page 55 you must consider some of the evidence to decide whether or not its main aims have been achieved.

1   Has squalor been eliminated?

Beveridge saw this as a problem which related both to the needs of people and the ability they had to control their environment.

He was concerned about the quality of housing, for example:

Comment ▶ In the 1960s high-rise blocks replaced slum dwellings, which have subsequently been criticised for their quality. In 1981 The English Housing Conditions survey showed that there were 18m dwellings in England of which 1.1m were unfit for human habitation; 900,000 lacked basic amenities; 1m required repairs costing more than £7,000.

(Average p.a.)	
1945–54	10,000
1960–64	70,000
1981–82	12,000

Slum clearance. Houses demolished (Eng. and Wales).

2   Has disease been controlled?

Notification of infectious disease (1000s)		
	TB	Whooping Cough
1951	50	192
1961	22	27
1971	10	19
1981	7	30

Infant mortality rates Deaths of infants under 1 year per 1000 live births	
1870–72	150
1900–2	142
1910–12	110
1920–22	82
1930–32	67
1950	31
1960	22
1975	15
1980	12

Life expectation		
	Males	Females
1901	48	51
1931	58	62
1951	66	71
1961	67	73
1971	68	75
1979	70	76

Infectious diseases have caused fewer deaths in recent years (although there are occasional epidemics).

Improved medical care and health facilities have reduced infant mortality rates and increased life expectancy.

Hospital medical staff (Full time 1000s)			
1972	1975	1977	1981
32	36	38	42

3   Has ignorance been eliminated?

% pupils remaining at school after minimum leaving age as % of age group.

Age	1950	1960	1980
16	14.1	21.5	19.00
17–18	6.6	11.1	18.0

Pupils leaving school with low CSE grades or no qualifications.

	1971–2	1981–2
Girls	204	185
Boys	221	215
Total	425	400

Number of university students

in 1000s	Males	Females	Total
1938–9	38.3	11.6	50.0
1981–2	189.5	118.8	308.3

Comment: The evidence indicates improved educational standards since the reforms introduced in 1944.

4   Has idleness been eradicated?

In his plan, Beveridge assumed that there must be an employment policy which would eradicate idleness. 'The maintenance of employment is wanted for its own sake and not simply to make a plan for social security work more easily . . .' He wished to ensure that those who could not work should not be unduly penalised.

Unemployment rates (millions)

1935	2.0
1945	0.1
1955	0.4
1965	0.3
1975	0.6
1980	1.7
1985	3.2
1987	2.9

Comment: Since the early 1970s there has been a decline in world trade, changes in technology and in economic policies in Britain. Unemployment rates have increased. Benefits are maintained at levels intended to discourage idleness. Critics argue they are too low to maintain families in basic comforts.

5   Want

The aim of Beveridge was to produce a scheme to ensure that everyone in the community would always be free from want. This is why he advocated three systems of benefit:

(a)   social insurance payable on a contractual basis
(b)   social assistance payable on a test of need

(c)   children's allowances payable to all without means test.

To achieve these ends the plan was:

(a)   universal, covering every citizen regardless of size of income

(b)   equal benefit to all for equal contribution

(c)   those whose needs were not met through the social insurance scheme would be able to claim extra benefit if they could prove need. He assumed that such a group would gradually diminish. By these means he hoped that his plan would eliminate poverty, help in the redistribution of income and increase social equality.

There were some studies in the early 1950s (notably Rowntree) which suggested that this may have been the case, but later work in the 1960s and subsequently into the 1970s and 80s (especially Townsend) has seriously questioned this view. For details see: poverty, distribution of income and wealth and social equality.

Is the welfare state necessary?

The answer you give to this part of the question will depend on the arguments you have presented in your essay (see also the debate on equality, page 61).

Has the welfare state increased equality and eliminated poverty?

1   The aim of increasing social equality.
    The answer that you give to this aspect of the question may depend on the perspective you adopt.
2   The aim of eliminating poverty.

View that the welfare state has achieved this aim	View that the welfare state has not achieved this aim
1. If poverty is defined in an absolute way (see page 277) then the improved living standards and diets of most people must reduce the numbers in poverty.	1. Townsend and other researchers have redefined poverty in their studies dating from the 1960s. They use a concept of relative deprivation. On this basis the numbers in poverty have increased steadily.
2. Since the welfare state has provided people with greater security in the face of economic and other problems they may be less inclined to see themselves as 'poor'. There may be less subjective poverty.	2. Even on an objective basis the numbers who claim SB (the Government's poverty line) is increasing.
3. Before the introduction of the welfare state the elderly and the unemployed, in particular, had no means of avoiding poverty. Now they can live above the level of destitution.	3. The welfare state can only offer limited resources and these are generally inadequate.
	4. Poverty is deep rooted and a complex problem. Coates and Silburn (*Poverty: the Forgotten Englishmen*) say it is not just shortage of money. It is a deprived lifestyle aggravated by poor housing, poor job prospects and permanent insecurity. The welfare state has not defeated these problems.

Have the aims of the welfare state been achieved?

Analysis in terms of different perspective and theories.

You should notice how questions which have a similar central theme ('to what extent have the social and political aims of the welfare state been achieved?') can be phrased in slightly different ways. You must recognise the emphasis of the question to ensure that you are answering it adequately. The phraseology will often enable you to answer from a particular perspective or theoretical position. This is helpful because it enables you to impose a clear structure on your answer.

▶ For example, some questions may put a functionalist point of view:

The role of the welfare state is to maintain existing levels of social inequality in a legitimate form. Discuss.   (AEB)

This is asking: do you think that it is true to say that the function of the welfare state is to maintain order and harmony in a society where major inequalities might otherwise cause disruption, by reducing their effects? In this way social inequalities are accepted by people as legitimate. Even those who do not do well in the system are given some help and assistance.

▶ Some questions put a Marxist perspective:

It has been claimed that the strongest continuing influence in the development of the welfare state has been the successful attempt of the dominant social groups to buttress the existing social and economic order. What do you understand by this claim? To what extent do you think it adequately accounts for the development of welfare provision?

This question is asking you to consider the idea that the introduction of the welfare state has been to help disguise the extent and effect of social inequalities which in reality cannot be eradicated in a capitalist economic system. Welfare provisions have helped buy off possible discontent. Other questions may ask for a discussion of a liberal or

▶ Weberian position:

Evaluate the contention that the welfare state is an attempt to resolve the divergent interests of different classes.

To answer such questions you should be familiar with the following ideas:

Three theories of social justice and social equality: Functionalist, Marxist and Liberal/Weberian

Functionalist	Marxist	Liberal/Weberian
Social justice: In every society there must be a hierarchy of power. Those at the top are the most privileged and they are responsible for the dispensation of social justice by being responsible for the welfare of those below them. Members of every social stratum have a function to fulfil. This hierarchical arrangement of power is recognised as legitimate so long as power-holders are seen to exercise their responsibilities for the welfare of others in some clear way. The structure of the welfare state is one way in which this is achieved. It is therefore functional in promoting order and harmony in society. **Social equality:** This is seen as an unattainable myth. It would be neither feasible nor desirable for everyone to share everything in society equally. People have different talents and abilities which help sift them into their class and status positions. The aim of the welfare state is just to promote order in society not equality.	**Social justice:** This can only be achieved in a society when the hierarchy of power based on class differences has been abolished. The superstructure of society is organised in such a way as to promote the interests of the owners of the forces of production. From this point of view, even the welfare state operates to buttress the interests of this group by the provision of welfare for the poorest sectors of society. **Social equality:** Holman (*Poverty*) makes the point that social deprivation means lack of access to certain resources. Any commitment to counting these involves a belief that equality is possible. This would mean that it would be impossible for some to have advantage over others as a result of family connection, inheritance etc. Those who suffer social and cultural deprivation lack equality. In an equal society everyone would have equal access to economic resources and to valued goals and happiness.	**Social justice:** This view, like the functionalist/ conservative interpretation, also accepts the inevitability of a hierarchy of power, but regards it as legitimate only if it has been arrived at from a position of initial equality. The liberal position is one which opposes privilege, but not necessarily inequality. **Social equality:** From this point of view social equality does not necessarily mean that everyone will become identical and share everything in the society equally. People have different talents and abilities. In this sense it is impossible to make everyone equal. The concept is best seen in terms of 'equal opportunity'. Everyone should start with the same chances of obtaining desired goals, but only those who show the most ability will achieve them. In an equal society, which is promoted by a welfare state, everyone should have an equal chance to develop their talents. Holman says complete equality is not possible but is a goal worth pursuing.

THE CHANGING ROLE OF WOMEN IN SOCIETY

CONTENTS

Questions on this topic tend to fall into the following broad areas:

1 The influence of culture and biology on the division of labour between the sexes in the home and in work.
2 Changes in the domestic role of women and men in modern Britain.
3 Changes in the pattern of female employment.
4 The causes of changes in the pattern of female employment.
5 Some of the consequences of the changes in the pattern of female employment.
6 Some of the problems faced by women in employment:
   (a)   the equality package
   (b)   the effects of legislation.
7 Theoretical perspectives accounting for the position of women in society.

THE EFFECTS OF CULTURE AND BIOLOGY ON SOCIAL ROLES

Distinguish between gender roles and sex roles.
Are the cultural influences more significant than the biological with regard to the role of women in society?

Kessler and Mckenna (*Development Aspects of Gender*) suggest that the term sex should stand for the biological differences between males and females. Gender stands for:
(a)   the social and cultural differences between men and women
(b)   the personal and psychological characteristics associated with being a woman or a man (namely femininity or masculinity). Many of these characteristics may be 'assumed' to be biological (such as natural male dominance or female intuition) although there may be some evidence to indicate the significance of cultural influences.
The debate is about:
(a)   whether the biological facts of a person's sex cause their social (or gender) roles to follow a certain pattern
(b)   the extent to which there is inequality between men and women in contemporary society and the ways in which inequalities have been shaped by social factors, including the way society is structured and people's cultural expectations.

  Morgan (*Gender*) points out that just as in French 'there is nothing naturally feminine about a table (*la table*) or masculine about wine (*le vin*) . . . so this should serve to remind us that in sociology we are dealing with social rather than natural classifications . . .'

A role is a pattern of behaviour associated with a person's social status or social position in a group. The individual tends to behave in accordance with what is expected of someone in that position (e.g. doctor and patient; lawyer and client). Roles are learned in the family, in school and in the workplace. This is part of the *socialisation process*, which is the way in which people:

(*a*)   gain a self-image and sense of identity
(*b*)   gain values, attitudes and beliefs
(*c*)   learn the wider values of society
(*d*)   learn appropriate patterns of behaviour
(*e*)   learn their gender roles: i.e. a set of expectations about what behaviour is appropriate for people of one gender.

There is much evidence to show that there are differences in the ways in which boys and girls are raised in families and the way that people respond to them in everyday life. But studies of the socialisation process do not necessarily explain the source of such gender differences. These may be divided between two perspectives:

Biological arguments

These are based on the view that it is the biological facts of sex difference which determine role behaviour. Stress is laid on the significance of physiological factors.
1. In the Victorian period there was a belief in phrenology: that head bumps indicated personality. Those in females indicated love, dependence, and domesticity; in males, aggression and ingenuity.
2. It was believed that measures of brain size showed males to be more intelligent because of their larger brains (later shown to be inaccurate).
3. Early psychologists, such as Galton and Burt, believed that women were emotionally unstable, less logical than men and had a greater facility for simple repetitive tasks.
4. In more recent years the 'split brain theory' suggested that the left side of the brain predominates in women giving them superior skills in the use of language; in males the right side predominates giving them superiority in spatial skills (science and engineering).
5. Some anthropologists have argued that because most of man's history has been as hunter and gatherer the role of the woman was to bear children and care for them. People have become genetically adapted to this way of life. Specific patterns of behaviour have become imprinted on human nature. Any attempt to abolish gender roles would be to run against nature. Power and politics is a male province, domesticity and child care that of the females in society.
6. Some functionalist writers have accepted the biological differences as the source of social inequalities between men and women. This is because it is the most functional way of organising society. The biological differences are not genetically programmed but they have led to practical differences in the organisation of society.

Cultural arguments

These emphasise the fact that behaviour is learned in social groups. The traditional division of labour in the home and in the place of work is justified by the values and beliefs which predominate in the society. These will vary to some extent from one culture to another. Many sociologists raise objections to the biological arguments because:
1. They are too deterministic. They assume that differences are inevitable and unchangeable. They justify the *status quo*.
2. Much of the biological 'evidence' comes from animal studies and it may be unwise to generalise from this about human behaviour.
3. There may be fewer women scientists than male because the image of 'a scientist' (an eccentric in a white coat) does not match the female self-image.
4. Girls may be diverted from science as a result of teacher expectation i.e. they are not expected to perform well and so are given less time and attention.
5. Women have not had access to higher education until comparatively recently.
6. Opponents of the biological views argue that there are examples of societies in which there is no clear-cut division of labour based on sex differences. Morgan refers to the Kung who lived in bands of about 35 persons. There was much overlap in work activities. Hunting was seen as being as much a matter of luck as of prowess and the skills required in foraging for food fully recognised.
He notes how in other societies 'knitting, weaving and cooking sometimes fall into the male province, while such things as pearl diving, canoe handling and house building turn out to be women's work . . .'
7. Oakley notes how in some societies there are no rules about the sexual division of labour and the roles of father and mother are not clearly differentiated. In contemporary USSR, China and Israel women are important members of the armed forces and women are involved in many heavy manual jobs.

CHANGES IN THE DOMESTIC ROLE OF WOMEN

Despite the dramatic changes in the position of women over the last 100 years, the family is still the primary institution through which women participate in British society. Discuss.

There are frequent claims that women in the modern family hold a more democratic position (Willmott and Young: *The Symmetrical Family*). This suggests that men take a greater part in the domestic duties of the household. It also assumes that because of major legal, demographic and educational changes, women have greater opportunity to choose whether to spend their lives independently, as housewives, as mothers, as companions or as careerists in dual-career families.

Legal changes For example, those which have provided greater opportunities to obtain divorce or separation and to receive economic protection (even if cohabiting).

Demographic changes These have included the decline in family size, improved methods of contraception, an increase in the number of nuclear families and greater opportunities for social mobility.

Educational changes These have resulted in better opportunities for women to improve their education. Many more have been able to gain access to higher education and therefore to worthwhile careers.

Economic changes There has been a steady increase in the number of women in the work force, which has risen to about 41% in 1985. (52% of women are married).

However, some writers oppose this 'democratic' image.
2   Oakley emphasises the extent to which 'housework' is part of the feminine gender role even in contemporary society.
(*a*)   She argues that a full-time housewife without children will work a 40–60 hour week; those with one child: 70–80 hours per week. They would spend another 40 hours per week in paid employment.
(*b*)   The increasing dependency on drugs, tranquillisers and the high incidence of female shoplifting are all evidence of the sense of alienation and anomie suffered by many women.
(*c*)   Women are socialised into the equation 'femininity = domesticity'. Through this socialisation housework becomes an accepted part of their role. Yet they cannot conceive of housework as 'work' in the same sense as what their husbands do is work.
(*d*)   This attitude is validated by society's refusal to place an economic value on housework and to assign any status to the housewife.

2   Oakley (*Mothers and Children in Society*) argues that major inequalities remain in the home.

(*a*)   Time-budgets in many industrialised countries show that men are not participating in housework and child-rearing to the extent that is commonly believed.

(*b*)   We do not live in a unisex society and most families have a division of labour according to which running the home and looking after children remain the wife's responsibilities.

(*c*)   The image of the ideal woman who is capable of perfection as mother, wife and employed worker is subversively presented in the mass media, particularly advertising.

3   J and E Newson (*Patterns of Infant Care*) present a more optimistic view of the role of the father in the modern nuclear family. They rated highly participant fathers as those who would do anything for their children; those who performed three or more functions were rated as 'helping' and those with a score of less than three as 'sometimes helping'. Classing them into groups of participant, moderate and non-participating it was found that only 21% were non-participant, 27% were moderate in their help and 52% were highly participant. They conclude that thirty years before their study the number of fathers rated as highly participant would probably have been negligible.

NB: it is interesting to note that this study was conducted in the 1960s before the advent of the feminist movement and its more critical perspective of what constitutes help in the family.

CHANGES IN THE PATTERN OF FEMALE EMPLOYMENT

There are a variety of questons asked on this topic. Some are concerned with the facts and their interpretation with regard to changes over a period of time. Others may test your understanding of more specific causes and consequences of the changes; and the success or failure of legislation designed to promote equality.

Outline and discuss the major changes which have occurred in the pattern of female employment since 1930 in Britain.

There are two points of view to consider, one which sees a steady improvement in the economic position of women and another which takes a more critical view.

▶   The improvement view:

(*a*)   The demand for women's labour has fluctuated over time but has increased steadily since 1971. It has fallen back slightly in the 1980s as a result of increasing unemployment.

(*b*)   Almost 60% of women of working age have a paid job.

(*c*)   They form about 40% of all wage earners.

(*d*)   The passing of legislation in the 1970s, especially the Equal

Women aged 15–59 in paid employment between 1931–66		Women aged 16–59 in paid employment between 1971–81	
1931	36.5%	1971	56.8%
1938	29.5%	1972	57.6%
1940	34.0%	1973	59.9%
1942	43.4%	1974	61.5%
1943	45.4%	1975	62.0%
1944	44.5%	1976	61.5%
1946	36.0%	1977	61.8%
1948	36.2%	1978	61.9%
1951	45.1%	1979	62.4%
1961	51.2%	1980	61.4%
1966	58.5%	1981	58.3%

Source: *Annual Abstract.*

Pay Act and the Sex Discrimination Act, have helped ensure the improvement in women's earnings relative to men's.

(*e*)   Women are increasingly holding positions of importance in contemporary Britain (e.g. there is a female monarch; Prime Minister etc.).

(*f*)   Women's opportunities in the labour market are constantly improving.

(*g*)   Record numbers of women applied for and were accepted by universities in 1984. Women form 41.3% of the undergraduate total.

▶ The deterioration view:

(*a*)   Women tend to occupy the least well-paid jobs. They are those with fewest fringe benefits and opportunities for promotion. Two out of five women are in part-time jobs which are among the lowest paid. Studies by the EOC suggest that women earn less than two thirds of men's wages despite legislation.

(*b*)   Women tend to be concentrated in particular fields of work, especially textiles, catering, health, clerical and educational.

(*c*)   Women tend to be encouraged into 'male' fields of work at times of national crisis (e.g. wartime) and discouraged in times of prosperity.

(*d*)   By 1981 women were falling back to the position they held in the labour market in the 1970s, despite legislation designed to increase their opportunities.

(*e*)   The proportion of women in top professional jobs remains low.

Bank managers	1%
Accountants	2%
University professors	2%
Architects	5%
MPs	5%
Sergeants in police	2%
Senior teachers	20%

THE CAUSES OF INCREASING FEMALE EMPLOYMENT

What are the major causes and consequences of the increasing female employment?

(OX)

These can be analysed in particular time periods (according to the dates which may be specified in the question) and in terms of economic, demographic and social influences (see statistics).

1939–51 During this wartime period and post-war re-building of Britain there was a high demand for labour. Women entered factories as part of the war effort and many subsequently remained. This helped set the trend which showed that women were capable of such heavy work.

1951–71 The economic boom continued. Women workers helped satisfy the increasing demand for labour. Living standards increased and there was a steady demand for new household appliances which their extra incomes could provide. Demographic changes also occurred in this period. Birth rate began to fall in the mid 1960s following the introduction of the pill. Family size began to fall making it easier for women to return to work earlier. Social attitudes also began to change. The Women's Movement encouraged more to seek careers after marriage. The educational system was expanding. New universities, polytechnics and colleges of higher education were producing more women with high-level qualifications.

1971–5 The Equality Package was introduced. This was intended to provide equality for women with men in work. The result may have been to encourage more women to enter the work force.

1975–85 Although there was a down turn in the economy, women continued to seek work in order to supplement family incomes (especially if the husband was unemployed). The revolution in leisure which started earlier in the 1960s meant that people had come to expect frequent holidays and access to regular entertainment. The additional income that women in the household could provide enabled this need to be satisfied. Many employers preferred to take on women employees since they accepted part-time work, and loop-holes in the Equality Legislation enabled employers to pay lower rates than males would accept.

▶ Useful studies:

1 Mallier and Rosser (*The Changing Role of Women in the British Economy*) note how prior to industrialisation evidence indicates that women played an essential role in agriculture and domestic production. Industrialisation led to more women being employed in factory work and domestic service and their numbers in the economy expanded:

(a)   In recent years less time is spent on domestic chores.

(b)   If a woman has been employed prior to marriage it is likely that she will take the opportunity of returning to work because psychological barriers are removed.

(c)   Once increasing numbers of women return to work this will encourage others, setting a trend.

(d)   The advent of commercial TV may have been significant in creating a more consumer-minded society in which additional income is highly regarded.

(e)   A fall in birth rate and improved child-care facilities have freed more women for work.

2   Martin and Roberts (*Women and Work*). Their study was the first full Government survey of women and employment since 1965. They found:

(a)   Although it is the norm for women to work before and after having children, men are still the main family wage earners. Working women still do more housework and child-care than men.

(b)   Most women who take part-time work are mothers with young children.

(c)   Most of the wives questioned thought that it was financially important for women to work. Few worked only 'for the pin money'.

(d)   Overall, an increasing number of women are spending more of their lives in employment. Few adopt the male pattern of continuous lifetime employment as a full-time worker.

(e)   Only a minority of full-time women workers shared domestic work equally with their husbands.

(f)   Only 20% of full-time working wives have the same or a higher rate of pay than their husbands.

An interesting and contrary point of view has been put forward.

3   Hakim (Principal Research Officer in the Department of Employment) argues that the rise of the working woman is a twentieth-century myth:

(a)   By re-analysing data she found that the proportion of women working in 1861 was the same as in 1971.

(b)   The census of 1851 noted that 25% of all wives and 66% of all widows had a specific occupation other than domestic work in the home. Between 1901 and 1931 that declined to one in ten married women. By 1951 it had again risen to 25%. This suggests that women were typically involved in work in the mid nineteenth century and then excluded from it in the early part of the twentieth.

(c)   She also argues that there has been little or no change in the type of work women have been expected to do in the work force since the turn of the century. They have always been confined to typically 'female jobs.'

(d)   There is no evidence of a trend towards greater integration of the sexes in work. Much will depend on the equal opportunities legislation to reverse the problems faced by women.

| CONSEQUENCES OF THE CHANGING PATTERNS IN FEMALE EMPLOYMENT |

This century has been described as 'the woman's epoch'. Discuss some of the consequences of increasing female employment.

Divorce rates Some writers (e.g. Hart) have suggested that the increasing divorce rate has been significantly affected by the growing numbers of women in paid employment. They can achieve greater economic independence.

Living standards Martin and Roberts have suggested that most women who work do so to improve their family income and not for 'pin money.'

A study entitled 'Families in the Future' found that without women's earnings four times as many families would live in poverty. For one in seven retired households women are the sole or main breadwinner.

Male hostility Glucklich and Snell (*Women, Work and Wages*) found that many men continue to resent and resist the possibility of women moving into male jobs and narrowing pay differentials, especially at times of economic difficulties. The trade unions are criticised for failing to help to promote measures to benefit women, especially those in the lowest paid sectors. (Women form about 60% of the lowest-paid workers).

They are the most easily discarded workers Analysis of unemployment statistics suggests that because women are more frequently employed in part-time work they are more easily made redundant as the economy becomes more depressed. They are caught under the 'last in, first out' rule because breaks for child-care reduce their length of service.

Stress Cooper and Davidson (University of Manchester) found that women executives suffer greater stresses and strains than their male counterparts. The woman manager with children at home has to cope with the additional workload and conflicting demands of career, marriage and family. Discrimination appears as a potential cause of stress in work. This may deter many women from entering or remaining in managerial positions.

The effects on children Yudkin and Holmes (*Working Mothers and their Children*) found that:
(*a*)   The vast majority of mothers of pre-school children made adequate arrangements for the care of their children whilst at work.
(*b*)   A review of the literature on the subject 'shows dogmatism and relatively little evidence about long-term effects . . .'

(c)   They argue that among school-children there was some evidence to show that they developed more independence and maturity where mothers worked.

(d)   There was no correlation with mothers working and rates of juvenile delinquency.

(e)   They suggest that full-time work with a child under three in the home is less desirable unless very good care arrangements have been made.

An increase in the number of dual-career families Fogarty et al. found that:

(a)   There was an increase in the number of dilemmas which faced such couples; these related to domestic duties, child-care arrangements.

(b)   There were often more strains in the marriage.

(c)   Where the partners were well adjusted and could compromise, then a successful dual-career arrangement was possible and successful.

Increased social mobility of women Heath (*Women Who Get On in the World*) argues that:

(a)   The average working-class home is now more likely than at any other time in its history to have one of its members in a white collar job and to be exposed to middle-class influences.

(b)   We may be witnessing a gradual transformation of the class structure as a result of the increasing employment of women in white-collar jobs.

(c)   This could also have other effects; for example, it could affect voting patterns in the future. The mobility of women may weaken traditional party allegiances and produce a more calculating electorate.

THE PROBLEMS FACED BY WOMEN IN WORK

What factors inhibit the achievement of equal employment opportunities for women in modern Britain?

(a)   Women have traditionally been a source of cheap labour in the British economy. Wages councils were introduced in 1909 to establish and maintain 'a reasonable standard of remuneration for workers concerned.'

(b)   Since the turn of the century the number of women in the economy has expanded in wartime and again in times of economic boom.

(c)   Few women have achieved high positions of authority in Britain until recent years. The equality package 1970–75 was intended to improve women's opportunities in this respect. However, studies continue to cast doubts on its success.

▶ Useful studies:

1 Foggarty et al (Women in Top Jobs)

   (a) Employers tended to see women as less reliable and assumed that maternity would end their career plans.

   (b) Women in top jobs found they were not easily accepted by male colleagues as equals.

   (c) Many older men had strong and outright anti-feminist attitudes.

   (d) Women were generally less successful than men because fewer were recruited for top positions; fewer were promoted and many were confronted by hostile attitudes.

   Studies prior to 1970 showed that the majority of women workers were involved in the lowest-skilled and lowest-paid jobs.

Representations of women in trade unions

Union	Membership			Executive members		Full-time officials		TUC delegates	
	Total	Women	% Women	Total	Women	Total	Women	Total	Women
APEX..............	95,049	50,594	53.2	15	3(8)	47	2(25)	13	5(7)
ASTMS...........	390,000	87,750	22.5	22	2(5)	95	6(21)	28	3(6)
BIFU..............	154,579	78,765	50.9	32	4(16)	37	7(19)	19	4(10)
CPSA..............	190,347	137,369	72.2	29	4(21)	14	3(10)	30	9(22)
GMBATU........	766,744	258,739	33.7	38	1(13)	287	12(97)	86	4(29)
NALGO...........	766,390	390,859	51.0	71	20(36)	191	20(97)	72	23(37)
NUPE	680,000	455,600	67.0	26	10(17)	180	12(120)	34	10(23)
NUT	250,499	180,179	71.9	41	8(29)	27	2(19)	37	10(27)
NUTGW..........	76,509	69,319	90.6	15	8(14)	38	4(34)	13	10(12)
TGWU............	1,490,555	228,750	15.3	42	1(6)	500	9(765)	92	9(16)
USDAW	392,307	239,170	61.0	18	1(11)	122	10(74)	35	5(21)

(Figures in brackets show how many women there would be if they were represented according to their share of the membership.)
Source: All figures have been supplied by the individual trade unions.   Quoted in *The Guardian*. Aug. 1985.

The Equality Package

1. The Equal Pay Act 1970	Equal Pay for broadly similar work.
2. Employment Protection Act 1975	Women become entitled to maternity leave.
	Pregnancy is no grounds for dismissal.
	It requires employers to give back jobs to mothers within 29 weeks of childbirth.
3. Social Security and Pensions Act 1975	Abolished lower rates of sickness and unemployment pay for women.
4. Sex Discrimination Act 1975	Stated that it is unlawful to discriminate in the following areas:
	a Education b Employment c Housing, goods and services.
	The Equal Opportunities Commission was set up to offer legal advice and assistance.

2   The EOC 2nd Annual Report showed that three years after the Act:
    (*a*)   Women earned on average two thirds as much as men each week.
    (*b*)   The rate of progress towards equality was decreasing.
    (*c*)   Firms still tended to segregate jobs in order to retain lower rates of pay for women by showing that they were not doing 'broadly similar work to men'.
    (*d*)   Of 575 firms surveyed only 39% had analysed their work force by sex and only 2% had taken positive action on their findings.
3   The EOC 5th Annual Report said that:
    (*a*)   Women would continue to earn about 73% of men's pay unless there were substantial changes in the Equality legislation. Otherwise there is the possibility of growing disenchantment with the relevance of legislation.
    (*b*)   'Since the war there has not been a five-year period more unhelpful . . . to the task of promoting equal opportunities for women.'
4   The EOC 10th Annual Report (1985) shows that on average women's hourly earnings have remained at around three quarters of men's since 1975.
5   An EOC Report 'Women and Public Bodies' stated that:
    (*a*)   The 'old boy network' is keeping women from being appointed in significant numbers to public bodies.
    (*b*)   Not only is it unfair that women should not be equally represented on policy-making bodies whose decisions affect all the population but there is a failure to exploit fully the resource of talent vested in half the population.
6   The Local Government Operational Research Unit (*Developing the Neglected Resource*: 1984) found that:
    (*a*)   1.75 million women are employed in local government. There is only one woman Chief Executive (Deeside District Council).
    (*b*)   Only 1 per cent of chief officers are women.
    (*c*)   Many councils who call themselves 'equal opportunities' employers have done little so far to turn policy into practice.
    (*d*)   In 1985, ten years after the passing of the Sex Discrimination Act, a project to assist women who have been sexually harassed was established. This was because the SDA did not outlaw this form of harassment and it was not until 1985 that a court made a decision on the subject. Ethnic minority women have been particularly troubled by a combination of sexual and racial harassment. The new group will offer advice and counselling.
7   In 1985 areas in which the anti-discrimination laws have failed to gain much success include:
    (*a*)   Building societies which may still refuse to take the higher earning wife's income as the basis of a mortgage.
    (*b*)   Equal pay: the national average wage is approximately £180 per week. One woman in 20 earns less than £80 per week. Of 9,842 employers found breaking the law by underpaying women workers, only two were prosecuted.

The Low Pay Unit (1984) found that 40% of employers in Britain were breaking the law in paying below the £70 a week fixed under the Wages Council regulations.

(c)   The movement of women into non-traditional areas of work. Numbers in engineering, public administration, science etc. are still very small.

(d)   The Guardian's Naked Ape Column continues to provide regular examples of the negative ways in which women are viewed in contemporary Britain:

She's a bit like the barmaid at the local. Not exactly pretty. Not unattractive either. But she's got that sort of odd 'something'. The 'something' that would make you want to take her off to the woods, and sort of, see what she's like. If you know what I mean. *Description of a motorcycle in Hondaway magazine.* (Lydia Duemmel, West Lobe, Cornwall).

'BATTERED divorcees tend to turn their new, placid husbands into wife beaters.' *Dr John Williamson, Doctor magazine.* (Sue Solis, Kent).

'THE cost of each shower should not exceed 3p. This is, without question, the most inexpensive method of keeping your wife and children clean.' *Popular DIY magazine.* (D. J. Bruce Durie, High Wycombe).

'IN SPITE of the fact that most candidates were girls, the maths and science results were excellent.' *Report by J. Almond of the Academic Board meeting at Hardenhuish School, Chippenham, Wilts.* (Margaret Jensen, Sue Wiskin, Chippenham).

'THEY at first thought the driver was a woman as it was being reversed with difficulty and the lights had not been switched on.' *Crime report in Newcastle Evening Chronicle.* (Anon.)

Mr Suthee said that corruption in Thailand has three root causes: legal loopholes, power abuse and bad wives. *New Sunday Times, Kuala Lumpur* (David Nelson).

'. . . the new arrangement is primarily intended for the uninitiated reader who, understandably, is often put off by such mundane chapters as 'The Cow' or 'Woman' . . .' *N. J. Darwood's introduction to Penguin Classics' Koran.* (Corinne Gretton, Hadleigh, Suffolk).

Mrs ZITA KELLY, who from today is Lady Provost of Glasgow, came across in her interview with my colleague Jessica Barrett yesterday as a quiet, gentle, self-effacing person with little interest in politics.
    And these are indeed pleasing qualities in a woman.
    Her husband, Dr Michael Kelly, is clean and tidy, young and personable, intelligent and articulate. *Charles Graham, 'Scotland's most penetrating writer,' in the Glasgow Evening Times, May 8 –* (Peter Taylor, Glasgow).

QUESTIONS in the Southwestern CSE examining board's English comprehension paper for May:
    Women always panic more than men in a crisis.
    It was even more difficult than usual to make women obey.
    It was even more difficult than usual to guess how women would behave. (Tilly Mortimore, Dracott, Somerset).

WHY is it that women are such bad drivers? . . . If you see a car travelling at twenty miles per hour along the middle of a main road so that no one can overtake, you can be sure the driver is a woman!' *Royal Society of Arts Examinations Board, passage for aural comprehension.* (Claire Taylor, London NW5).

Source: Guardian.

8   A 1988 survey by Research Services of 8,604 top executives in Europe showed that only 15% were women. In Britain there are only 10% compared to 22% in France.

THEORETICAL PERSPECTIVES

Contrast sociological accounts of the position of women in society.

The Functionalist view

1. Since the isolated nuclear family is the most functional unit for modern society, in the family the woman is primarily responsible for socialising the young.
2. Mothers bear and care for the young and so have the closest and most important bond with them.
3. Scruton (a philosopher) criticises feminism as an ideology because it fosters the idea that all social institutions are dominated by males. It seeks to make a person's sex irrelevant in determining social identity.
4. He says it is an inescapable and beneficial part of the human condition that the sexes are socially distinct and perceive each other differently.
5. The sexual division of labour and of social roles reflects the differences in relationships between men and women.
6. In considering who benefits from the division of labour, the functionalist would argue that everyone does.

The Weberian view

1. Harris (*Women in the Women's Movement*) took the view that to understand the position of women in society it is best to see how women interpret their own situation.
   She obtained her evidence from building up a picture of attitudes through conversations, in-depth interviews and notes from discussion groups. Her conclusion is that sexism (the belief that it is acceptable to treat people differently according to their sex) permeates the whole fabric of society.
2. She says that women have internalised male definitions of themselves (i.e. that they are less able in technical matters). This is a kind of 'slave mentality'.
3. She adds that as long as women accept this view they will always be open to exploitation and manipulation.
4. As to who benefits from the present division of labour in society, she concludes that it is primarily men who do so, since they hold power.

The Marxist view

1. Female subordination in society results from the emergence of private property.
2. Monogamous marriage developed to protect the institution of private property.
3. Men need to control women to maintain power and to ensure the legitimacy of their heirs.
4. Marxists would reject the view that women's apparent economic independence outside the family gives her more power within it.
5. Because women tend to enter the lowest-paid occupations in the labour market this helps reinforce their inferior status in society as a whole.
6. Also, in entering the labour market women help to reinforce the power of the capitalist economic system. They become a 'reserve army of cheap labour'.
7. In work women are less militant than men, subject to sexist attitudes and powerless to retaliate.
8. Gender consciousness and female solidarity are necessary for change to occur.

THE FAMILY

CONTENTS

Questions on this topic cover a wide range of areas:

1 Problems of definition:
   (a)   Cross-cultural studies.
   (b)   Analysis of different types of family structure.
2 Changes in the structure of the family in industrial societies:
   (a)   Research studies illustrating variant forms.
   (b)   Historical and contemporary perspectives.
3 Family relationships:
   (a)   The significance of family networks.
   (b)   The significance of social class.
4 Some feminist perspectives on the family.
5 Theories of the family:
   (a)   Functionalist.
   (b)   Marxist.

PROBLEMS OF DEFINITION

'The major problems of any comparative study is that of arriving at an agreeable definition of the family.' Discuss.   (LON)

How universal is the family as a social institution?   (Wel)

1   Murdock's definition:
The family is a social group characterised by common residence, economic co-operation and reproduction. It includes adults of both sexes, at least two of whom maintain a socially approved sexual relationship, and one or more children, own or adopted, of the sexually cohabiting adults . . .'

Problems of this definition:

(a)   It does not allow the use of the term 'family' about those headed by one parent.
(b)   Those in which a couple have no children.
(c)   Parents who live in a commune (such as a kibbutz) where the children grow up separately from them.

Comment: Whether or not the family is a univeral institution depends to some extent on the definition that is used. If 'a family' is defined in a specific way, then there will be examples drawn from cross-cultural studies to indicate that it is not a universal institution. If it is defined more broadly, then it is harder to find exceptions.

2   A family is a social unit made up of people related to each other by blood, birth or marriage.

Problems of this definition:

It allows a married couple without children to be described as a family, but not an unmarried couple who are living with each other in a permanent union.

Comment:

This wider definition does meet the problems arising from Murdock's description.

3   A family is a social unit made up of people who support each other in one or several ways; for example socially, economically or psychologically (in providing care, love, affection etc.) or whose members identify with each other as a supportive unit.

Problems of this definition:

It is now so broad that it is difficult to conceive of exceptions to the existence of some form of family in every society.

Comment:

This wider definition would allow the term 'family' to be applied to:
(*a*)   A cohabiting couple of the same sex.
(*b*)   Unrelated members of a cohabiting group, such as a Children's Home, commune etc. whose members regard themselves as 'a family'.

EXAMPLES FROM CROSS-CULTURAL COMPARATIVE STUDIES

1   The nuclear family in Britain.
(*a*)   The small size of the unit, living independently of wider kin, is related to economic factors: income, housing and job opportunities. Children are emphasised more for what they can achieve rather than for their economic value.
(*b*)   The main advantages of living in small units is in terms of the economic structure of advanced capitalist societies where there is emphasis on geographical and social mobility.
(*c*)   The concept of monogamy is built into the Christian moral code and supported by the existing legal system. It is assumed to be 'the correct and best' system.
(*d*)   The independence of young married couples and of the elderly also results from the expectations and norms which people share in modern Britain. This ethic of 'independence' is sustained to some extent by the existence of the welfare state which provides support for people.

2   The nuclear family in pre-industrial society: Firth (*We, the Tikopia*) describes family life on the island of Tikopia.

(*a*)   The average population of a village is about fifty persons. There are strong incest taboos; marriage with a kinswoman closer than second cousin is frowned upon.

(*b*)   The nuclear family is always a recognisable unit. Even when two families live together in one household, each has its own section of the floor, and 'when visits are paid to other households it is this little group that moves together . . .'

(*c*)   Husbands and wives who work in the gardens or fishing co-operate in the preparation of cooking meals and also in the care of children.

(*d*)   Overall authority and the ownership of land is in the hands of the male since it is a patrilineal society.

(*e*)   However, there are strong ties of extended kinship in the society also. The links with kindred by marriage tie members into a clan which provides strong subjective family associations. These ties of kinship are more widely used than in contemporary Britain where tasks beyond the nuclear family are carried out by institutions which are not associated with kinship.

3   The extended family: Yorubaland, Nigeria.

(*a*)   The extended family is the norm. They consist of as many as a hundred people, all closely related kin, sharing homes within close proximity to each other.

(*b*)   The family structure is based on polygamy. There are two main advantages:

> (i) Economic: The people are mainly farmers who require a large, cheap labour force.
>
> (ii) Status: In this society a man who can support many wives has high social prestige.

(*c*)   The existence of an extended family system has many advantages:

> (i) There is no welfare state. The extended family provides welfare, assistance, training etc.
>
> (ii) It helps reduce the level of social conflict. Problems are resolved in the family and not by law.
>
> (iii) People develop a strong sense of attachment and identity to a group and an area.

4   The family in a commune.

About 4%–5% of the population of Israel live in kibbutzim settlements. They have been in existence for more than sixty years, since the first was established.

(*a*)   No money changes hands on a kibbutz. Members are provided with food, accommodation, clothing etc.

(*b*)   All wealth produced from the sale of goods goes to finance the kibbutz.

(*c*)   Marriage is monogamous.

(*d*)   Children are generally raised apart from their parents, in 'age groups', with other children. They are cared for by trained nurses and other staff.

(e)   Children grow up with a greater commitment to 'the community' and the kibbutz than to the individual family.

(f)   Although this does not meet Murdock's definition of 'family' it could be seen as 'an extended family' from a more subjective perspective.

Concluding points: The view that the family (especially the nuclear family) is a universal institution is based on the argument that every society has some social organisation which regulates the permanent relationships between adults so that important functions are fulfilled:

(a)   The reproduction of the population.

(b)   The care of the young.

(c)   The stabilisation of relationships between adults.

(d)   The transmission of the social culture from one generation to the next.

The view assumes that the structure of the institution of the family is always broadly the same in every society.

However, critics point out that:

(a)   There is no universal definition of the family.

(b)   It may not be the case that every society has an institution which is recognisable as a family. For example, in some, the relations between adults is not based on a permanent conjugal arrangement (e.g. Ashanti of Ghana). In others, the child's parents may have no understanding of how children are procreated and therefore they feel no need to care for them as a 'family unit' (e.g. Nayar of India and the Trobriand Island of the Pacific).

(c)   While there are institutions concerned with various aspects of domestic life they vary in structure from one society to another.

CHANGES IN FAMILY STRUCTURE

How has the structure of the family changed in Britain over the last hundred years? Indicate the social implications of the changes.   (WEL)

The modern nuclear family is uniquely well adapted to meet all the requirements of industrial society. Examine this proposition and evaluate the evidence for it.

THE NUCLEAR FAMILY   There is debate as to whether the nuclear family developed as a result of industrialisation in the eighteenth and nineteenth centuries from a pre-industrial extended type, or whether both have always been and continue to be significant family structures.

THE VIEW THAT THERE HAS BEEN A CHANGE AND THAT THE ISOLATED NUCLEAR FAMILY IS NOW DOMINANT

1 Parsons (*The Normal American Family*) argues that the American family structure has been undergoing a process of major change.

(*a*)   There has been an increase in divorce rates.

(*b*)   There has been a change in social and moral values.

(*c*)   There has been a decline in birth rate.

(*d*)   The family in industrial societies has fewer functions to serve.

(*e*)   The nuclear family is becoming the typical structure in industrial societies.

(*f*)   Relationships with wider kin are based on choice not obligation.

(*g*)   There is a functional relationship between the isolated nuclear family and the economic structure.

(*h*)   The nuclear family becomes the most functionally suitable structure. This is because family members are increasingly socially and geographically mobile; the nuclear family is small and economically self-sufficient.

(*i*)   The extended family cannot be functional in an industrial society since it tends to tie members to a specific area; conflicts can arise in a family where sons achieve higher status than the father in an inflexible and immobile family unit.

(*j*)   He concludes that the structural isolation of the nuclear family ensures that it remains functional for an efficient industrial society.

2 Linton (*The Family in Urban Industrial America*) also argues that in modern industrial society the extended family has lost its traditional functions. This is because:

(*a*)   There have been major changes in geographical and social mobility.

(*b*)   New technologies have been developed requiring higher levels of skill.

(*c*)   New systems of transport have made mobility easier.

He suggests that kinship ties are ignored when people can do without them. 'City dwellers recognise extended ties only in sending Christmas cards and occasional visits . . .'

The effects on the nuclear family have been:

(*a*)   To weaken marriage ties. There are fewer pressures on people to conform to traditional norms.

(*b*)   Life in urban areas is more anonymous and marriage breakdown more socially acceptable than in smaller close-knit communities. He points to a series of factors which have helped to undermine the traditional family structure:

(*c*)   Increased urbanisation which provided the chances of better houses and jobs.

(*d*)   Increased industrialisation which enabled more women to enter the work force and encouraged smaller families.

(*e*)   Increased secularisation which meant the decline in the influence of the church in people's lives, allowing contraception, divorce etc. to become more widespread and socially acceptable.

He concludes that the family may now be less stable than before, adding 'the revolutionary effects of these . . . on the family . . . can scarcely be overrated . . .'

3 Willmott and Young (*The Symmetrical Family*) put forward a theory to describe the development of the family from pre-industrial to contemporary times. They discuss four stages of development:

(a) The pre-industrial family: the family is the unit of production; all members work as a team. This type was displaced by the industrial revolution, although some examples persist to the present day.

(b) The family of the industrial revolution: individual members were employed primarily as wage earners. The family became a support unit for its members, especially the least successful. Among the poor in urban areas, the extended family again became a significant structure. This only declined with the improvement in living standards and the development of the welfare state. Some examples remained however, as Willmott and Young found in their study *Family and Kinship in East London*.

(c) The nuclear family with which we are familiar in contemporary Britain has emerged from stage 2 and has become the dominant type. The authors argue that it originally epitomised the emerging middle-class family structure. But since the norms of those at the top of the social hierarchy gradually influence those at lower stages, then this structure predominated throughout society. This stage describes the symmetrical family in which husbands and wives take up equal share in the domestic duties of the household.

(d) A possible stage 4 family is described, which is asymmetrical. They suggest that the attitude of those at the top of the occupational hierarchy towards work is that it is a central life interest. These values are likely to filter through society so that families will become less privatised *as more men become involved in responsible and absorbing jobs and wives revert to a more domestic role*.

Points of criticism:

1 Studies of the affluent workers suggest that they do not absorb the attitudes and norms of those in higher social classes.

2 This part of the theory is based on a small sample of 190 managers.

3 Statistics indicate that in the 1980s there are more, not fewer women entering the work force.

4 Studies suggest that the workers whose jobs are affected by new technologies are not necessarily finding them more rewarding (see page 334).

5 Increasing levels of unemployment are likely to increase the levels of home-centred activities.

Has the extended family been replaced by the isolated nuclear family? (OX)

THE VIEW THAT THE EXTENDED FAMILY REMAINS SIGNIFICANT IN MODERN BRITAIN

▶ *Historical perspectives:*

1   Laslett (*The World We Have Lost*)
His work, based on an analysis of parish registers between 1564 and 1821, showed that:
(*a*)   Only approximately 10% of households contained kin beyond the nuclear family in the period.
(*b*)   There was no evidence that the extended family was the dominant structure which was replaced by the nuclear type as a result of the industrial revolution.
(*c*)   He suggests that it may have been the presence of the nuclear family which enabled the industrial revolution to develop rather than the reverse (e.g. members of small family units were already potentially more geographically mobile).

2   Anderson (*Family, Household and the Industrial Revolution*)
He argues that among the poor sector of the population the industrial revolution tended to encourage the strengthening of ties with wider kin. He found in his study of Preston in 1951 that about 23% of households contained kin wider than the nuclear family. This was probably because families needed to support each other in times of depression. The family acted as a welfare system. This is the type of structure found by Willmott and Young in Bethnal Green in the 1950s.

▶ *Contemporary perspectives:*

1   Rosser and Harris (*The Family and Social Change*)
Their study of Swansea in the 1960s confirmed that there were high levels of contact between related kin who were dispersed widely in an urban area.
(*a*)   They found a form of extended family system operating. Kin were in contact by visits, letter and telephone.
(*b*)   Services were exchanged beyond the nuclear family, both economic and social.
(*c*)   This was true for both working- and middle-class people. The extended family provided a focus of identity in a similar way to those reported by the respondents in the Bethnal Green studies.

2   Sussman and Burchinal (*The Kin Family Network*)
They argue that the views expressed by Parsons and Linton rest on a theoretical analysis. This is coloured by their functional perspective. Sussman and Burchinal present evidence to show that the extended family (or a form of it) continues to operate in industrial America. They challenge the view that the isolated nuclear family has resulted from the urban industrial revolution.
(*a*)   Most people do receive varius forms of aid from kin after marriage. Even among upper-class families substantial financial aid flows from parents to off-spring (i.e. nuclear families are not isolated).
(*b*)   Other gifts, advice, job opportunities may flow from other kin members.
(*c*)   Kinship visiting is a primary activity of urban dwelling.

(d)   Desire for kinship visiting is strong, especially among middle-class families.

(e)   The extended family structure still performs important recreational, ceremonial and economic functions.

(f)   The view that the extended family disintegrates because of lack of contact is unsupported by evidence.

3   Litwak (*Geographic Mobility and the Extended Family*)

He has developed the concept of a modified extended family to deal with the difficulty of describing the family structure of contemporary industrial societies. It is composed of nuclear families bound together by affectional ties and by choice. The modified extended family functions to facilitate the achievement and mobility goals of the various families involved. He concludes that the extended family as a structure does exist in modern urban society in the sense that family members may not live in close proximity to each other, but they do have frequent contact and supply mutual aid to each other. Sussman and Burchinal comment that this concept of a modified extended family should now emerge as the one to replace the misleading one of the isolated nuclear family.

The phrase 'the typical British family' is stereotypical and is misleading.

(a)   Why is this so?

(b)   What are the consequences of this use of this stereotype?   (AEB)

Examine the view that significant changes are taking place in the family in contemporary Britain.

When people use stereotypes they are building an image which they believe to be true, of the person, group or institution. It is based on a few pieces of information and helps to make a complex issue simple and understandable. The stereotype of 'the typical British family' in the last quarter of the twentieth century would be two parents and one or two children living independently of their relatives. The family unit is democratically managed with a proportion of wives going out to work . . .

The stereotype of the Victorian family is of a large family unit headed by the eldest male, stable and unified.

This is misleading because research suggests that there never has been a time when there has been a 'typical' structure.

1   See Laslett's study (page 87).

2   Anderson in a paper in 1983 examined six popular myths about the family in the Victorian period:

(a)   The view that in that period the community was more stable. The 1851 census showed that more than 50% of the population were not living in the community in which they were born.

(b)   The view that the family was more stable.

He suggests that death created about the same proportion of broken homes as divorce does today. There were probably more broken families with dependent children in 1826 than in 1983.

(c) The view that there was more affection towards children in that period. He argues that before the late eighteenth century there was little love and affection in relations between spouses and parents and children. The novels of Dickens suggest that children had many problems in this respect in the nineteenth century.

(d) The view that Victorians were more moral.

He suggests that the illegitimacy rate was about the same as today. Also, approximately 60% of women bearing their first child in the early nineteenth century had conceived before marriage.

(e) The view that all Victorian families were large.

In 1750 the average household contained 1.8 children, in 1850, 2.0 children and in 1970, 1.1. (These figures are lower than birth-rate statistics because in earlier periods there were higher infant mortality rates; a large number of children left home early to go into service or find other work). But in the 1850s approximately 8% of households contained three or more generations. In 1970 about 4% contained three generations.

(f) The view that the modern family has less concern for the elderly. In 1906 about 6% of the population over the age of sixty-five were in poor law institutions. The majority were looked after by relatives. In 1983 about 5% are in institutions.

3   Chester (*The Family*) describes variant forms of family structure which add weight to the view that there is no 'typical' British family. In 1979 12% of families were one-parent type, of which 95% were female-headed.

Divorce is one of the major causes of variant forms.

Housing conditions of lone parents

Rented	72%
Flats	28%
No central heating	48%

(a) At the community level such families tend to suffer many problems: They are more likely to be stigmatised; to be more vulnerable to intervention by neighbours, officials etc.; to suffer social isolation; have low living standards.

(b) The re-constituted family: re-marriage is the commonest outcome of divorce. But where children are concerned this creates step-relationships. These, too, have problems of social credentials. They may appear 'odd' through an incongruous collection of children or because of complications of surnames and kin networks.

(c) He concludes that failure to adapt to the consequences of these changes means that confusions and ambiguities in concepts of the family, which produce social problems, will remain.

What are the factors which affect the conjugal role relationships in the modern family?

Using information drawn from any studies describe and account for the relationships which sociologists have observed between family life and social-class membership.

Bott (*Family and Social Network*) analysed different relationships between husbands and wives in relation to their family networks. These are the connections that each spouse has with friends, organisations, place of work etc. She distinguishes between two types:

(*a*) Segregated roles in which husband and wife carry out most of their leisure activities independently of each other.

(*b*) Joint conjugal roles in which they share most activities and equality in all their dealings. In the home there is much division of labour, shared interests and friends in common.

▶ *Factors affecting role relationships and patterns of behaviour in the family*:

1 Network theory suggests that the degree of segregation in role relationships varied with the connectedness of the family networks. The more this was connected, the greater was the segregation of roles. The more this was dispersed, the greater was the likelihood of joint or shared roles between husband and wife.

Points of criticism: (*a*) The sample was very small (twenty families in greater London).

(*b*) Measures of connectedness are hard to establish.

(*c*) The class factor may be relevant in analysis.

2 Many studies have been conducted to try to establish the significance of social class in conjugal relationhips.

▶ *Working-class families*:

1 Willmott and Young (*Family and Kinship in East London*).

They noted that localised working-class extended family groups spread over two or more nearby houses was a distinctive feature of kinship in the East End. Families had long-standing roots in the area. There was a strong stress on the mother-daughter tie, manual workers seeming to have more need for the extended family as 'a woman's trade union'. Roles were largely segregated.

2 Kerr (*The People of Ship Street*)

She notes how the pattern in this working-class area was for the woman to take her husband home to live with or near her mother. 'I couldn't get on without me mother . . . I could get on without me husband. I don't notice him . . .'

3 Klein (*Samples from English Culture*)

She says that just as industrial conflict is endemic, so is conflict in the home in lower-working-class families. Disagreements were often found to be concerned with money. The wife's role was defined in terms of her husband's convenience, much as his role was defined in terms of management's convenience. She noted that there tended to be a lack of give and take in relationships and an unusually rigid division of labour in the household.

▶ *Middle-class families*:

1 Willmott and Young (*Family and Kinship*)
Their study also included an analysis of middle-class families and conjugal relationships in Woodford. They noted that far fewer people there lived close to their parents. There was less day-to-day inter-action between them. The population was more geographically mobile and relationships between spouses more democratically based.

2 Hubert (*Kinship*)
He found that the informants (and particularly the women in the sample) tended to be independent of parents before they married. This contrasted with the working-class situation, in which a girl tends to live at home until married. He suggests that middle-class children are taught the virtues of independence at an early age, which encour-ages mobility.

3 Bell (*Middle-Class Families*)
He also found that young middle-class couples asserted their independence, making help between mother and daughter less likely, but a greater sense of companionship between spouses more so.

Concluding points:

1 There is a danger of over-stating the differences between middle- and working-class families. Rosser and Harris (see page 87) found little difference in patterns of behaviour between the two groups.

2 The concept of class is a complex one and authors need to specify more clearly which social groups they are including in their categories.

3 Although 'independence' from kin seems to be a dominant norm among middle-class families, Lupton and Wilson (*The Social Back-ground of Top Decision-Makers*) have shown that among upper-class families kinship ties are important and 'alliances' between rich families are frequent through marriage.

4 In child-rearing, classes 1 and 2 are likely to be better informed and more able to seek advice and act on it, and to attend parent-teacher meetings etc.

5 It is a complex problem to interpret the effects of social factors on behaviour but there is evidence to show that class values do vary and that the differences have important consequences for the relation-ships between husband and wife and parents and children.

6 Some feminist writers dispute the extent to which conjugal roles have become more democratic even in middle-class families.

SOME FEMINIST PERSPECTIVES ON THE FAMILY

'The most important influences in the sociology of the family in recent years have come from the work of feminist writers.' Outline and discuss some of their contributions.

1   Oakley has presented a range of arguments in several of her books and articles which seek to explain the exploited position of women in contemporary society:

(*a*)   She presents evidence to show that gender roles are culturally not biologically determined.

(*b*)   There is no evidence to show that there are some tasks solely performed by women in all societies (except childbirth).

(*c*)   Although there has been a steady growth in the number of women in the work force they are still expected to maintain their role as housewife, which has remained their primary role.

(*d*)   The role of men has always been more important outside the home, so encouraging their position as 'breadwinner'.

(*e*)   Women's primary role as 'housewife' ensures that they remain subordinate to men, making it difficult for them to pursue careers.

(*f*)   This also leads to the increasing geographical and social immobility of women.

(*g*)   The housewife role, which is exclusively allocated to women, has no status, is unpaid and alienating and takes precedence over all other roles.

(*h*)   Her conclusion is that the only way that women will gain freedom and be able to develop fully as individuals in society is for the abolition of the role of housewife, the sexual division of labour and the family itself as it is presently understood and structured.

2   Barnard (*The Future of the Family*) sees marriage as a key factor limiting the potential of women:

(*a*)   Marriage is particularly beneficial for men. They are more likely than single men to have successful careers, high incomes and high-status occupations.

(*b*)   Wives, on the other hand, are found to express marital dissatisfaction more frequently than men, since they gain least. They suffer more illness than single women. They initiate divorce proceedings more frequently than men.

(*c*)   It is invariably the wife, rather than the husband, who makes the adjustments and compromises in marriage. Her self-image deteriorates as she accommodates to her husband's needs at the expense of her own.

3   Sharpe (*Just like a Girl*) discusses the significance of the educational system in shaping a girl's self-image.

(*a*)   The school curriculum is gender based.

(*b*)   Girls are discouraged from studying science subjects by the attitudes of teachers as well as of male pupils.

(c)   The girls' eventual attitude to work is reflected in their school experiences. They favour office work, bank work, nursing, shop work. They do not select engineering, top professional occupations etc.

(d)   She found that the girls in her study tended to 'lack confidence, opportunity and desire to challenge the strict divisions of work . . .' They were inhibited by the dominant norms of what was and was not considered to be 'women's work'.

4   Friedl (*Women and Men*) puts forward a possible explanation for the male dominance in families and for the sexual division of labour, based on anthropological data.

(a)   She notes that in societies where certain tasks are assigned to males they carry more prestige than the same tasks assigned to females in other societies.

(b)   She argues that male dominance arises from the fact that they have greater access to highly valued roles in the society and they can control the exchange of goods and materials.

▶   *Comment*:

The work of these female writers (some of whom have a strong political commitment to change in the social structure of society) may be considered to be too ideological and not sufficiently value-free or objective. However, the same argument may be raised against those male writers whose work has previously predominated. In this respect the women researchers do present an alternative to the more traditional view of, for example, Talcott Parsons, that the 'expressive female role' in the family (to provide love, care and affection for members) is a functional necessity for its stability and cohesion and that this justifies their submissive and subordinate role in society and in the family.

THEORETICAL PERSPECTIVES

The picture of the family as functional both for its members and for society has come under strong criticism. Outline the functionalist analysis of the family and discuss major criticisms of this analysis.

THE FUNCTIONALIST PERSPECTIVE

1   The effectiveness of the family is seen in relation to its ability to carry out functions which are essential to the maintenance of the stability and perpetuation of society.

2   The essential functions include:
(a)   caring for the emotional needs of members
(b)   the provision of a secure home
(c)   the socialisation of the young
(d)   the reproduction of the species

(e)   the stabilisation of adult personalities.

3   As society becomes more highly evolved so institutions specialise in fewer functions. The state introduces specialist organisations which remove some functions from the family (e.g. schools, hospitals).

4   The social system is in harmony when all the parts function efficiently. There is said to be a functional relationship between the isolated nuclear family and the economic system. This is considered to be the most functional unit for modern industrial society.

5   The isolated nuclear family provides a socially and geographically mobile work force to meet the changing economic needs of society.

6   It is also functional in that members gain status from their levels of achievement and success. These are crucial in an industrial society. In a 'static' extended family differentials in levels of achievement between family members could give rise to conflict, which would be dysfunctional.

7   The role of the woman in the family is functional when she plays an 'expressive' role, providing care and affection for members.

8   Because the family is isolated from wider kin this ensures closer and warmer relations between husband and wife (joint conjugal roles).

9   The family becomes more specialised in its functions (although some writers, such as Fletcher (*Family and Marriage*) have argued that the family's functions have increased in modern society since there are more duties and obligations to be fulfilled).

Points of criticism of the functionalist view: 1   The concept of the isolated nuclear family may be over-stated (see Litwak).

2   There is evidence to show that the extended family has not disappeared in the way predicted by functionalists in modern society (see Sussman and Burchinal; Rosser and Harris).

3   It may be that industrial societies do not require greater geographical mobility than non-industrial societies. Many workers commute long distances to their places of work.

4   There is some evidence to suggest that there were large movements of population in pre-industrial times.

5   Some research suggests that levels of social mobility are limited in modern industrial society, especially in times of high levels of unemployment.

6   Short-range social mobility may have been more common in pre-industrial times than functionalists assume.

7   The view that there is greater joint conjugal role relations in modern industrial society may be over-stated (see comments of Oakley).

8   There is evidence that the nuclear family was a prominent form of family organisation in pre-industrial England.

9   The view presents a conservative stance and suggests that the nuclear family must be the best possible organisation. Such authors start from a committed defence of the family.

THE MARXIAN VIEW

How far do you agree with the claim that the nuclear family is a bourgeois entity based on private gain and oppression?

---

1   During the earliest stages of human development the forces of production were communally owned and the independent family unit did not exist. The society was the family.

2   As a result of evolutionary development the family slowly emerged as a social institution together with the concept of private property and class divisions.

3   The defence of the family by religious doctrines and legal enactments was encouraged by the ruling elite. Structures were necessary in order to ensure the transmission of wealth usually through the male line, to direct family members. The male domination of the family helped ensure the paternity of off-spring.

4   In contemporary society the family is seen by Marxist writers as a means of producing a supply of labour; women remain a particularly exploited group working to maintain the home and in the lowest-paid occupations in the economy.

5   The role of the woman is to maintain the household and to ensure that her husband works efficiently. She helps absorb his frustrations and disappointments in work.

6   The need to support a family ensures that workers act in responsible ways. They have duties and responsibilities.

7   The home provides a place in which the worker can relax away from the dangers and discontents of work.

8   Children are socialised into the norms of the capitalist system. They learn to be passive and not to be critical of the social structure.

9   In recent years some attention has been focussed on the extent to which the blue-collar worker has become more 'privatised' (home-centred). This can also be interpreted by Marxist writers as a means of ensuring the survival of the existing society. Lack of interest in communal activities inhibits the possibility of frequent dangerously unsettling collective action.

▶   *For Marxists, the solution may lie in*:
    (*a*)   Changing the family structure. Leach (*A Runaway World*) argues that what is needed is a more communal type of structure in which children could grow up in larger units with more emphasis on the community.
    (*b*)   Changing the social structure. Cooper (*The Death of the Family*) argues that the family acts as 'an ideological conditioning device' and that an exploitive family produces an exploitive society. He suggests that only in an egalitarian society can people be truly free to develop themselves and their talents fully.

Points of criticism: 1   All Marxist writers start from an ideological position that condemns the family as an agency of capitalist values.

2 There is always an emphasis on the needs of the individual rather than society as a whole.

3 Such writers advocate a new social order without specifying how social life will be organised when this is achieved.

4 The view assumes that there will be a natural orderliness in social relations arising out of those previously imposed by forces of exploitation.

5 All the social ills of society are seen to stem from the destructive aspects of the family system, which is an institution operating in the interests of the ruling class. This can be regarded as a narrow view of the sources of disorder.

6 The view does not explain the similarities in family structure in capitalist and non-capitalist societies and why divorce and violence occur in them also.

MARRIAGE AND DIVORCE

CONTENTS

The questions on this topic tend to relate to the following areas:

1   The social significance of marriage:
    (a)   Pre-industrial societies.
    (b)   Industrial societies.
2   The problems of assessing the stability of marriage in modern society.
3   Factors affecting increasing divorce rates:
    (a)   Opportunities to escape marriage.
    (b)   Increased conflict in families.
    (c)   Changing values with regard to marriage.
4   Variations in divorce rates between different groups:
    (a)   The factors associated with these variations.
    (b)   The possible consequences of divorce.
5   Trends in divorce:
    (a)   Contemporary data.
    (b)   Theoretical perspectives.

THE SIGNIFICANCE OF MARRIAGE

From a comparison between at least two different types of societies what would you say is the sociological significance of marriage?   (Lon)

Every society must have its population replaced by new generations. Marriage is an institution which ties two people (in some societies where polygamy is practised, more than two) by legal or customary bonds which establish rights and duties between them. It is a means whereby the population is reproduced in a socially acceptable way in some societies. In others (e.g. Tikopia) a marriage follows the birth of the first child. When the woman becomes pregnant then the couple settle down in a permanent and recognised union.

Non-industrialised societies

1   In some, marriage serves the interests of the entire family group. It helps to establish alliances between them and to ensure their survival. (This may also be true to some extent among the very rich families of industrial societies. See Lupton and Wilson.)
2   In societies where marriages are arranged and the husband's family must pay a large sum for his wife to her family, then the marriage

bond may be even more significant. Such marriages are difficult to break because of the complications in their arrangement.

3   In some patrilineal societies, such as Tikopia, a marriage is important as a means of ensuring off-spring who help to expand kin groups. All land is passed through the male line. When a man has left behind him sons who have settled down and have left descendants, the group is recognised as 'a house'.

4   In other patrilineal societies there is a custom called the 'levirate'. If a married man dies his widow may be taken over by one of his brothers or some other close kinsman. The wife is still regarded as being married to her dead husband and any children she may later have are regarded as his. If the wife dies at a young age then one of her sisters may be taken as a replacement.

5   In such societies marriage is important as an institution which serves the interests of the social group not those of the individual.

Marriage in industrial society

1   In modern Britain the emphasis is on the benefits for the individuals concerned.

2   Attitudes towards marriage are different in that people expect emotional gratification, companionship and security, rather than simply the production of heirs. These expectations are not always met, which may help to account for the high divorce rate.

3   However, where there are children these may be raised by both parents, in a democratic arrangement, by a single parent or by the mother and daughter in close harmony (as described by Willmott and Young).

4   Statistics from OPCS show that 95% of women and 91% of men have been married by the age of forty.

5   In Britain monogamous marriage ('a voluntary union of one man with one woman for life') has traditionally been defended by the Christian moral code and the legal system. It is therefore significant as a long-standing central institution which affects social roles, attitudes and behaviour. It is marked by a wide-ranging set of rituals.

6   The Finer Committee on One-Parent Families (1974) commented that 'marriage must be drawing into the institution large numbers who lack any evident vocation for it. . .'

7   The popular and stereotypical image of the family as a married couple with one or two children is mistaken. This now only represents about 25% of all households. About 15% of households are occupied by single pensioners and about one in eight families are one-parent households.

8   Although marriage remains a popular institution (the proportion of marriages involving the previously divorced is one in three in 1985), nevertheless there is evidence that an increasing number of people are choosing to cohabit rather than marry.

Concluding points: Marriage serves different functions in different types of society. Its strength and fragility may also vary. In pre-industrial societies marriage is primarily a means for strengthening links between kin groups. In industrial societies the needs of the individual are more to the fore. The stability of the marriage may be related to the lack of expectations about love, affection and companionship; for example, where the marriage is arranged and large sums of money are involved. Instability is more likely in marriages which link individuals in a more personal way; in relationships based on choice. This may be unfortunate in view of the norm that most married couples are expected to produce children.

THE STABILITY OF MARRIAGE IN MODERN BRITAIN

Assess the view that increases in rates of divorce, illegitimacy, the growing acceptance of pre-marital sex, common-law marriages and homosexual unions are all indicative of the impending breakdown of family life in modern society.

It is always difficult to assess the extent to which marriage and family life is more or increasingly less stable now than at some time in the past. The main problems are:

(*a*)   Finding an adequate measure of stability.

(*b*)   Knowing enough about families of the past in order to make useful comparisons.

(*c*)   The difficulty of using statistical measures in that they may be hard, if not impossible, to obtain. For example, it is doubtful if the number of homosexual unions is recorded. Also, where they are recorded they may not have been collected for long, making comparisons with earlier historical periods almost impossible.

CHANGING ATTITUDES TOWARDS MARRIAGE

1   Urwin (*Can the Family Survive?*; 1944) wrote 'the family in the modern world, by many signs and tokens, is in a perilous state. Critical observers declare that it is disintegrating and tending to disappear . . .' He saw the disintegrating influences as the demand that women were making for equality in work, the 'modern preoccupation with sex . . . almost amounting to an obsession . . . and the decline in the influence of the church.'

These comments suggest that every generation is concerned that the family is becoming less stable.

2   Divorce rates have increased for many reasons. But it cannot be assumed that marriages were necessarily more stable when there were fewer divorces. We do not know how many unhappy and unstable marriages existed which were not broken by divorce.

3   Other measures may be equally difficult to interpret.

	1901	1921	1951	1961	1971	1976	1980	1981
(1000s) Decrees absolute granted (UK)	1	3	30	27	80	136	160	157
Marriages	300	360	400	387	447	396	409	388
Crude birth rate (per 100 live births)	30	23	16	18	16	12	13	13
Average family size	3.3	2.23	2.3	2.2	2.0	1.9	2.0	2.0
Women workers as % of labour force	19.0	29.0	30.0	32.0	36.0	40.0	42.0	42.0

The statistics are open to a range of possible interpretations. But as far as the future of the family is concerned:

1 Marriage rates have fluctuated over a long period. But the decline in the birth rate that started in the mid 1960s will mean that there is a reduction in the number of people of marriageable age for the rest of the decade.

2 There was about a 5% fall in the number of marriages between 1980 and 1981.

3 Average family size has remained stable for a long period even though the number of women in the work force has steadily increased.

Extra-marital conceptions	1971	1981
Total number of illegitimate births	208,000	245,000
% of births conceived before marriage	38%	20%
% of illegitimate births	35%	36%
% of abortions	26%	43%

These statistics indicate that:

1 Between 1971 and 1981 the total number of conceptions outside marriage in Great Britain rose. This reflects an increase of about 25% in the population of single women rather than an increase in rates of extra-marital conceptions.

2 There has been little change in the proportion of extra-marital conceptions which end in illegitimate births over the period.

3 The fact that there has been an increase in the number of abortions does not necessarily mean less family stability, since it could be argued that the birth of an unwanted child could subsequently increase the chances of instability in later relationships.

4 Dyer and Berlins (*Living Together*) suggest that there has been an increase in the numbers of people cohabiting and forming 'common-law' marriages. Statistics from OPCS suggest that couples marrying

in the late 1970s were three times more likely to have lived together before marriage as couples who married at the beginning of the decade. One in ten of all non-married couples are thought to be cohabiting (an estimated 330,000 women under the age of fifty.) However, the authors suggest that marriage frequently becomes an acceptable option to such people, especially if they decide to have children. The institutions of state tend to recognise personal relationships only through a marriage contract.

NB: A point not raised in the question but which could be debated as another possible indication of instability in family life is the level of conflict and violence which has been observed. Consider the material discussed in relation to the following question.

VIOLENCE IN THE FAMILY

How can violence in the family be explained sociologically?

1   Dobnash and Dobnash (*Violence Against Wives*) argue that:
    (*a*)   Attacks by husbands on wives are increasingly common. About 25% of all serious assaults in the criminal statistics of indictable offences are of this type.
    (*b*)   The statistics may underestimate the full amount since many attacks may go unrecorded.
    (*c*)   The police are often reluctant to intervene in domestic disputes.
    (*d*)   The penalties for such attacks are relatively low.
    (*e*)   Such violence could be explained in terms of 'power relations' in a marriage. In using aggression of a physical sort men are displaying their power. This is supported by widely accepted social norms which tend to accept that the male is, and ought to be, the dominant partner. The association between masculinity and self-esteem promotes in a working-class culture sexist attitudes to women in the home.
    (*f*)   Violence against women can also be seen as a reflection of the wider social inequalities that exist in the society between the sexes.
    (*g*)   This would be a line of argument supported by such writers as Oakley and Freidl and one that runs counter to the views of Willmott and Young in *The Symmetrical Family*.

2   Laing (*The Politics of the Family*) argues that violence in a family can stem from the complicated relationships which develop. He is particularly concerned with the psychological violence that results in the destruction of personalities. Bizarre behaviour may be the individual's response to an intolerable social situation. It is labelled as 'madness' because it makes no sense to observers, although it may have meaning for the actor.

3   Leach (*A Runaway World*) puts forward the view that the stress and conflict between husband and wife and parents and children arises

from life in small nuclear families with their 'narrow privacy and tawdry secrets'. He argues that the result is that when parents and children are forced to live in this oppressive way, they take too much out of each other, 'the parents fight, the children rebel'. His theme was directed to the conclusion that contemporary family life incubates hate which finds expression in conflict. Writing more recently (1982) he confirmed his earlier view when he wrote of present family life resulting in 'claustrophobia for all' and that 'the English continue to rear their children cooped up in boxes like battery hens. . .'

4   NSPCC Report 1985. This stated that marital conflict was the biggest single factor in child abuse. Parents often seemed ignorant of the effect of their quarrels. Between 1977 and 1983 the NSPCC found that marital discord featured in 57% of their cruelty cases.

5   See also the points raised in the theoretical perspectives.

FACTORS AFFECTING INCREASING DIVORCE RATES

Examine the major causes of the increasing frequency of divorce in Britain.

There are four categories of marital breakdown:

Divorce This is the legal termination of marriage following a decree absolute. The couple are then free to re-marry.

Legal separation The partners separate but the marriage continues to exist. There are no reliable statistics available.

Desertion One partner leaves the family. The marriage remains until a decree absolute is obtained. Reliable figures for desertion are also difficult to obtain, but Chester (*Divorce*) suggests that separations and desertions are both increasing.

Empty-shell marriages The couple live together but there is no love, affection or economic support provided by either partner.

In answering any question it is always useful to look for a structure which you can impose on the question in order to ensure your material is well organised. In this case there is a useful analysis by Hart which offers such a structure.

Hart (*When Marriage Ends*)

She suggests that there are three factors to consider in an analysis of increasing divorce rates.

THE OPPORTUNITIES TO ESCAPE MARRIAGE

Increases in trends in divorce have tended to follow changes in divorce legislation. At the turn of the century divorce was still comparatively expensive and therefore available mainly to the rich. The poor tended to rely on separation orders.

1909 The Royal Commission on Divorce recommended a simplification of procedure and an extension of grounds for divorce.

1923 Matrimonial Causes Act enabled a wife to obtain a divorce on the grounds of her husband's adultery, without having to prove some other offence in addition, which had been the case since 1857.

1937 The Herbert Act further extended grounds, to include incurable insanity, cruelty and desertion for three years or more.

1949 The Legal Aid Act enabled those with low incomes to be provided with assistance to cover legal costs.

1950 Matrimonial Causes Act introduced new grounds for a decree of nullity of a marriage (e.g. non-consummation; being of unsound mind).

1969 Divorce Reform Act. This introduced the concept of the 'irretrievable breakdown of marriage'. This occurs when:
(a)   The partners have ceased to cohabit for two years and neither objects to a divorce.
(b)   They have separated for five years and one person has objected to a divorce. This objection is then overruled.
(c)   Where there is conduct which a husband or wife cannot reasonably be expected to endure.
(d)   But the Act states that no divorce can be obtained until the court is satisfied that the best possible arrangements have been made for the children of the marriage.

1970 The Matrimonial Proceedings and Property Act. This provides guidelines to judges in the award of financial settlements. It is based on the idea that the parties should be placed in the financial position in which they would have been if the marriage had not broken down.

1984 The Matrimonial and Family Proceedings Act. This removed some of the maintenance obligations on husbands to former wives. Now maintenance may be for a set period and may relate to the conduct of the parties. Under this Act there is an absolute bar of one year before any couple can apply for a divorce. The main consideration remains the welfare of the children.

Comment: It is not so much that legislation causes divorce rates to increase but more that the increase results from the fact that the couple who are not happily married can now obtain grounds for a divorce. The new law provides a solution to a marriage that has already disintegrated.

OPPORTUNITIES FOR INCREASED CONFLICT AND STRESS

These could be examined under the following headings:

Industrialisation The adaptation of the family to the requirements of an industrialised economic system may have generated more stress.

Work may be increasingly difficult to obtain; for those in work it may lack intrinsic interest; expectations for higher living standards may increase; there may be more pressure on women to run a home and seek employment.

Urbanisation Cities are often overcrowded and housing is unsatisfactory. There are problems in travelling to work and school on busy roads. There may be less sense of community and greater alienation and anomie in cities (see pages 000). See also comments of Leach and Laing (pages 000).

Secularisation The decline in the significance of religion in people's lives may have helped divorce to become more socially acceptable. Marriage loses its 'sacramental' quality. In 1977 there were more civil than church weddings for the first time since records started in 1832.

CHANGING VALUES CONCERNING MARRIAGE

There are some functionalist writers (e.g. Fletcher: *The Family and Marriage*) who argue that people are increasingly expecting more from marriage than couples in the past. There is an emphasis on companionship and shared experiences. Those who fail to achieve these may be more inclined to break the marriage in order to attain them with another partner. On this view a high divorce rate reflects the high standards which people have of marriage.

Oakley argues that the benefits that men and women gain from marriage are different. Whilst there is inequality in wider society then there will be inequality in the home. One result is that women's changing role is also a significant factor in the rising divorce rates. Women file more than two thirds of all petitions for divorce. Ross and Sawhill conducting research in the USA found that the higher the wife's annual income the greater the probability that the couple would separate.

Comment:

It could be argued that it is not the employment of women that necessarily causes divorce. It may be more likely that this makes it possible, in that women who are unhappy in their marriage are more likely to look for satisfaction in their occupation. Having a well-paid job gives them economic independence which makes divorce feasible if the couple are unhappy in their marriage.

VARIATIONS IN DIVORCE RATES

Account for variations in the divorce rates between different groups. What have been the major social consequences of these increases?

The occurrence of divorce is unevenly distributed in society. It affects different classes, age groups and occupational groups in different ways. These variations can be discussed in terms of the social structure of society. The problems of the consequences of divorce are open to different interpretations according to the perspective from which it is viewed. Functionalists may have one answer and Marxists another.

▶ Variation in divorce rates:

Age at marriage The younger the age of marriage the higher the rate of divorce. Teenage marriage is especially vulnerable.
(*a*)   Young married couples face greater economic difficulties than older people.
(*b*)   A high proportion of these are to legitimate a pregnancy.
(*c*)   As they grow older they may be more inclined to grow apart with different interests and expectations.

Class differences The highest divorce rates occur among those groups at the bottom of their respective social classes. The highest rates are found in the lower middle class and lower working class. This may be because members are subject to more economic and social pressures.

Cultural differences The chances of marital breakdown are increased if spouses have different social or cultural backgrounds. It may be difficult for cross-class or cultural marriage partners fully to appreciate or understand aspects of behaviour, belief etc.

Occupation Studies have indicated that there is a relationship between occupations requiring frequent separation from a spouse and high divorce rates (e.g. travelling salesman, lorry driver etc.). It may also be true among those who have a high involvement in their work and a low involvement in their home life (e.g. executives, lecturers, artists etc.).

Children in the family There is debate among researchers as to this factor. Thornes and Collard (*Who Divorces*?) found that marriages which end up in divorce were twice as likely to be childless as those which did not. However, Dominion and Abrams (Social Science Research Council) suggest that there is a sharp fall in happiness once children arrive, which is never recaptured.

THE POSSIBLE CONSEQUENCES OF DIVORCE

Chester (*Divorce*) argues that society has never fully accommodated itself to the consequences of mass divorce because it has not resolved its attitudes towards the phenomena itself. Governments seem undecided about how to cope with the fact that life-long monogamy is no longer pursued by about one third of the population. The result, he says, is a succession of contradictory policies.

1   There is a need to re-structure social services to meet the needs of mass divorce; although it could be argued that this could be seen as the abandonment of the family.

2   Social security schemes seem uncertain as to whether they should encourage remarriage, employment or the full-time care of children.

3   From a functionalist perspective, the family may be seen as less stable since individuals are not able to find security, identity and *emotional satisfaction*.

4   Studies by Bloom and Lynch in the USA claim to have found correlations between broken marriages and high levels of stress; increased health problems; increased psychiatric problems as well as higher rates of alcoholism and suicide.

5   Wallerstein and Kelly (*Surviving the Breakup*) note high levels of disturbance in young children whose parents divorce. They claim that in the USA, of children appearing in psychiatric clinics, more than 80% come from broken families.

6   Illsley and Thompson (*Women from Broken Homes*) argue that the term 'broken home' must be interpreted with care. There is no general agreement as to what constitutes a broken home. It can result from death, desertion, separation, imprisonment, hospitalisation or divorce. Some are broken permanently, some for brief periods. Little is known about the extent or significance of these different types of broken home. Effects may vary between age, sex and type of broken home.

    As far as the consequences of divorce are concerned they argue that:

    (*a*)   Broken homes of this type do not possess the monopoly of childhood unhappiness.

    (*b*)   Some children may be better off when removed from an unhappy home atmosphere and placed in a stable one-parent family.

    (*c*)   In general, where parental relationships are disturbed then those between parents and children are also likely to be unsatisfactory.

7   There will be an increase in the number of one-parent families. In 1984 one family in eight (with 1.5 million children) is of this type. Also numbers in care have increased from 62,000 in 1961 to 105,000 in 1981.

8   A further consequence of the increase in the divorce rate may be to increase the tendency to avoid marriage.

    (*a*)   Dyer and Berlins (*Living Together*) conducted a survey which indicated that there was an increasing tendency towards cohabitation rather than marriage. Their survey estimated that in 1979 more than one third of a million couples were living together unwed. Nearly a quarter of single women and two thirds of divorced women marrying between 1977 and 1979 had lived with their husbands before marriage.

    (*b*)   Chelin (*Marriage, Divorce and Remarriage*) also notes the rise in cohabitation, not only in Britain but other European countries also. In Denmark, one in three of all people in their early twenties are living with someone. The figure is higher in Sweden. In the USA it is estimated that there was a 40% increase in the numbers between 1977 and 1979.

▶ Their explanations for these changing attitudes include:
(a)   A loss of belief in the value of marriage.
(b)   Marriage is no longer seen as an ultimate objective in a relationship.
(c)   Financially, it can pay to remain 'single'. The tax system works to their advantage.
(d)   A break in such a relationship is easier to achieve than the complications and expense of a divorce.
(d)   Having children is seen less and less as a reason for marrying.
(e)   There is less opposition and social stigma attached to cohabitation.
(f)   Common-law wives can claim a share in the family home following a break in the relationship, if they can show that they have made a contribution to it, by paying a part of the mortgage for example.

9   Chester concludes that the main problem facing Britain is not the high rate of divorce but the failure of our society to organise itself to meet the problems raised by marital breakdown.

TRENDS IN DIVORCE

Outline some of the trends in divorce in recent years. Is divorce functional?

To answer any question on the trends in divorce you must be familiar with the statistics. Apart from relevant points already mentioned you should also note the following details:

1   In recent years divorce seems to have levelled off at about 150,000 p.a. (one marriage in three).
The reasons include:
(a)   Fewer teenage marriages.
(b)   Fewer early births in marriage.
(c)   Fewer pre-marital conceptions.
(d)   Increased rates of cohabitation.
(e)   The high rates of unemployment in the 1980s makes separation or divorce difficult, since jobs, housing etc. are hard to obtain.

2   In 1981 for the first time in thirty years the number of marriages involving at least one divorced person dropped. In one marriage in six both partners were remarrying.

3   There is a continuing trend towards later marriage (men 24.1, women 21.9).

4   Between 1971 and 1981 the median duration of marriage ending in divorce remained at about ten years. In that period there was about a 4% increase in divorce among those over thirty-five.

5   In 1980 more than £5 million was paid out each week in SB to about 250,000 families unsupported after separation or divorce.

6   The OPCS (1984) noted that the divorce rates among the unemployed were almost double the national rate among those under the age of forty and nearly four times the national average in families where a husband lost his job within fifteen years of retirement.

In order to answer the second half of the question it is useful to contrast two theoretical perspectives:

The Marxist view of divorce

1. In a capitalist economic system it is women in particular who are exploited. Divorce is an important means of escaping from the limitations of marriage.

2. In such an economic system, people's material aspirations are raised which encourages more women to go out to work. This places more stresses on the relationship and leads inevitably to conflict and divorce.

3. Children would not suffer the traumas of the divorce if they were brought up in a more communal environment rather than in independent nuclear families where they often become a pawn or scapegoat in the battle between the parents.

4. Marriage is seen as a bourgeois concept which is the product of the need in a capitalist society for a stable workforce, in which the ideology of the ruling class is transmitted form one generation to the next. Divorce is seen as a necessary institution.

The functionalist view of divorce

1. Divorce is functional in that it allows unhappy people to separate in a socially accepted way, providing protection for the partners and the children. It would become dysfunctional if the divorce rate reached exceptionally high levels, since it might then lead to social instability.

2. In general, policies are needed to protect the family and marriage in order to ensure a balance between the needs of the individual and those of society.

3. Vogel and Bell (*The Emotionally Disturbed Child as the Family Scapegoat*) argue that family conflict may be functional in that where it is directed at an emotionally disturbed child it provides a scapegoat for parental tension. Although this may be harmful to the child the relations between husband and wife may be strengthened. They can then perform their normal roles in the community. The problems their child is causing may draw them closer together.

STRATIFICATION

CONTENTS

Questions on this topic tend to fall within the following areas:

1 Forms of stratification.
2 Ways of assessing class membership.
3 Changes in the occupational structure.
4 Changes in the class structure:
   (a)   The fragmenting class structure.
   (b)   The position of white-collar workers.
   (c)   Changes in the working class.
   (d)   Changes in the middle class.
5 Theories of social stratification:
   (a)   Marxist.
   (b)   Weberian.
   (c)   Functionalist.

FORMS OF STRATIFICATION

How do slavery, caste and estate differ as forms of social stratification?   (Cam)

Cuber and Kenkel (*Social Stratification*) define stratification as 'a pattern of superimposed categories of differential privilege'. Mayer (*Class and Society*) defines it as a system of differentiation which includes 'a hierarchy of social positions whose occupants are treated as superior, equal or inferior relative to one another in socially important respects. . .'

These definitions indicate that stratification describes a society which is divided into different strata of groups whose members share similar levels of status, power or privilege. There exists a system of social inequality between the groups forming the various strata.

A society can be stratified according to a number of factors, of which class division is one associated particularly with industrialised societies; in pre-industrial societies caste, slavery and estate are predominant.

Caste stratification

(a)   The most developed case is found in Hindu India (although there are examples found elsewhere). Caste is sanctioned by religion. This legitimises the concept of 'pollution'. This means that those in an 'unclean caste' have come into contact with others in a higher caste, whose purity is thus violated. Religious rituals are necessary in order to become cleansed.

(b)   In India the main castes are the Brahmins, Rajputs, Vaishyias, Sudras and the untouchables. A person's caste determines every aspect of life: their place in the division of labour, whom they may marry, where they may live etc.

(c)   A member of a caste is never allowed to break through its rigid social and economic barriers.

(d)   In the southern states of the USA and in South Africa caste-like structures are found, and in Japan there remains a group who suffer from being regarded as social outcasts, known as the Burakumin. In Britain, many gypsies are regarded as a 'pariah' group.

Estates stratification

(a)   This was found in feudal systems of stratification.

(b)   Feudal society was characterised by a hierarchy of authority headed by a king (or emperor or pope in Europe) followed by the nobility and the commoners. These formed the three main estates.

(c)   These estates were legally defined (members having specific rights and duties); they had specific functions to perform in the society and they had political significance.

(d)   Although the system had religious backing, this was less prominent than in the case of caste society.

(e)   The system was transformed in Europe into a class system as feudalism fell into decline. Intermarriage and individual mobility between the estates was possible.

Slave society

(a)   This was found in Ancient Greece and Rome. It also became a lucrative business in the sixteenth century when Europeans transported thousands of Africans to the USA.

(b)   Slaves have no legal rights. They are the chattels of their owners.

(c)   The system represents an extreme form of legal and social inequality.

(d)   Slaves performed important economic functions, providing free forced labour.

(e)   Slavery fell into decline as it became recognised as an inefficient and immoral method of organising labour. It was abolished in British colonies in 1834 and in the USA in 1865.

Social class

(a)   MacIver (*Society; Its Structures and Changes*): 'any portion of a community which is marked off from the rest . . . by a sense of social distance'.

Weber (*Economy and Society*): 'class are aggregates of individuals who have the same opportunities of acquiring goods and the same exhibited standard of living'.

Hughes (*The Concept of Class*): 'a class is simply some collection of things grouped on the basis of at least one characteristic held in common by all members of the collection or class. . .'

Reid (Social Class Differences in Britain): 'social class is a grouping of people into categories on the basis of occupation'.

(*b*)   In summary, there is stratification by class whenever the population is divided into groups which can be ranked in superior or inferior positions on the basis of some difference of power, privilege or status. The concept of class implies something about social relationships, values, lifestyles and life chances. There is some mobility between the classes on the basis of achievement, which is not possible in a caste, slave or feudal society.

WAYS OF ASSESSING CLASS MEMBERSHIP

How far is social class position determined by level of income? Illustrate your answer with empirical evidence.

How far is occupation the major determinant of both social class and status in industrial societies?

Assessing a person's social class is a complex matter. In using the term social class, sociologists are referring to broad groups of people who can be ranked in socially superior and inferior positions on the basis of some criteria. The difficulty is agreeing on the criteria to be used. The three significant rewards of high social class are power, privilege and prestige. There are several factors which could be considered: occupation, income and wealth, status, lifestyle and life chances, family background.

OCCUPATION

However, the major criterion which has been used in most research is occupation. This has been found to be correlated to most other factors associated with class.

(*a*)   Occupations are differentially rewarded.

(*b*)   A person's occupation is a good indicator of their economic situation.

(*c*)   It takes up about two thirds of a person's life and places the individual in social situations in which there is interaction with others of a similar social type.

(*d*)   It is likely largely to determine their type of home and place of residence.

(*e*)   It tends to influence leisure activities, favoured entertainments etc.

(*f*)   It may influence the type of clothing worn.

(g)   Knowledge of a person's occupation helps us to 'make sense of them'. We 'know' how to treat them and what to expect of them.

(h)   It influences the kind of role a person plays in society and this in turn influences patterns of behaviour.

In these ways occupation is a good single indicator of a whole range of characteristics. Knowing that someone is 'a doctor' or 'an unskilled labourer' helps us make good guesses about their level of education, their likely voting behaviour, their lifestyle, life chances, income and wealth, family background etc.

For the purposes of research, the class structure is normally assessed in terms of the Registrar General's classification. Since the census of 1911 occupational groups have been grouped into a number of broad categories:

Class 1	Professional	Accountant; architect; clergyman; doctor; lawyer; university teacher.	5%
Class 2	Intermediate	Aircraft pilot; chiropodist; MP; nurse; police officer; teacher.	14%
Class 3a	Skilled non-manual	Clerical worker; draughtsman; secretary.	10%
Class 3b	Skilled manual	Driver; butcher; brick layer; cook	44%
Class 4	Semi-skilled	Bus conductor; postman; telephone operator.	17%
Class 5	Unskilled	Labourer; messenger; cleaner; porter.	6%

Source: *From Birth to Seven* Davie et al 1961

Some modifications are sometimes used which provide a finer gradation and a more comprehensive classification.

Occupational status level

1.a	Higher professional	5.	Skilled manual
b	Landed proprietors	6.	Relatively skilled manual
2.a	Intermediate professional		
b	Substantial farmers	7.	Semi-skilled manual
3.a	Lower professional	8.	Unskilled manual
b	Small proprietor		
4.a	Supervisory, service employee		
b	Self-employed (no employees)		

(Adapted from Goldthorpe *et al.: The Affluent Worker*.)

Some surveys do take account of other factors. For example, the National Survey of Health and Development classified respondents by the father's occupation as well as the social background of the mother.

INCOME AND WEALTH

There are wide differentials of income and wealth in Britain (see page 118). However, it is difficult to assess a person's class purely on the basis of this factor:

(*a*)   Many low-status occupations may provide higher rates of pay than those more highly classified by the RG (e.g. skilled manual workers may receive more than clergymen, nurses, teachers etc.).

(*b*)   High income may give high status in a particular social environment but this is not necessarily the same as high social class (see page 128).

(*c*)   Class is a complex concept which involves norms, values and attitudes. These cannot be changed or absorbed by someone overnight, so that to win the pools may not mean a change of class.

(*d*)   Some research studies suggest that this is recognised by the public: Butler and Stokes asked a sample to describe the characteristics which best established a person's class:

Middle class	% of respondents	Working class	% of respondents
Occupation	61	Occupation	74
Income	21	Income	10
Attitudes	5	Attitudes	5
Manners	5	Manners	5
Education	5	Education	5
Others	3	Others	3

(*e*)   Atkinson (*Unequal Shares*) argues that income and wealth are good indicators of class membership. He shows that the top 1% of wealth-holders own 25% of all the wealth in Britain. The top 5% own 25% of all the wealth. The bottom 90% own about 35%. These great wealth-holders form the highest social classes and hold power as a direct result of their wealth and income.

(*f*)   Lockwood (*The Black-Coated Worker*) suggests that income is not so relevant in assessing class position. In his study he wished to see how the position of the clerk had changed over time. Between 1900 and 1930 clerks earned more than manual workers. But since that time their financial position has deteriorated. Nevertheless, the clerk retains a higher social class position. He has better job security, shorter hours and more fringe benefits.

(*g*)   More recently, Townsend (*Inequality in the Work Place*) confirmed that manual workers, although often high earners, continue to suffer major disadvantages in the work place in comparison with lower paid white-collar workers.

Personal wealth

	1966	1971	1976	1979	1980	1981	1982
Percentage of wealth owned by:							
Most wealthy 1% of adult population	33	31	24	22	21	21	21
Most wealthy 2% of adult population	42	39	32	28	28	28	28
Most wealthy 5% of adult population	56	52	45	40	38	40	41
Most wealthy 10% of adult population	69	65	60	54	51	53	56
Most wealthy 25% of adult population	87	86	84	77	76	79	81
Most wealthy 50% of adult population	97	97	95	95	95	96	96

Distribution of adult population by individual net wealth

Percentage of adult population with:

	1966	1971	1976	1979	1980	1981	1982
less than £5,000	91	85	69	55	48	49	51
over £5,000	7	12	23	26	27	26	24
over £15,000	1.7	2.7	6.8	16	22	21	20
over £50,000	0.4	0.4	0.9	1.7	2.4	3.1	3.9
over £100,000		0.3	0.4	0.7	0.9	1.2	1.4
Total adult population – millions	39.2	39.8	40.5	41.1	41.4	41.9	41.9

Source: Inland Revenue

The Royal Family Official Budget

Her Majesty The Queen	£3,850,000
The Queen Mother	£334,400
HRH The Duke of Edinburgh	£186,000
Prince Andrew	£20,000
Prince Edward	£20,000
Princess Anne	£116,200
Princess Margaret	£113,100
Princess Alice	£45,800
Duke of Kent	£122,700
Duke of Gloucester	£91,100
Princess Alexandra	£117,200
Total	£5,016,500
Reimbursed by Queen	£331,000
Total	**£4,685,500**

1984–1985 Civil List: 3.5 per cent rise agreed for 1985–86

Comments:

1   The authors of *Social Trends* (14) comment that there were substantial reductions in the shares of marketable wealth of the richest groups in the early 1970s (largely because of the fall in the prices of stocks and shares). During the following years there was little change in the pattern of ownership of wealth.

2   Atkinson and Harrison argue that between 1924 and 1972 there was a trend towards greater equality in wealth distribution. This trend has been reversed since 1979.

3   Atkinson (*Unequal Shares*) argues that where there has been redistribution it has been primarily between the very rich and the rich. It is his view that the reason why wealth remains more unequally distributed

than income is because of the significance of inherited wealth in the pattern of wealth-holding.

4   In 1988 Britain's highest paid directors were Sir Ralph Halpern, £1.35m; Christopher Heath, £1.33m; and Lord Hanson, £1.2m. Where their salaries have risen they have been well ahead of inflation (5%) or average earnings (9%).

CHANGES IN THE OCCUPATIONAL STRUCTURE OF BRITAIN

Assess the effect of changes that have occurred in the occupational structure of Britain on the class structure.

Higher-grade professions There has been an overall increase in the number of males in this category, especially between 1951 and 1971. The number of females has remained fairly static, showing a slight increase in the decade 1961–71.

Employers and proprietors There has been a decline in the number of males in the category and a slightly smaller decline in the number of women within it.

Administrators and managers There has been an increase in the number of males in the group but the number of females declined between 1921 and 1931 and subsequently increased in recent years.

Lower-grade professionals There has been a steady increase in the number of males in the category, especially after 1951. There has been a similar increase in the number of women employees.

Supervisors, foremen There has been a steady increase in the number of males and females in this category.

Clerical There has been a very small increase in the number of males but it is an occupational group which has seen the greatest increase in the number of women employed.

Sales personnel and shop assistants The employment of males has fluctuated and numbers have declined since 1931. For women, there was a steady increase until 1961 when a small decline became apparent.

Skilled manual The number of skilled manual workers remained fairly constant until 1971 when the figure dipped below 30% for the first time. There has been a marked decline in the number of female workers in this group.

Semi-skilled There has been a small decline in the number of semi-skilled males but a much greater decrease in the number of females in this category.

Unskilled Whilst there was a marked rise in the number of unskilled male workers in the 1920s, there has been a subsequent falling off in their numbers to a figure below that for 1911. The number of unskilled female workers has remained fairly constant throughout the period described in the statistics.

Population trends 37 (1984): This noted large changes in the British work force over the decade 1971–81. Some of these were:

(a)   There was a significant rise in unemployment, from 1 million in 1971 to 3.2 million in 1981. It was particularly high in construction and mining (18%) and among men aged 16-19 (20%) and girls 16–19 (17%).

b Decrease in employment 1971–81		Increases in employment 1971–81	
Energy	11%	Banking and finance	26%
Agriculture	19%	Services, government and politics	6%
Food, drink, clothes, paper manufacture	22%		
Metal goods, vehicle manufacture	24%		
Mineral products, chemical manufacture	28%		

General conclusions:

There has been a growth in the highest classes. The proportion of men in classes 1 and 2 rose from 23% to 29% and of women from 17% to 22%. However, the increase in the number of women in the economy has mainly been in the clerical, lower-grade professional, supervisory and sales personnel categories. Their numbers have declined in the manual occupations. The industries that have lost jobs have been those which mainly employ males.

CHANGES IN THE CLASS STRUCTURE

Is the British class structure becoming increasingly fragmented or is class consciousness increasing?

In this century there have been many changes in the occupational structure of British society (see above).

1   Marxists have argued that society is becoming increasingly polarised between rich and poor, the proletariat and the bourgeoisie (see page 122).

2   Functionalists have argued that class divisions, although inevitable and functionally useful, have narrowed and become increasingly blurred (see pages 122–3).

3   Weberians have argued that classes are so flexible that cohesion is never likely. They form and disperse over specific issues (see pages 123–4).

CLASS CONSCIOUSNESS

1   For Marxists, class consciousness means that members of the proletariat become fully aware of their common identity and the levels of exploitation that they face. In becoming 'a class for itself' revolutionary action to obtain change becomes possible.

2   Critics of this view argue that this is becoming less true in modern Britain. For example:

(a)   Lockwood *et al* (*The Affluent Worker*) showed that manual workers were becoming more privatised; more concerned about improving their own living standards, but not necessarily by union or other mass action.

(b)   Hill (*The Dockers*) also found that dockers, like the car workers in Lockwood's study, were not class conscious and politically motivated. Although they were an example of 'the traditional working class' they also saw their work in instrumental terms, but also had a fairly home-centred private life.

Such studies suggest that among both the new and the traditional working class there is no strong evidence of radical attitudes towards class conflict in the way Marx predicted.

▶   However, in reply, Marxists might argue:

(a)   There is a problem in assessing attitudes of workers. The answers they give to questions about class attitudes may depend on the way questions are framed, who asks them and under what conditions.

(b)   Answers may also be open to a range of interpretations. These may depend on the ideologies of the interviewer and research team.

(c)   Workers may give answers which are influenced by the prevailing ideology of consensus which predominates, especially in the mass media, which tend to portray strikers or those on the left as potential social threats.

▶   Functionalists or Weberians might argue:

(a)   Even if these survey results are not accepted, there is no evidence that class consciousness is developing among working-class people in present day-to-day life. The recent miners' strike failed to unify all the miners in a concerted effort to win their case. Many miners continued to work throughout the entire year-long dispute.

(b)   Roberts (*The Fragmentary Class Structure*) has said that whilst the working class may remain an unstable and continuing challenge they do not appear to be a revolutionary threat.

Technological change has transformed the office worker into a white-collared proletarian. Do you agree with this assessment of the current class position of the white-collar worker?

There has been much debate about the class position of certain white-collar workers, especially those clerical workers who tend to be classified in Class 3a of the Registrar General's scale. Are they part of the middle or the working class?

The proletarianisation thesis

The view is put by Marxist writers that there are groups of workers whose class position is objectively working class (because they do not own the means of production) even though they may appear to be in bourgeois occupations (such as clerical workers) and have middle-class identifications. The opponents of the view argue that self perception is an important aspect of class identification, as well as the fact that the work of such groups is largely different from that of manual workers in factories.

Westergaard and Resler (*Class in a Capitalist Society*) argue that low-level white-collar workers are among the broad mass of ordinary labour 'and indeed are often well down towards the bottom of the pile. . .' They dispute the view that changes in the occupational structure have led to any major changes in the class structure of modern Britain. They would accept that the modern office worker is a white-collared proletarian, and focus particularly on the more negative aspects of technological change in the office.

▶ Some disadvantages of technological change:

(*a*)   Modern office equipment often requires fewer skills in its use.

(*b*)   There is often much noise and impersonal work conditions in large open-plan offices, where people are tied to their desks, often doing repetitive tasks.

(*c*)   Personal skills (shorthand, personal relationships etc.) are often minimised and there is less contact between the secretary and the professional for whom she works.

(*d*)   Modern technology may reduce the demand for secretaries with much training or hopes of promotion.

Opponents of the proletarianisation thesis

1 Lockwood (*The Black-Coated Worker*)

   He argues that the number of clerical workers has steadily increased throughout the century. However, the clerk appears to be in an intermediate position, trapped between classes above and below. Although there are some similarities between the work of the clerk and that of the manual worker, Lockwood suggests that the clerk has a stronger identification with the middle class, although he accepts that the position of the male clerk in particular is an ambiguous one.

2 Weir (*Wall of Darkness*)

   He notes how white-collar workers have always put high emphasis on secure and steady jobs which provide adequate income and chances of promotion. These attitudes tend to distinguish them from the more instrumental attitudes of blue-collar workers.

3 Wier and Mercer tested the thesis in a study of white-collar workers in Hull. They indicate dual findings. For many of the women workers

there was some evidence of proletarianisation, especially where they had low qualifications and suffered many of the disadvantages of the modern office. They tended to have little contact with the professional management. However, for the majority of males the reverse seemed to be true. They were more likely to enjoy chances of promotion and to identify with and have more middle-class contacts. They were less likely to be involved in routine work.

Some possible conclusions:

1 From a Functionalist Weberian perspective it could be argued that for women from a working-class background with minimum qualifications and skills, the new technologies in the office do not enhance chances of upward mobility. For others with more qualifications and skills, working in a modern office where these are valued and utilised, the chances of upward mobility are increased. This is particularly true for males.

2 From a Marxist perspective such arguments would be seen as examples of false class consciousness.

There is no working class in Britain. There are only different groups of working people. Discuss.   (Ox)

The answer to the question depends on the perspective that is adopted.

1 Marx predicted that the working class in industrial societies would become more unified as exploitation increased. Therefore, working people who do not own the means of production do form the proletariat or working class.

2 Those sociologists who tend to follow the Weberian perspective in their analysis would accept the implication of the question that the whole class structure (and not just that of the working class) has become more fluid and heterogeneous.

   (*a*) There have been major changes in the occupational structure, which has resulted in the traditional working class becoming divided into several categories whose members have little in common. Each has a different status and degree of power in the market place.

   (*b*) Dahrendorf (*Class and Class Conflict in Industrial Society*) argues that traditional class divisions are disappearing. There has been a decline in traditional working-class industries and there has been a growth in the middle-class occupational groups, especially among the bureaucrats and professions. All this makes the class picture more complex.

   (*c*) Butler and Rose put forward the embourgeoisement thesis to suggest that as affluence increased among the traditional working class, so the classes were likely to merge. Increased mobility may therefore have increased the flexibility of the class structure (see page 127).

   (*d*) Lockwood (*The Black-Coated Worker*) emphasised the importance of the subjective element in class identification. Often people identify with a class to which objectively they may not appear to belong, but nevertheless this may help to shape their behaviour (e.g. voting).

(e)   There have been both economic and social changes in the lives of people in Classes 3b, 4 and 5 which may have affected their self-perception and to some extent their objective position. For example, many have improved living standards, the opportunity to buy their own homes (including council houses); they have access to more material goods, greater legal protection in work, and higher expectations about their opportunities and quality of life.

(f)   At times of high unemployment many people may suffer downward mobility. That is, they may take work for which they are overqualified. The question then arises, are they in the class established by their present occupation or that of their first?

These arguments lead to the view that it is not possible to speak of 'the working class', since this would encompass about 60% of the population (Classes 3b, 4 and 5). Within these categories there are a range of attitudes, values and social norms.

Arguments that the classes have not merged

1   Some critics argue that all manual workers tend to suffer similar problems even though they may not have developed a unified class consciousness. They are more likely than white-collar workers to be made redundant, laid off or put on short time. Unemployment rates are higher. They have more serious illness: e.g. in 1982 35% of males and 42% of females in the unskilled category reported long-standing illness, compared with 23% of males and 21% of females in the white-collar section.

2   Sennett and Cobb (*The Hidden Injuries of Class*) are critical of the claim that workers are melting into a homogeneous society. They describe the emotionally damaging effects of social class of blue-collar workers in the USA. They note the low self-esteem with which many manual workers describe themselves. 'These feelings amount to a sense that the lower a man defines himself in society in relation to other people, the more he seems at fault. . .'

3   Lockwood and Goldthorpe (*The Affluent Worker*) reject the embourgeoisement thesis. This claims that the more affluent sections of the working class are losing their identity as a social stratum and are becoming merged into the middle class. They argue that all the factors that contribute to a person's social class have not been taken into account. They say that income and wealth are not in themselves useful measures of class position. The other factors to be considered are:

(a)   The economic aspect: manual workers have less job security etc.

(b)   The relational aspects: there is no social intermixing.

(c)   The normative aspect: the manual workers do not share the same norms or values as the white-collar workers.

(*d*)   The political aspect: the manual workers tend to see the Labour Party as the party of the working class.

The main areas of convergence between the classes is in terms of their shared preference for increasingly privatised lifestyles. These workers are described by the authors as 'the new working class'.

It is now more realistic to talk about the middle classes rather than the middle class. Explain and discuss this view.

This question, like the previous one, invites a discussion between those sociologists who argue that there is an increasing polarisation of the classes, so that they are becoming more homogeneous, and those who dispute the view and argue that they are becoming more heterogeneous.

▶   The view that the middle class is becoming more fragmented

1   Roberts *et al.* (*The Fragmentary Class Structure*) put forward the view that it is not realistic to speak of *the* middle class since there is an increasing division into a number of different strata.

(*a*)   The results of their survey indicated that 27% of respondents had a 'middle-mass image' of society. They saw themselves as part of a middle class which made up the bulk of the population. They were trapped between a small and powerful upper class and a comparatively poor lower working class. They were mainly in the middle range income bracket.

(*b*)   19% saw themselves as a 'compressed middle class'. They perceived themselves as a narrow, threatened group, who were squeezed between two powerful classes above and below. This view was held mainly by small businessmen.

(*c*)   15% subscribed to a type of class imagery in which the social hierarchy was portrayed as a 'finely graded ladder'. No single stratum was recognised as numerically dominant. This view was most common amongst the more highly educated respondents.

(*d*)   14% held a 'proletarian image'. They tended to define themselves as working class and saw themselves as part of the largest class at the base of the stratification structure. Those holding this image were mainly routine white-collar workers. The authors argue that it is unlikely that workers will become more bourgeois in the future:

(*i*) Whilst it is true that there are factors which favour the development of middle-class attitudes amongst manual workers, none is sufficiently powerful in isolation to guarantee a bourgeois outcome.

(*ii*) The appearance of middle-class attitudes only becomes possible when a constellation of favourable circumstances coincides, but their interconnection is rare. In the researchers' sample there were only eleven such cases: i.e. a worker was affluent, an owner-occupier; had few close friends in work and had strong white-collar connections.

(*iii*) Whilst some of these features are likely to become more widespread, there seemed no grounds for believing that other favourable circumstances were increasingly common.

They concluded that the trends were not so much towards increasing middle-class attitudes and values among affluent workers, as the maintenance of working-class ethics with less emphasis on class awareness.

THEORIES OF SOCIAL CLASS STRATIFICATION

**THE MARXIST
PERSPECTIVE**

The origin of class is in the division of labour. Discuss.

1   It is the economic infrastructure which is the foundation on which the social superstructure is built.
2   The group which controls the forces of production controls the form of superstructure.
3   Classes arise from inequalities in the economic structure of society. When the means of production are in private hands this is the group which holds power.
4   Classes appear where there is the production of surplus goods in the economy whose distribution is controlled by the non-producers for their own gain.
5   Where there are no surpluses, as in simple societies, no classes can develop.
6   In a capitalist economic system the exploitation of the work force is known as alienation. Although the worker is legally free (compared with those in slave society) the workers are controlled by the employer, the pace of the work and the technology of production. There is the seed of class division in alienation.
7   Class is rooted in the economic structure of society and class conflict becomes a major source of social and historical change.
8   Class therefore refers to a whole set of relationships (economic, social and political) which determine the individual's position in the whole society.
9   Membership of a class is an objective fact, but it requires class consciousness to develop in order for people to act in a unified way to seek change.

Points of criticism:

1   There is much evidence to suggest that the manual workers of Class 3b, 4 and 5 do not form a homogeneous group; nor do they have common status, common interests or live in similar ways with similar norms and values. They do not have a common enemy in an all-powerful ruling class.
2   In contemporary society there is an increasing level of cultural home-

geneity, in that there is a common culture which cuts across classes, through television, radio, newspapers etc. The mass media help to impose shared vales.

3   Marx oversimplified a complex situation by combining together a large number of disparate people called 'the working class' (proletariat) and the 'bourgeoisie'. In fact different strata have distinctive qualities, as shown by Roberts *et al*. in *The Fragmentary Class Structure*.

4   Marx presents a model based on economic determinism. He does not allow for subjective impressions nor for the effects of status differences influencing opportunities in society.

THE WEBERIAN VIEW OF CLASS AND STATUS

The concentration of power in early capitalist society has given way to a contemporary diversity of competing groups among which none is supreme. Examine and evaluate this view.

1   Classes arise from the inequalities in the distribution of power (that is, the ability to achieve desired ends against the opposition of others).

2   Power varies between people in three key spheres:
(*a*)   Economic.
(*b*)   Social.
(*c*)   Political.

3   A person's class is determined by the position held in the economic sphere. This market position is important in explaining why some people have greater access to scarce resources than others.

4   People are in the same class when they share the same chances in the market of obtaining the scarce resources of jobs, income and property.

5   This view allows for the existence of many classes whose membership frequently changes. For example there may be:
(*a*)   Property classes (as described by Rex and Moore).
(*b*)   Acquisition classes (these will arise where people can exploit their particular skills in the economic market).
(*c*)   Educational classes (where people can exploit their intellectual skills in the market).

6   It also leads to the view that there are various types of working- and middle-class groups which emerge according to their skills and levels of power. The class position of their members is not based on any hereditary rights; it is a fluid and flexible process.

7   There are no necessarily permanent groups. The market is a place of transitory goals; groups dissolve once they are able to achieve their ends.

8 Class conflict is not an inevitable feature arising from a desire to produce a more equal society.
9 The Weberian view leads to a more pluralistic view of class than the Marxian.

Weber's concept of status

1 This refers to differences in the social sphere. It relates to a person's prestige in the eyes of others.
2 A person's social power is determined by social prestige.
3 'Status groups are stratified according to the principles of consumption of goods as represented by special styles of life. . .'
4 Class and status are different facets of the stratification system. A person with high economic power does not necessarily have high social status.
5 A person's status may be more relevant than his class in obtaining important scarce resources. Two people in the same class may have different levels of social status. It may be that the person of higher status is able to obtain the job or house.
6 Groups are not likely to form in a permanent way around status factors.

Points of criticism:
1 Weber's concept of pluralistic classes may be thought to reduce the significance of class as a tool of social analysis, since it becomes difficult to make any clear statement as to distinctions between the life chances of middle-and working-class groups.
2 His emphasis on the subjective element in class analysis means that it is the subjective perception of the individual that is relevant in assessing class membership. If people doing unskilled, low-status work claim to be middle class, then this must be considered to be relevant.
3 Weber assumes high levels of social mobility in industrial societies, making class cohesion unlikely. However, at times of high unemployment mobility is limited, which might suggest that class consciousness will develop.
4 Although Weber wishes to distinguish between class and status, critics would argue that the two correlate closely in the economic and social spheres of everyday life.

Examine the view that social stratification and social inequality are permanent, necessary and inevitable features of human society. (AEB)

Notice how this question raises arguments about the functionalist perspective. You must remember that this is only one possible interpretation. You must therefore present the functionalist views, but also some points of possible criticism, and then reach a conclusion. Consider the following points:

THE FUNCTIONALIST VIEW

1 The various parts of a society must be seen in relation to the whole to see how they contribute to the maintenance of the entire system.

2 A society has certain needs which must be fulfilled to ensure its survival. Even a system of stratification must be functional otherwise it would not exist.

3 The system of stratification derives from common social values. It is a social norm that some people are valued more highly than others. Those who perform the most important functions most effectively will gain the highest rewards and esteem.

4 Stratification is an inevitable feature of all human societies. Different forms of stratification result from the way that people are ranked according to the values of the society.

5 Such systems are valuable because they are examples of shared social values and they provide a means by which people can be motivated to achieve higher esteem in their society.

6 Inequalities in power are legitimate and socially necessary; without them societies would be inefficient.

7 Social stratification by class is the device by which the most important positions in society are filled by the most able and qualified people. Since some positions in society are more functionally important than others, they require more skill and technique. These positions must therefore have higher rewards attached to them.

Points of criticism:

1 Critics ask how it is possible to assess which positions in society are the most functionally important? Is someone earning £50,000 p.a. five times more important than someone who earns £10,000 p.a.?

2 There are many people in low-paid jobs who are functionally very important for society (e.g. nurses).

3 Differentials in pay seem more likely to be related to differences in power rather than functional value.

4 It may be that social stratification actually inhibits mobility rather than being a source of encouragement. (The unskilled worker may believe he lacks the ability to improve his social position.) The functionalist view tends to assume that it is easy for someone to step outside their cultural norms and respond to 'the incentives of the market place'.

5 Social stratification may not integrate people more closely into their society, but widening inequalities may become dysfunctional, encouraging conflict and distrust.

Thomas (Guildhall Lecture, 1982) said that Britain should prevent an under-class being created in its cities. He pointed out that in the USA such a group, largely comprising members of minorities, had emerged despite progress in racial advancement in the past two decades. People were trapped in a continuing web of poverty; the members could become a menace to people and property, and hostility to all under-class stereotypes was created.

6 Consider a Marxist interpretation, which denies that class divisions are inevitable or necessary.

CHAPTER EIGHT

SOCIAL MOBILITY

CONTENTS

Questions on this topic cover the following main areas:
1   The problems of definition and of measuring the extent of mobility.
2   The trends in mobility (statistical details).
3   The effects of mobility on the class structure.
4   The influence of education on mobility patterns.
5   Theoretical perspectives: is Britain an open society?

THE PROBLEMS OF ASSESSING THE EXTENT OF SOCIAL MOBILITY

Define social mobility. Examine the problems that sociologists face in studying patterns of social mobility.

In some systems of stratification people tend to be chained to a role and a category entered into at birth (e.g. caste). In others the social system appears to offer opportunities for social movement, either up or down the social scale.

Social mobility refers to any movement in the class structure over a short or long period of time. It can involve either upward or downward movement. There are normally two main types identified:

Intergenerational mobility The position of a son or daughter is compared with that of their parents. This is movement between generations, based on occupation.

Intragenerational mobility The position of individuals is compared at particular points in their careers to see whether they are moving up or down the social scale. This is movement within a generation.

There is a third type that has been discussed by some authors:

Stratum mobility While an individual may not be mobile, his social stratum might be. For example, without leaving his social class the working-class son of a working-class father may be in a social stratum which is improving its social position relative to other groups. By raising levels of admission to the occupation it may achieve higher social status.

PROBLEMS IN MEASURING MOBILITY

1 Intergenerational mobility raises the following difficulties:

(a)   Individuals do not necessarily have stable patterns of development throughout their careers. There are not likely to be consistent increases or decreases in income, status. This makes it difficult to know at what point to make the comparison between the generations.

(b)   People constantly encounter changes of fortune in their careers. They are often quite erratic and shaped by unforeseen developments and subject to crises which may divert them in different directions from that intended at the outset.

2 Measuring intragenerational mobility raises the difficulty of deciding at which point in a person's career the comparison should be made:

(a)   With their first job: but this may have been of a temporary nature in a relatively low-status occupation which would give a false impression of the extent of mobility.

(b)   With their first regular job: this may have been the prelude to a career which required experience and further qualification and which was at the bottom of a ladder subsequently climbed.

(c)   At the height of their career: this may have been in an exceptionally high-status position which was not subsequently maintained.

(d)   At the end of their career: the person may have become disillusioned by this stage and failed to develop all their potential.

3 The problems of measuring stratum mobility are:

(a)   How to assess the extent to which a group has increased (or lost) status over time.

(b)   Comparison between occupational groups in terms of their relative status over time is also difficult because from time to time there are official re-classifications of occupations. This occurred in 1961. The result was an apparent change in the social structure of Britain. Of 25% of Class 1 who were re-classified, 20% went into Class 2 and 5% went into Class 3.

Concluding points:

1 The amount of mobility may depend on the measure used.
2 The measure used depends on the operational definition used in the research project.
3 Care must be taken when making comparisons over time, between generations and between what appear to be occupations of similar social status in those time periods.

THE TRENDS IN SOCIAL MOBILITY

Examine the trends in social mobility in Britain since 1945.

Lipset and Zetterberg (*A Theory of Social Mobility*) have pointed out that from Plato to the present, occupation has been the common indicator of stratification. Occupations are differentially esteemed and studies show a remarkable agreement as to how they rank in esteem. There is also substantial agreement among the rates from different areas of the country, different sizes of towns, different age groups, different economic levels and different sexes. There also appears to be a great deal of international consensus about the occupational prestige classes.

▶ *Some useful studies*:

A Glass (*Social Mobility in Britain*); an intergenerational study. He used the following classification of class groups:

Class 1:	Professional and administrative.
Class 2:	Managerial and executive.
Class 3:	Inspectional, supervisory and other non-manual higher grade.
Class 4:	Inspectional, supervisory and other non-manual lower grade.
Class 5:	Skilled manual and routine non-manual.
Class 6:	Semi-skilled manual.
Class 7:	Unskilled manual.

His analysis revealed the following:

Table 1: **The social class of fathers of men in class 1 (in 1949)**

49% of respondents had fathers in Class 1
16% of respondents had fathers in Class 2
12% of respondents had fathers in Class 3
11% of respondents had fathers in Class 4
14% of respondents had fathers in Class 5
None of respondents had fathers in Class 6
None of respondents had fathers in Class 7

Table 2: **% of men (1949) having fathers in the same class as themselves.**

Class 1	49%
Class 2	25%
Class 3	20%
Class 4	24%
Class 5	50%
Class 6	24%
Class 7	25%

Comment:

1 Recruitment within a class was highest in Class 1 and Class 5.
2 It is lowest in Class 3.
3 The highest levels of social mobility were in Classes 2,3,4,6 and 7.
4 Extreme movement across class lines was rare. Only 3% of sons of fathers in Classes 1 and 2 had joined Classes 6 and 7.
5 None of the sons in Class 1 had fathers in Classes 6 and 7.
6 There was more mobility within class groups (e.g. 5–7; 1–4) than between them.

B　Harris and Clausen (*Labour Mobility in Great Britain 1953–63*)
They conducted an intragenerational study and used the Registrar General's classification. They studied the careers of 4,062 men and 1,304 women and found:

Class 1:	94% remained in the class between 1953 and 1963. 5% went down into Classes 2 and 3a. 1% went into Class 4.
Class 2:	86% remained. 0.5% moved up into Class 1. 7% went into Class 3a. 6.5% moved into the manual working class.
Class 3a:	76% remained in the class. 12% moved into Classes 1 and 2. 12% moved into Classes 3b, 4 and 5.
Class 3b:	78% remained in the class. 9% moved into Classes 3a, 2 and 1. 13% moved into Classes 4 and 5.
Class 4:	73% remained in the class. 7% moved into Classes 2 and 3a. 14% moved into 3a and 6% fell into Class 5.
Class 5:	68% remained in the class. 2% moved into Classes 2 and 3a. 30% moved into Classes 4 and 3b.

Comment:

1　There were high rates of self-recruitment in Classes 1 and 2. There was little downward mobility into manual working classes.
2　Mobility in 3a was balanced between upward and downward movement (12% in each direction).
3　There was greater downward mobility from Class 3b.
4　Only 7% moved into white-collar occupations from Class 4.
5　There was even smaller movement from Class 5. Only 2% moved into white-collar work.
6　In general, most movement was found to be short-range and within rather than across class lines.
7　There was very little long-range mobility from the top to the bottom of the class structure or vice versa.

The mobility of women.

Class 1:	There was only a small representation of women in this class in 1953 (4%) and the numbers remained much the same over the ten-year period. 1% had fallen into Class 2.
Class 2:	86% remained in the class. 7% fell into manual occupations.
Class 3a:	84% remained in the class. 6% rose into Class 2 and 8% fell into manual occupations.
Class 3b:	65% remained in the class. 9% rose into white-collar work. 26% fell into Classes 4 and 5.
Class 4:	8% rose into white-collar work but 9% fell into Class 5.
Class 5:	70% remained in the class. 5% rose into white-collar occupations. 25% rose into Classes 3b and 4.

Comment:

1　Women in Classes 1, 2 and 3a tended to remain secure.
2　Women already in manual occupations tended to move between classes rather than across them.
3　There were comparatively high rates of downward mobility among the women. This may be because they lacked opportunities, there was discrimination against them in promotion etc., and they were

more likely to have breaks in their work for child-rearing which made it difficult to make progress in a career.

C   Halsey (*Origins and Destinations*) and Goldthorpe (*Social Mobility and the Class Structure in Modern Britain*) produced data based on an intergenerational study. The class categories they used were:

Class 1:	Higher professional, higher-grade administrators, managers in large industrial concerns and large proprietors.
Class 2:	Lower professionals, higher-grade technicians, lower-grade administrators, managers in small businesses and supervisors of non-manual employees.
Class 3:	Routine non-manual, mainly clerical and sales personnel.
Class 4:	Small proprietors and self-employed artisans.
Class 5:	Lower-grade technicians and supervisors of manual workers.
Class 6:	Skilled manual workers.
Class 7:	Semi-skilled manual workers.

Their studies revealed the following:

Table 1:   **The social class of fathers of men in Class 1 (1972).**

25% of respondents had fathers in Class 1
13% of respondents had fathers in Class 2
10% of respondents had fathers in Class 3
10% of respondents had fathers in Class 4
12% of respondents had fathers in Class 5
16% of respondents had fathers in Class 6
12% of respondents had fathers in Class 7

Table 2:   **% of men (1972) having fathers in the same class as themselves.**

Class 1	25
Class 2	12
Class 3	11
Class 4	27
Class 5	17
Class 6	42
Class 7	37

Respondents were classified according to their present occupations while their fathers were classified according to the occupation which they held when the respondent was fourteen.

Short-range mobility was defined as any movement in or out of Classes 3, 4, 5 or 6 (since they are all much at the same level).

Long-range mobility is that from the top to the bottom and vice versa.

Comment: **1**   It is difficult to make direct comparisons with the 1949 study because the researchers have not used the same system of classification, although some general conclusions may be drawn.

2   It appears that in 1972 there was more long-range mobility.

3   There appeared to be more chance to enter Classes 2,3 and 4. This may be the result of the falling birth rate, especially in the highest classes.

4   There is a picture of a more open class structure than earlier, although other research suggests that Class 1 remains more highly self-recruiting than others. For example, Giddens (*An Anatomy of a British Ruling Class*) notes that:
    85% of Bishops of the Church of England
    86% of high-ranking military officers
    85% of major judges
    76% of Conservative MPs (1979)
    attended public school

5   The number of positions which are of high status and which are highly rewarded has expanded in the occupational structure.

6   The proportion of middle-class employees from working-class backgrounds remained at about 50%.

7   There was some evidence of less downward mobility.

8   Exactly how much mobility and stability are found depends on the number and size of the categories distinguished. Heath (*Social Mobility*) comments that if the sample was divided into two, Class 1 and all the rest combined into a second category, it would be found that few people experienced intergenerational mobility. He suggests that there is still more short-range than long-range mobility in Britain.

    Less than 10% of men from Class 1 dropped to low-level manual work, but about 25% dropped the short distance to Classes 3–6.

    About 15% achieved long-range upward mobility, but about 50% made the smaller distance to Classes 3,4,5 and 6.

9   The evidence suggests that qualifications improve a person's chances of obtaining better-paid jobs. Families from the middle and upper ranges of the social structure seem more able at securing these or finding alternative routes if they fail the first time.

THE EFFECTS OF MOBILITY ON THE CLASS STRUCTURE

What effect has social mobility had in the twentieth century on the British class structure?

Kerr (*Industrialism and Industrial Man*) argues that the industrial society is an open community encouraging occupational and geographic mobility. In this sense industrialism must be flexible and competitive . . .

The view is that industrial society must be 'open' and 'meritocratic'. There must be increasing opportunities for movement into higher social status levels. The emphasis is on achieved rather than ascribed status. However, there are critics of this view.

In debating the question, consider the following points:

1 Class stratification involves social inequality.

2 If a society has a system of social mobility this does not necessarily remove the inequalities.

3 Entry to a social class is a complex matter, involving changes of value, belief, attitude and patterns of behaviour.

4 It is likely that classes do become more distinct when there is limited mobility. Therefore, an 'open' society should make distinctions less clear.

5 From 1945 to 1979 there did seem to be some evidence of a trend towards greater economic equality in Britain.

6 The mobility studies of 1949, 1963 and 1972 indicate that there is not a great deal of long-range mobility. However, there is debate as to whether the stratification system in Britain is becoming more homogeneous or more heterogeneous. Goldthorpe (*Social Stratification in Industrial Society*) suggested that there was evidence, with the emergence of a new working class, that the system of stratification was becoming less well integrated. 'There is evidence of cultural and in particular of 'social' barriers still widely existing between 'working class' and 'middle class' . . . middle incomes have not resulted in the generalisation of middle-class ways of life or middle-class status.'

7 Roberts *et al.* (*Fragmentary Class Structure*) located a fragmented middle class, but also a 'proletarian' working class located at the foot of the social scale who saw society as divided between 'us' and 'them'. They held fairly radical political views. They were strongly integrated into their local community, were often members of trade unions and lived in council housing. They were immersed in a blue-collar network and seemed unlikely to be subject to the effects of social mobility.

8 Scase (*Conceptions of the Class Structure*) conducted a comparative study in England and Sweden to compare attitudes. He noted how Swedish workers considered an individual's class position was determined by economic circumstances and level of education. Among English workers there was more emphasis on family background. Education was given less weight. Asked whether they thought that many people moved from one class to another 70% of the Swedish workers answered yes, compared with 42% of the British sample. He concluded that in Britain the class structure is still largely seen to be shaped by a number of traditional factors and there was less belief in the possibility of mobility than in Sweden.

Concluding points:

(*a*) Social mobility may not have a direct effect on the class structure. It depends how much mobility is available.

(*b*) It is convenient to measure mobility by comparing occupational positions at various points in a person's career or by comparing one person's occupation with another. But there are difficulties in doing this.

(*c*) Rates of mobility are affected by the extent to which particular occupations are accessible. (Some become more closed as entry qualifications become more demanding).

(*d*) At times of high unemployment mobility may become more limited and the occupational class structure becomes less open.

THE INFLUENCE OF EDUCATION ON MOBILITY PATTERNS

Assess the influence of education on mobility. (OX)

1 Miller (*Comparative Social Mobility*) argues that patterns of mobility are not understood simply in terms of the occupational structure and occupational opportunities. It is also necessary to consider more variable aspects of the social structure, such as its educational institutions. One of the interests in research into mobility has been the factors which promote or restrain mobility, as well as the extent to which modern stratification systems are open or closed. Generally, in modern industrial societies there is increasing emphasis on achievement rather than ascription, for which education is assumed to be a prime source.

2 Runciman (*Towards a Theory of Social Stratification*) points out that having a designated number of years' schooling is relevant to individual mobility only if it is accompanied by an increased availability of more privileged positions to which the education will gain preferential access.

3 Raising educational levels ought to generate greater mobility as new technologies increase opportunities and demands for greater skills in the market place.

4 If occupation in a society is determined largely by education and education by social-class background, then the chances of increased mobility will be reduced if educational opportunities are not available in an expanding economy.

5 Stratification will become increasingly closed unless there is a sufficient expansion of opportunities to develop high-level skills and to utilise them. In some societies (e.g. South Africa) a closed stratification system is maintained by limiting the educational opportunities of black children. This can help to develop the emergence of an under-class of those who have no hope or chance of mobility. It can also help to develop greater class consciousness.

6 From a functionalist perspective, since the reorganisation of secondary education, further education and higher education, the opportunities have been greatly increased for people to improve their qualifications and their social status. The tripartite system (1944), the comprehensive system (after 1964), the expansion of universities and polytechnics (including the Open University for those with no formal educational opportunities) must have increased chances of mobility.

7 Neave (1973) showed that the number of children from working-class backgrounds who entered university was increasing with the development of comprehensive education.

8 Halsey (*Towards Meritocracy. The Case for Britain*) argues that if a person's father is drawn from the highest managerial classes, they stand an eleven times greater chance of getting a university degree than someone from Classes 4 or 5 (RG's scale).

Industrial societies are reducing the proportion of unskilled jobs required and expanding the professional and technical occupations. The direct effect of the class hierarchy of families on educational opportunity has risen since 1945.

He concludes that the expansion of educational opportunity on its own is not enough to make significant inroads into the class-biased educational disadvantages. 'Social and educational policies have not successfully seized on the enlarged occupational opportunities since 1945 to realise either an egalitarian or a meritocratic society.'

THEORETICAL PERSPECTIVES

Is the rate of social mobility a satisfactory indicator of the openness of society?

(Ox)

Functionalist view

1 The dominant ideology of mobility is that everyone has an equal chance of mobility since this is based on achievement.
2 Education is a primary source of such mobility.
3 A primary reason for wishing to see high rates of mobility is to increase economic and social efficiency.
4 Societies must allow for the most able people to fill the most important positions.
5 The class structure is an open system, a ladder of opportunity exists. People can choose the rung to which they wish to ascend.
6 A fluid society is an open society. The level of mobility is therefore a good measure of how open it is.
7 Miller has said that a society which is relegating to lower-status groups sons born in an advantaged stratum is more open than one which safeguards the privileges of the already advantaged.

Weberian view

1 Relatively high rates of social mobility are important in a society because they provide a political safety valve, diminishing frustration and conflict.
2 Class conflict becomes less likely when educational and occupational opportunities exist to increase levels of status and power.
3 People have the chance to influence their desire for improved status by joining power groups, such as trade unions etc.
4 Class solidarity is also unlikely in a fluid open society because people form and disperse around short-term aims in competition for scarce resources.
5 Evidence for the openness of a society is the extent to which educational survival rates of children from different backgrounds is increasing in the society.

Marxist view

1 There is no strong evidence of long-range mobility across class lines. It is primarily short range and within classes.
2 Upward mobility into the ruling elite is impossible since this is a closed group.
3 There is evidence that the lower working class is increasingly homogeneous and there is no embourgeoisement process underway.
4 There is also a large sector of the middle class which has an identification with the proletarian sector.
5 Bowles (*Unequal Education*) argues that unequal schooling reproduces the division of labour. It does not compensate for inequalities generated elsewhere in the capitalist system.
6 Distinctive class subcultures remain. Those at the bottom are unable to improve their social position because there is an unequal distribution of political power.

MASS MEDIA

CONTENTS

Questions on this topic include the following main areas:
1 The ownership and control of mediums of communication.
2 Theories: (a) Marxist (b) Functionalist.
3 The impact of the media:
   (a)   Attitude formation.
   (b)   Reporting news.
   (c)   Deviance amplification.
   (d)   Violence and TV.
4 The mass culture debate.

THE OWNERSHIP AND CONTROL OF THE MASS MEDIA

Some questions asked on this topic require a general discussion of ownership and control:

Examine the relationship between the ownership, control and production of mass media.
(AEB)

Others can be interpreted from a specifically theoretical perspective:

'Control of the mass media is an important part of elite power'. Discuss.   (AEB)

This is putting a Marxist view for discussion.

'The mass media constitute an important source of knowledge and belief for members of society'.   (AEB)

This question could be examined from a functionalist viewpoint, or in terms of the sociology of knowledge.

Definition The mass media are those mediums of communication by which information, ideas, opinions and knowledge are transmitted to large numbers of people in the population at the same time and which have been introduced since the development of mechanical and electronic technologies. Gould and Kolb (*A Dictionary of the Social Sciences*) defines mass media as 'all the impersonal means of communication by which visual and/or auditory messages are transmitted directly to audiences. Included among the mass media are TV, radio, cinema, newspapers, magazines, books and advertising.'

The mass media clearly include a range of different mediums but those most frequently discussed in terms of the question of control and influence are the press and to a lesser extent TV. The audiences for these are very large and in terms of their political, economic and social influences, their potential is very great.

Concentration of ownership

1   Reed International (R. Maxwell) owns:
Daily Mirror; Sunday Mirror; Sunday People and Scottish newspapers; IPC (which publishes over 200 women's magazines, comics and journals.

2   News International (R. Murdoch) owns:
Sun; News of the World; The Times; The Sunday Times; Times Supplements; *Today*.

This company is also the largest shareholder in London Weekend TV.

3   The Thompson Organisation owns a large chain of regional newspapers and has an important interest in Scottish Television.

4   Trafalgar House (Lord Mathews) owns:
Daily Express; Sunday Express; Daily Star; London Standard.

5   Associated Newspapers (Lord Rothermere) owns:
Daily Mail; Mail on Sunday and several provincial newspapers.

This company also has an important interest in Southern Television and commercial radio stations.

6   Pearson Longman owns:
The Financial Times and *The Economist*. The company also has an important interest in Penguin and Longman books.

Only the *Guardian* and *The Daily Telegraph* are not owned by UK conglomerates or foreign-based multi-national companies which publish 80% of all national and regional papers in Britain.

Comment: Some writers are critical of the apparent concentration of ownership among a few powerful companies which are frequently controlled by a few rich and influential men. Others see no conflict here and argue that rich individuals cannot necessarily influence the content of papers or TV programmes. The wealth of the companies and the individual owners is evidence of their economic efficiency.

1   Sheridan and Gardner (*Media, Politics and Culture*) argue that:
(a)   The concentration of power has been misused. All journalists are influenced by the audience they write for, the owner they work for and their colleagues who give them feed-back.
(b)   All the material written derives from a social context and serves particular ends, namely the ideology of the owners.
(c)   Six independent TV stations are partly owned by one of the major newspaper companies. This means that there is a great concentration of ownership of the most powerful media by a few individuals

who can impose their attitudes on the content. This must have the effect of limiting media freedom.

(d) The support of advertisers is crucial to the success of the press and commercial TV. They pour money into the media because advertising is successful. But this lowers the standards of press and TV because the largest audiences are attracted by the most trivial content. The concentration of advertising helps to strengthen the control of the media in a few hands.

2 'Attitudes to the Press' (Report 1984) on readers' attitudes to the press based on interviews with more than 2,000 people found:

(a) Many respondents were critical of the standards of journalism.

(b) There was little knowledge about the extent of the ownership and control of the press or TV stations.

(c) There was much ignorance about the economics of the newspaper industry and its watch-dog, the Press Council.

(d) Women's magazines were said to provide a vital network of social welfare services for women. They helped to inform and educate women in significant matters relating to family welfare.

(c) There was some criticism of magazines for girls which did little or nothing to help the young come to grips with social realities.

3 Some writers argue that there is a separation between ownership and control. Control of output is said to be in the hands of professional editors; the owners simply manage the financial aspects of the company.

(a) Lord Thompson, once the owner of *The Times*, said that 'I have my views on various subjects . . . but I never see them appear in the paper unless the editor agrees with them . . .' Robert Maxwell, owner of the *Mirror*, has recently made a similar point.

(b) Wintour (an ex-editor) has said 'in general advertising influence is negligible and where it is not it is harmless . . .'

(c) Shareholders would not accept constant interference from rich owners since profits might fall.

(d) The battle for a free press, independent of interference from owners and Government, has been a long one in Britain.

(e) People do not buy papers for their political content alone. Papers must entertain. Often readers are not aware of the political views of their paper. (Many people think the *Sun* supports the Labour Party).

THEORIES

Control of the mass media is an important aspect of elite power. Discuss.

The Marxist view

1 The majority of the national press and television news editors report events in terms of the *status quo*. There is wide support for the Conservative Party. Serious matters are not dealt with adequately: there is emphasis on the trivial. Those who control the media mould public taste and opinion.

2 Because the media operate in the interests of a ruling elite the audience has no real choice to assess competing ideologies (e.g. Northern Ireland).

3 Advertisers largely determine the content of papers and TV programmes. This accounts for the low level of serious content.

4 Those who own and control the press and TV stations are likely to be men whose ideological values range between conservative to reactionary. The content of the media will reflect these views, ensuring that negative attitudes will be attached to those people and events defined as 'hostile'.

5 The media propagates a bourgeois concept of reality. It describes a picture of the world which fits that of a particular class. Any apparent sense of freedom to select alternative models of action or belief is illusory.

6 There is seldom any account of the evolution of major events in media reports. They tend to appear as random eruptions of conflict. Their causes (often arising from exploitation) are seldom discussed.

7 Critics argue that the Conservative media use the term 'Marxist' as one of abuse. It conveys illegitimacy and a powerful image of an alien force. It is a means of suggesting threat, subversion and hostility. Most people are unfamiliar with the philosophies or ideals of Marxism.

Myers (*Media Hits the Pits*) argues that those who own and control the means of mass communication were marshalled in opposition to the NUM. The Glyn Report which put the union position got little mention during the dispute.

8 The Glasgow Media group argue that they have found strong evidence of right-wing bias in the content and presentation of news stories on TV.

The Functionalist view

1 The media are not allied to one party nor do they necessarily sensationalise or trivialise. Journalists cater for what people want. The media, therefore, reflect events, attitudes, tastes etc.

2 In a free market people do have choice and there is a range of papers from extreme left to extreme right.

3 A major outlet for advertising, the media keep people informed as to the availability of products and competition ensues.

4 It is a mistake to assume that those who own mediums of communication necessarily control the content of the messages which are disseminated.

5 Fearing (*The Influence of the Movies*) suggests that in the cinema the individual learns to reaffirm the norms of his culture or group; the area of significant meanings is enlarged, as is an awareness of the range of possibilities.

6 Rosengren and Windahl (*Mass Media Consumption as a Functional Alternative*) argue that the media serve important functions as a source of news, facts, information etc. which enables people to make informed judgements.

7 The media help to provide a greater sense of commitment to the society by promoting cultural values and by identifying areas of conflict and opposition.

The function of entertainment is an important one, helping people to relax after work and refreshing them.

Those who wish to express dissenting views can do so and such reports are available for those who wish to read them.

8 This group is accused of being too ideologically biased, failing to examine their data with sufficient impartiality.

THE IMPACT OF THE MEDIA

ATTITUDE FORMATION

Do the mass media of communication change or merely reinforce attitudes and behaviour?

Questions are sometimes asked which focus on attitudes towards race, politics, violence etc. In such cases you must ensure that you relate your material to the specific issue raised in the question.

An attitude is a unified set of beliefs which are strongly held. It helps the individual to explain and make sense of events. To hold an attitude implies:

(*a*)   an emotional response (a person *feels* strongly about something

(*b*)   a rational element (the person has a *reasoned belief* based on evidence)

(c)   a behavioural response (the person *behaves* in accordance with beliefs).

Those who wish to change attitudes include politicians, advertisers, and reformers. They are faced with the problem of changing existing attitudes from positive to negative or vice versa. This can be described as an incongruent change. Or they may wish to intensify an existing attitude (i.e. make someone believe something more strongly). This can be termed a congruent effect.

▶ *Research findings*:

Research indicates that it is a complex process to form attitudes and equally difficult to change them. They are learned responses which people develop so they become fixed over time.

Trenaman and McQuail (*TV and the Political Image*) suggest that the most common effects on an audience are either minor changes or a reinforcing tendency. This arises as a result of three factors:

(a)   selective exposure (people are selective in their choice of paper, programme etc. and tend to avoid those which might give rise to conflict).

(b)   selective perception (people tend to perceive information which fits existing expectations).

(c)   selective retention (people tend to retain information which supports existing attitudes and they ignore that which presents conflicting views).

It is therefore difficult to achieve an incongruent change. The communicator would have to:

(a)   be someone the audience accepts as credible

(b)   present new evidence in a clear and simple way

(c)   raise new questions in the minds of the audience.

REPORTING NEWS

Reporting news is inevitably partial, selective and biased. Discuss.

Much research has been conducted into the way that news is gathered and selected for communication. There is much debate as to whether it is done in an entirely objective way by impartial journalists or whether there is unintentional bias.

1   Radio and TV channels are under an obligation established by Act of Parliament to ensure fair and balanced coverage of political issues from all points of view, especially during an election campaign. (The exception is where 'the public interest is involved'.)

2   The press are not faced with similar restrictions in their reporting of such issues. They are restrained in comments only by fear of legal action and issues of national security.

▶ *Research studies*:

1   Philo, The Glasgow Media Group (*Bad News; More Bad News*). This

group undertook a detailed content analysis of six months of news programmes. They are critical of the presentation of news on TV.

(*a*)   News is reported from the point of view of management/ government and seldom from the point of view of the work force or those in conflict.

(*b*)   Causal explanations seldom appear.

(*c*)   There is an inherent class bias among the journalists (middle class, university educated).

(*d*)   Strikers were generally portrayed in a negative light.

(*e*)   The impression created was that some industries were perpetually strike prone.

(*f*)   They found an increasing feeling among the audience that the BBC news was biased against the left (In 1960 96% thought it was impartial; in 1979 it was 78% who thought this).

(*g*)   The Glasgow group reject the idea that there can be objective, unbiased news reporting.

(*h*)   They reject the claim that journalists react to audience demands. In fact, broadcasters lead the audience into new attitudes.

2   Hartmann and Husband (*The Mass Media and Racial Conflict*) argue that if the media do influence events they seldom do so directly, but more through the way people think. They suggest that direct effects on attitudes following short-term exposure to media material are unlikely. But the media do play an important part in defining for people what the important issues are; 'they set the agenda for discussion'. As far as race is concerned this is in terms of 'numbers' (i.e. numbers entering the country each year). They also determine how people should think about them and interpret them. Because of the gate-keeping role of the news media some people have greater access to the media than others.

(*a*)   The British cultural tradition contains elements derogatory to foreigners (especially blacks). This stems from the colonial past.

(*b*)   The media operate with the culture and use its cultural symbols. This is exemplified in the use of cartoons, jokes etc.

(*c*)   Journalists work with specific news values: the criteria by which information about events is gathered, selected and published. The dominant values are those of conflict, threat and deviance. Events are more newsworthy when they can be interpreted within a familiar framework of existing images and expectations.

They conclude that the media tend to reinforce existing attitudes. The media do not intend to report in a biased way, they are simply following their normal procedures and applying their usual news values criteria. The authors suggest that the media should become more concerned with underlying causes and possible solutions to major issues.

**DEVIANCE
AMPLIFICATION**

Examine the role of the mass media in the amplification of deviance. Illustrate with examples. (Ox)

This question must also be considered in relation to a discussion of the concept of crime and deviance.

1 Becker (*Outsiders*) has said that 'society creates deviance'. This is done by making the rules 'whose infraction creates deviance'. An act becomes deviant when it is observed by someone who takes some action in relation to it and attaches a label of 'deviant' to the actor involved.

2 Wilkinson (*The Deviance-Amplifying System*) has described the sequence of events which results in an action becoming perceived as a serious form of deviance. He says 'the definitions of deviant behaviour relate to the information and cultural experience of the individuals making the definitions . . .'

3 Cohen (*Mods, Rockers and the Rest . . .*) examined the ways in which the mass media influenced the development of the mods and rockers phenomena in the mid 1960s. He considers how media reports:
(*a*) quickly shaped people's expectations
(*b*) provided the content of rumours that 'something was going to happen'
(*c*) publicised events and made them attractive to other youngsters
(*d*) established images and stereotypes of potential trouble-makers
(*e*) increased the problems by increased comment.

It is his thesis that newspapers do not intentionally exaggerate events, but in their use of sensational headlines, dramatic interviews and comment they sensitise the public to problems.

The use of stereotyped images helps people to make sense of ambiguous situations: people know who are 'the troublemakers' and a self-image develops among those so labelled.

Cohen's deviation-amplifying system

1 Initial deviation from valued norms leading to:
2 Punitive reaction by the community (which may lead to the segregation of groups and marking them as deviant).
3 Development of a deviant self-identity and behaviour appropriate to this identity.
4 Further punitive reaction etc.

Cohen (*Folk Devils and Moral Panics*) describes the process further when he explains how the media create moral panics as the amplification of deviance begins to spiral. The reports of an initially minor event gain wide coverage; the public are sensitised; the police may become involved; there are further detailed reports, often from the courtroom confrontations; these increase public concern;

troublemakers are identified as 'folk devils', who become increasingly alienated from the wider public. They are identified by dress, manner and other qualities of their 'youth culture'. Their expected behaviour leads to a 'moral panic' (concern by the public about what is seen as a serious moral and social issue).

Eventually, the panic subsides as another issue replaces it as a matter of media attention.

Assess the social impact of television.

VIOLENCE AND TV

One of the long-standing areas of debate is the extent to which there is a correlation between watching violent action on TV and violent behaviour in wider society. There is no clear evidence from research; part of the problem is defining the nature of 'violence'.

▶ *Research findings*:

1 Cumerbatch and Howitt (*Mass Media, Violence and Society*) The authors made fifteen studies on 2,000 children in comprehensive schools and reviewed and analysed 300 studies into media violence. They concluded that there was no direct effect, though they found much contradictory evidence in the studies. They argue that cartoons do not have a harmful effect on young viewers.

2 Surgeon General's Report (USA) (*TV and Growing Up*) This ran to six volumes and cost more than $1 million to produce. The conclusion was that TV violence does increase levels of aggression among child audiences. As many as 25% may be seriously affected. Of programmes classed as 'adult' 85% are viewed by young children.

3 Noble (*Children in Front of the Small Screen*) He found that for a small proportion of children with aggressive personalities viewing violence had a 'cathartic effect'. (They got rid of some of their own anger and frustrations by watching violence on TV.) But there may be some danger for children where there is no opportunity to discuss issues seen, with adults. Many delinquents were found to be avid TV watchers.

4 Pye Survey
This found that 45% of children aged 7–10 watched TV until 9 p.m. and one child in 100 watched until 11 p.m. 79% of families were found to exercise 'no control whatever over the number of hours their children watched TV'. On average each child was found to spend approximately twenty-two hours per week watching TV.

5 Katz (*Violence on TV*)
This BBC audience research report found that viewers do not worry much about violence on TV. 57% thought there was too much but only 18% actually perceived violence in the target programmes they were asked to monitor. The author suggests that perhaps the amount of violence has affected the viewers' threshold of tolerance so that they were so saturated they were no longer concerned about it. The author accepts that his report remains largely inconclusive.

6   IBA Research (*The Portrayal of Violence on TV*) This study suggests that the use of violence on TV may reinforce aggressive tendencies among the emotionally unstable. In a typical hour of TV programmes there would be at least two major sequences of violence involving death; one would be fictional and one real. The report states that 'TV is perhaps one of the most powerful mediums of mass communication . . . violent deaths should be reported in context and in relation to the importance of the event . . .'

7   Dunckley, commenting on the range of research findings, points out that there are many contradictory ones. He says, for example, that the BBC report does not provide a basis for concluding either that those who criticise TV for showing too much violence are justified or that there is no cause for concern. All the research indicates that the media can never be the sole cause of delinquent behaviour. Evidence is increasing that TV tends to reinforce existing attitudes, hence TV violence may tend to affect those in the audience who are already prone to aggressive behaviour.

THE MASS CULTURE DEBATE

Is there any evidence that the mass media of communication have created a mass culture?

Some writers have argued that there is a trend towards the development of a mass society. Although it lacks precise meaning the term 'mass' has come to be associated with undesirable changes in the structure of society. The suggestion is that a mass society shares a mass culture. The means by which this is disseminated among the population is the mass media. However, there are some who oppose the negative implications and argue that the media have beneficial effects.

McQuail (*Towards a Sociology of Mass Communication*) describes the debate:

1   Mass culture refers to the cultural products manufactured solely for the mass market. There is standardisation of product and mass behaviour in its use (Wilensky).

Mass culture refers to a whole range of popular activities . . . to entertainment, spectacles, music, books, films . . . and has become identified with the typical content of the mass media, and especially with fictional, dramatic and entertainment material (McQuail).

2   The *pessimists*, who associated the mass media with unwelcome societal tendencies:

(*a*)   Kornhauser: sees the development of a mass society in which democratic institutions are threatened and the conditions for totalitarianism result.

(*b*)   Bell: describes the increase in alienation, the erosion of traditional values as the ordered community and social life of the past breaks down. There is a decay in the popular art of a more stable society.

(c)   Arendt: the mass production of new cultural objects and consumer goods has resulted in a loss of originality.

(d)   T. S. Eliot: deplored the growth of mass culture because it threatened the existence of 'high culture', the culture of excellence. Mass culture is the culture of mediocrity.

(e)   MacDonald: mass culture mixes and scrambles everything together . . . producing what might be called 'a homogenised culture'.

(f)   Tumin: it encourages a 'cult of happiness . . .'

(g)   Rosenberg: 'at its worst mass culture threatens not merely to cretinise our taste, but to brutalise our senses.'

3   The *optimists* who do not see such dangers in the mass media:

(a)   Halloran: argues that the debate is marked by confusion as to the meaning of terms: high culture, mass culture, low culture. This leads to confusion and ambiguity, making consensus difficult.

(b)   Shils: suggests that the attack on mass media and mass culture is politically motivated and presents a one-sided critique of US society.

(c)   Williams: argues that 'majority culture' may not necessarily be in low taste. People are not sufficiently familiar with it; judgements as to what is good and bad depend on the values of a small minority of 'critics'.

(d)   Hoggart: makes the point that working-class culture may be just as valuable as middle-class culture but its qualities may not be recognised.

Conclusion:

The pessimists fear that in a mass society people become less concerned with the serious aspects of everyday life. Democratic values are threatened because people have less interest in them and they are therefore open to greater manipulation. Individuality is minimised. The traditional culture is replaced by one shared by the majority in the society. Tastes become more uniform. There is less interest in 'serious' culture. In a mass society, there is a mass culture and mass behaviour. People will act in a collective way; fashions, trends etc. predominate. People will act as a mass when there are similar needs or problems faced.

The optimists reject these views and see confusions arising out of a failure to establish the meanings of terms as well as the fact that the media can bring many benefits and introduce new values to the audience.

EDUCATION

CONTENTS

There are a wide range of areas covered in this topic. They include the following:
1 The educational structure:
   (a)   Mobility
   (b)   Meritocracy
2 Theories and perspectives:
   (a)   Functionalist
   (b)   Marxist
   (c)   Interactionist
3 Factors affecting educational achievement. Arguments in the debate:
   (a)   Biological
   (b)   Cultural
   (c)   The school
4 Education and social change.
5 The curriculum:
   (a)   Official
   (b)   Hidden
6 Education and gender.

THE EDUCATIONAL STRUCTURE: MOBILITY AND MERITOCRACY

Have the changes in the structure of the educational system since 1945 increased mobility and produced a more meritocratic society?

1 The changes in the educational system have included a move from the tripartite system (introduced by the Butler Education Act 1944) to the comprehensive; the phasing out of grammar schools; the slight growth of the independent sector. D.E.S. statistics indicate that this has increased from 5.6% in 1978 to 6.2% in 1983.
2 Rates of mobility in Britain are difficult to assess because it depends on the measure used. However, the general finding is that rates of long-range mobility seem fairly low. Rates of short-range mobility are higher but are mainly within classes rather than between them.
3 A meritocratic society implies that there is increasing equality of opportunity for those of similar ability. This means that people can achieve status position on merit. The educational system would act in

an unbiased way to select the most able people to fill the most important positions.

4   To a large extent the answer to the question depends on the perspective adopted.

The Functionalist perspective

(*a*)   Educational reform which promotes equality of opportunity must be a key to a more egalitarian society.

(*b*)   In modern Britain qualifications are available to all who aspire to achieve them.

(*c*)   The previously significant 'ascribed status' has given way to 'achieved status'.

(*d*)   Some form of social inequality is inevitable since there is a ladder of opportunity. Not everyone can climb to the top.

(*e*)   Social mobility is greatest in a society which operates on meritocratic principles. Those who obtain them can enter occupations which provide the highest rewards.

(*f*)   Schools help to stimulate individual talent and locate the most able people from all ranges of the class system to fulfil the most important tasks.

A more critical perspective

(*a*)   Although there have been major educational reforms the chances of educational success, in terms of high levels of qualification, for people of different classes, ethnic backgrounds and sexes do not seem to be achieved on merit.

Reid (*Social Class Differences in Britain*) shows that the chances of going to a university became greater for the non-manual classes during the 1970s. Admission statistics showed that in the number of entrants between 1970 and 1977 the percentage for Class 1 rose from 30% to 36% while that from Class 4 fell from 28% to 24%. Private schools maintained a virtual monopoly of top jobs. They comprise approximately 86% of high court judges; 83% of top directors; 80% of bank directors and nearly 70% of Conservative MPs.

(*b*)   Mills (*The Power Elite*) makes the point that access to top jobs is controlled by the members of the professions. They allow entry only from others in the same class. As a result levels of mobility into such occupational groups is tightly limited.

(*c*)   Halsey *et al.* (*Origins and Destinations*) studied 8,525 males educated in England and Wales. They found that boys from Classes 1 and 2 compared with ones from Classes 4 and 5 had:

forty times more chance of attending a public school; three times more chance of attending a grammar school; eleven times more chance of entering a university. (However, since the study was conducted in 1972 the comprehensive system has become more widespread). The conclusion reached at that time was that the educational structure had not established a more meritocratic society or greatly increased opportunities of mobility.

THEORIES OF EDUCATION

The major role of the educational system is not to promote equality, but to legitimate inequality. Discuss.   (AEB)

'To understand the behaviour of children it is necessary to examine their interactions with teachers'. Discuss.

Functionalist perspective

Functionalists ask two main questions:
a. How does the educational system promote order and stability in society?
b. What functions does it serve for the individual?
Durkheim said that society can only exist if there is a strong degree of social solidarity (value consensus). Education helps establish this by transmitting valued norms and beliefs to all pupils. These help integrate people more closely into the society. The education system also helps fulfil other needs of society by reacting to economic needs for a more skilled work force.

Parsons argues that the school is a vital secondary source of socialisation. By enabling the most able to rise to the top of the social hierarchy on merit, inequalities can be justified.

Marxist perspective

The Marxist also looks at society as a whole but examines its role in relation to the economic structure. The interest is particularly in the ways in which the values and ideologies of the ruling class are transmitted through the schools.
An example of such an analysis is:
Bowles and Gintis (*Schooling in Capitalist America*).
a. They argue that education serves to reproduce the existing social structure.
b. The fragmentation of work is mirrored in the fragmentation of the curriculum into tiny packages of knowledge.
c. The alienation of children in school is preparation for their later alienation in work.
d. Pupils are organised in a competitive hierarchical structure and prevented from gaining much intrinsic satisfaction from their work.
e. The conformists gain highest rewards.

Interactionist perspective

This perspective is based on the idea that social action arises out of interpretations and perceptions achieved in the course of interactions. The focus is on the relationships observed in the classroom.
Examples of studies using this approach include:
1. Cicourel and Kitsuse (*The Educational Decision-Makers*). They noted how teachers and councellors evaluated students and advised them in terms of their appearance, manner and patterns of behaviour, based on reports. They were responding to images, which made equality of treatment impossible.
2. Becker (*Social Class Variations*) found that teachers assessed pupils in terms of an 'ideal type' model. They perceived the children who approximated most closely to it as the most able. They tended to come from non-manual backgrounds.

FACTORS AFFECTING EDUCATIONAL ACHIEVEMENT

Educational attainment varies between different sections of the population. This cannot be explained wholly by the distribution of intelligence. What other explanations are there?

Critically assess sociological explanations of differences in educational achievement.

The question that has produced a great amount of sociological research and debate is why particular groups of children (especially those in Class 4 and 5) tend to be less successful in the educational system when there have been major changes in structure since 1944. (For differences in the educational attainments of girls compared to boys, see page 168; and for ethnic minorities, see pages 310–11).

Explanations tend to focus on three areas:

BIOLOGICAL/GENETIC

Explanation	Points of criticism
Intelligence: Although there is no precise definition it is usually taken to mean a capacity for learning or reasoning; an ability to think in abstract ways; to absorb new material quickly and process information. Some have argued that there is an IQ gene which is transmitted from parents. IQ tests were first devised by Binet (1905) to measure mental age. Terman's index of mental development was: $$\text{Intelligence Quotient} = \frac{\text{mental age}}{\text{actual age}} \times 100.$$ This established the 11+ test to select children for the appropriate school under the 1944 Education Act (Grammar, Technical, Secondary Modern).	1. An IQ gene has never been identified. 2. IQ tests may only measure cultural skills; they are often culture biased. 3. They tend to measure a capacity to conform to the testers' restrictions. Only the test-makers' answer is correct. They therefore ignore creative and imaginative skills. 4. IQ scores may be improved by coaching. 5. A child's future should not be based on the results of an unreliable test. 6. Knowledge of test scores by teachers may affect the way they treat children in the classroom. 7. The results of such criticisms led to the introduction of comprehensive schools.

CULTURAL (CULTURAL DEPRIVATION)

Many researchers have focused attention on the cultural background of the child as being a very important factor in determining attainment. This influences the child's attitudes, expectations and beliefs about what school is like and what value it may have, before entering at the age of five. After that, there is constant reinforcement of such attitudes. The culture of origin is seen to be more significant than any other factor. The following writers have discussed it:

Author Summary points	Points of criticism
1. Douglas (*The Home and the School*) noted a correlation between unsatisfactory housing, low parental interest and low levels of achievement. Middle-class parents paid more frequent visits to the school, had smaller families and exerted more choice in their child's school.	a. The reason why working-class parents may appear to show less interest is because they are in employment which makes visits to school difficult. b. It is difficult to measure 'positive' and 'negative' attitudes. c. Such parents may have high aspirations for their children but lack the knowledge about how best to advise them.
2. Prosser and Wedge (*Born to Fail*) found the disadvantaged children in their study (page 262) were less healthy and did less well in school. Their work suggested that such children could be identified at birth so that more social and educational provision was necessary, otherwise they had no chance.	a. The view that children are 'born to fail' as a result of their cultural deprivations suggests that a high proportion are 'doomed' and beyond redemption. Especially since more provision is unlikely at times of economic recession.
3. Halsey (*Educational Priority*) outlines a range of policies around the development of pre-schooling and community schools and their implications. He says 'not only must parents understand schools, schools must also understand the family and the environments in which the children live.' Teachers need to be sensitive to the child's social and moral climate of development.	a. More radical critics would argue that education cannot compensate for the inequalities in the wider social structure. 'Understanding' is not enough. There must be social change which promotes true equalities.

4. Newson (*Patterns of Infant Care*) There were found to be differences in child-rearing practices between manual and non-manual classes. Middle-class practices were found to provide later educational advantages. There was an emphasis on provision of stimulating home environment; discussion of issues between parents and children; all factors which help establish patterns of appropriate behaviour in school.

a. Interactionists would oppose the view that child-rearing patterns have a completely determining effect on future development. They would argue that people can change behaviour according to their interpretation of events, in the classroom, for example.

5. Bernstein (*Social Class and Linguistic Development*) argues that there are class differences in the use of language. Working-class children tend to use a 'restricted code'. Some characteristics:
a. short, grammatically simple sentences
b. often unfinished sentences
c. limited use of adverbs and adjectives
d. meanings often conveyed more by gesture
e. emphasis more on concrete not abstract ideas and meanings.
Middle-class children use a more 'elaborated code.' Its main characteristics include:
a. longer, more complex sentences
b. more extensive use of imaginative language
c. meanings more clearly stated
d. use of abstract concepts.
Bernstein has argued that the restricted code is inefficient in formal education. The elaborated code provides the power to allow more complex ideas to be conveyed. The child who uses only a restricted code is at an educational disadvantage, especially in examinations.

a. Rosen (*Language and Class*) argues that the terms 'elaborated' and 'restricted' may imply a qualitative difference between the classes themselves (Manual classes are inferiors), i.e. teachers may come to assume that because they teach many working-class children they have no chance of academic success.
b. Rosen says that working-class speech has its own strengths and it is not necessarily 'deformed or underpowered'.
c. Labov (*The Logic of Nonstandard English*) also denies that working-class children cannot express complex ideas, in his analysis of the speech patterns of black children. Theirs is also a very rich, verbal culture, and these children have the same capacity for complex conceptual learning.
d. The emphasis on restricted language may limit research into the shortcomings of the schools.

6. Sugarman (*Social Class Values and Behaviour in Schools*) suggests that there are differences in attitude and values between the classes. In the middle classes there is an emphasis on 'deferred gratification': they are encouraged to postpone pleasures and short-term aims for long-term goals. This would explain why there are more middle-class children remaining in school or higher education than working-class children who are socialised into an ethnic of 'immediate gratification'.

a. It may be an overgeneralisation to assume that members of the working class prefer instant gratification. Failure in school may lead to the view that things will not improve in the future, therefore it is best to take what is presently available.
b. Families with no history of higher education or qualifications among their members will not see their relevance.
c. The social norm of 'hard work' is expressed in terms of learning the job on the shop floor.
d. For middle-class children in higher education there may be a great deal of gratification, which is not deferred.

The educational status of young people aged 16–18 (1978–9)

Social class:	1+2	3a	3b	4+5
Males				
Full-time	55	45	25	20
Part-time	15	20	20	20
Not in	30	35	55	60
Females				
Full-time	60	50	30	30
Part-time	5	5	7	6
Not in	35	45	63	64

Source: Social Trends No 11

7. Bourdieu (*Systems of Education and Systems of Thought*) writes that just as the 'formal lecture . . . defines the right culture . . . so all teaching . . . will furnish a model of the right mode of intellectual activity . . .' He argues that the ruling elite impose their values and meaning on others. This enables them to set the agenda in establishing what counts as knowledge or intelligent behaviour. This cultural capital is accumulated by the dominant class and transmitted to others within it. The result is their academic success. They acquire the label 'intelligent' or 'gifted'. They appear to acquire valued knowledge more easily than others. The school thereby reproduces social inequality.

a. The theory rests on a Marxist analysis of power and domination.
b. There are examples of children from working-class backgrounds who have no such access to the cultural capital but who are subsequently able to achieve power and status.
c. Access to the cultural capital may assist a child in achieving an education in the private sector or in a selective school, but after that its effect may be less significant.
d. In contemporary society the most valuable knowledge may be scientific and computer-related skills. These may be increasingly available to all social classes.

THE SCHOOL

This aspect focuses on the extent to which children's level of achievement is related to what happens to them inside the school – the way it is organised in terms of its goals, rules, structures – as well as to teacher-pupil relations. This has been the particular (though not exclusive) concern of the phenomenologists.

Assess the influence of teacher expectations on their pupils' educational performance.

(Ox)

Schools do not merely react to children with varying qualities and capacities in a neutral way: they play an active part in creating children who are more or less educable, more or less knowledgeable, more or less manageable (Milton *et al.*). Explain and discuss.

(AEB)

Summary points

1. Hargreaves (*Social Relations in a Secondary School*) observed the normative structure of the pupils in their forms in a secondary modern school. He was concerned with the significance of the peer group in regulating patterns of behaviour. Teachers tended to assume that negative behaviour could be explained in terms of 'bad home-background'.

Hargreaves argues that this is an oversimplification. It ignores the crucial aspect of the pupils' sub-cultures as they develop in the process of classroom interaction. These tended to relate to the form the pupils were in and their stream. Those in the top streams had more positive attitudes than those in the lowest.

He concluded that the school can be regarded as a generating factor in development of delinquency. Teachers promote deviance by their treatment of the pupils, whose negative culture was a response to the problems they faced each day in the classroom.

2. Becker *et al.* (*Student Culture and Academic Effort*) describe some of the positive aspects of the development of cultural values among students. They state that subcultures develop best where a number of people are faced with a common problem and interest in the effort to find solutions. There is intensive interaction among students wondering what to learn, the worth of particular courses; how to deal with particular members of staff etc. The culture that arises among them provides them with a perspective and a pattern of responses; it provides a system of social support and patterns of shared understandings. Student culture is the cornerstone of many of the difficulties with students; it is one of the facts of life to which teachers must make some accommodation. For middle-class students it is a culture of coping, not opposition.

Points of criticism

Whilst Marxist critics of the methods of phenomenology would not be surprised by the findings they would argue that they can be explained in other ways. Reality is objective not subjective. The inequalities of wider society are reflected in the structure of the educational system.

In school, children are differentiated and stratified by streams and ability. The perception of children as bright or dull is not just something that arises out of the interaction process; the teachers are merely operating with the accepted normative values of wider society which sees the lower working-class as less valuable members. The education system is shaped by the economic system and must produce the kind of people required by the capitalist economy.

Teachers are the gate-keepers who can encourage or deter their entry into particular occupations.

Willis (*Learning to Labour*) describes how working-class subcultures are better described as 'counter cultures'. They evolve as cultures of opposition to the dominant middle-class values of 'academic success'. For males these counter cultures, found in the school and the work place, are not able to replace the middle-class ethics, but they enable the working-class boy to survive. They emphasise masculinity, toughness, aggression and sexist attitudes. He defines culture as 'the very material of our daily lives, the bread and butter of our understandings, feelings and responses . . .'

3. Keddie (*Classroom Knowledge*) is critical of the fact that explanations for educational failure are most often given in terms of pupils' ethnic and social class antecedents. She examines the defining procedures occurring within the school itself. She used observational techniques to establish the ways in which teachers evaluate pupils and establish their levels of ability. She found that they made use of their 'knowledge' of them in these assessments. Children were perceived to be most able where they readily absorbed the material presented to them. Those who offered 'irrelevant' knowledge were perceived as 'less able'. She concluded that the failure of high-ability pupils to question what they are taught contributes in large measure to their educational achievement. Classroom evaluation of pupils and knowledge are said to be socially constructed in the interaction process.

It is difficult to prove that meanings are constructed simply in the classroom as a result of interaction, rather than being culturally derived from wider society. If this were the only source of images then we would expect more variety in these to reflect the range of interactions that occur in the classroom.

It seems surprising that so many teachers arrive at the same interpretations about the same kinds of children, those from the working class being perceived in more negative ways than others. The meanings that are derived must have some origin. How do teachers know what class distinctions are likely to produce in the way of bad behaviour other than by their experiences in wider society? These expectations are carried into the classroom.

4. Rutter *et al.* (*Fifteen Thousand Hours*) The title refers to the number of hours spent by a child in school from the ages of five to sixteen. The study was carried out over six years in twelve inner London secondary schools. The authors examined:
a. attendance
b. academic achievement
c. behaviour in school
d. rate of delinquency outside it.

They concluded that different schools achieved varied results with children even when background differences were taken into account. Variations were related to what happened inside the school. Success was not related to smallness of school, use of resources, age of building. What did matter was:
a. the spread of ability among the intake;
b. a reasonable spread of ability was more significant than class of origin. A high proportion of low-ability children was associated with high delinquency rates;
c. the ability of the teachers to create and maintain specific norms. These included encouragement; consistency; acting as a good model for pupils;
d. the school ethos; rules set and enforced.

a. Heat and Clifford (*Oxford Review of Education 1980*) criticise the crude measures of class used: fathers' occupations were split into only three categories.
b. The failure to consider the effects of different primary schools.
c. The significance of class is underplayed.
d. Ethos is very difficult to assess or measure and is unlikely to be the source of success.
e. Action (*Educational Research*) accuses the researchers of 'cheating by putting in statistical cautions and then blandly ignoring them . . .'
f. Wragg (*Perspectives: Exeter University*) argues that the schools chosen were not typical. The twelve schools had 28% of fathers convicted of criminal offences; 51% of children were in overcrowded homes; 43% of the teachers were in their posts for less than three years.
g. Goldstein (*Journal of Child Psychology and Psychiatry*) said that the results should be treated with caution if not scepticism.

EDUCATION AND SOCIAL CHANGE

The power of the education system to transform societies has been much exaggerated. Discuss. (AEB)

Those who claim that changes in the educational system can produce changes in the structure of society would include many functionalist writers. They would argue:

1 There is a direct relationship between the educational system and the economic system. As the economy develops so an improved structure of education is required to ensure that workers have the appropriate skills.

2 The school-leaving age may be raised to retain a longer hold on pupils to prevent too many entering the labour market without the appropriate talents.

3   An improved educational system produces greater chances for social mobility, so transforming the class structure.

4   Education encourages greater personal development, enabling people to extend their full range of talents. This must ensure more harmony and order in society.

5   The principles of meritocracy and self-help are important values which promote the possibility of change towards a more open society.

6   The failure of many children to achieve their full potential can be explained in terms of cultural deprivation. Deficiences in culture result in poor socialisation.

Worton and Watson (*Compensatory Education and Contemporary Liberalism in the USA*) argue that the concepts of disadvantage and deprivation are often badly defined. They appear to focus on poor home background and lack of adequate language development in these children. Educational programmes have been developed to try to compensate for such deficiences:

(*a*)   Educational Priority Areas: these were introduced into Britain in the 1960s. The Government provided additional finance and other resources for schools in places designated as EPAs.

(*b*)   Operation Headstart (USA): in the early 1960s attempts were made to provide special programmes and assistance for children from poor homes (especially blacks) in their early years. It was later phased out, although some success was claimed.

Points of criticism: 1   Collins (*Functional and Conflict Theories of Educational Stratification*) argues that:

(*a*)   The educational system doesn't work as closely with the economic system as functionalist writers suggest. A high proportion of skills are learned in a practical way; many people have to undertake further training, provided by their employers, once appointed.

(*b*)   Many qualifications achieved by pupils are of no specific vocational use.

(*c*)   Obtaining high qualifications for entry into professional occupations is the means used for controlling its membership and status. The numbers obtaining entry are very small. There are still more children leaving school without a graded GCE or CSE exam than there are those having two or more A levels.

% distribution of achievement by school-leavers 1978/9 by sex

	Boys	Girls
2 or more A levels	14	12
1 A level	3	4
1+ 0 (A–C)	33	39
1+ GCE/CSE	33	31
No GCE/CSE grades	17	14

2   Marxist writers (e.g. Althusser) argue that the educational system

does not increase mobility or the chances of a meritocracy. It is a microcosm of wider society. The inequalities are reflected in the structure and organisation of the school. For the ruling class to survive the reproduction of labour power is essential. There is evidence of a decrease in equality of educational opportunity.

3   Bernstein (*Education Cannot Compensate for Society*)

(*a*)   He argues that the compensatory programmes would serve mainly to divert attention from the major inequalities in society.

(*b*)   He wrote 'I cannot understand how we can talk about offering compensatory education to children who in the first place have not, as yet, been offered an adequate educational environment . . .'

(*c*)   Such schemes imply that something is lacking in the family and so in the child.

4   Walsey (who directed the EPAs) said the scheme was intended to assist both children and schools, but it was never properly funded and the results were disappointing.

THE CURRICULUM

'The curriculum includes not only clearly defined teaching of subjects but also a hidden curriculum both of which transmit to young people a series of messages . . .' Briefly explain what is meant by this statement. With reference to other relevant sociological evidence outline some of the messages which might be transmitted in schools and describe the processes involved.

OFFICIAL CURRICULUM

Bernstein (*On the Classification and Framing of Educational Knowledge*) says that the curriculum defines what counts as valid knowledge. Evaluation counts as a valid realisation of this knowledge on the part of the taught.

Young (*Knowledge and Control*) argues that the focus of attention in the sociology of education has, for some, become an enquiry into the social organisation of 'knowledge' in educational institutions.

The question arises: what counts as knowledge, especially in the classroom? The answers given depend on the perspective or ideology of the observer.

William (*The Long Revolution*) has pointed out that 'education is not a product like cars and bread, but a selection and organisation from the available knowledge at a particular time which involves conscious and unconscious choices.' Sociologists endeavour to relate the principles that underly the curricula to their institutional and interactional setting in classrooms and in the wider society. He distinguishes four sets of educational ideologies which provide the basis for selecting the content of curriculum. These are related to the social position of those who hold them at a particular time:

Ideology	Social position	Policy
1. Liberal/Conservative	Gentry	The all-round educated man
2. Bourgeois	Professionals	Education for status
3. Democratic	Reformers	Education for all
4. Proletarian	Working classes	Relevance; choice

Shipman (*The Sociology of the School*) notes how all societies, whether capitalist or communist, have sets of beliefs which they wish to transmit to the future generations. Schools reflect these in the curriculum and teaching methods. Of each item on the curriculum it can be asked: does it serve a useful purpose and what priority should it have?

The Marxist view

1. The construction of a body of knowledge is inextricably linked to the interests of those who produce it.
2. The ruling elite develop their own self-justifying standards of evaluation.
3. Knowledge is what the gate-keepers of power define as knowledge. Reference to irrelevant facts in the classroom are ways by which teachers can distinguish the bright from the dull.
4. The curriculum is class based.

The Functionalist view

1. This presupposes an agreed set of societal values or goals which define both the selection and the organisation of knowledge in the curriculum.
2. The British educational system is usefully dominated by a set of academic curricula with a rigid stratification of knowledge. This provides status for the most able who are taught in ability groups and assessed by objective criteria.
3. The curriculum must change to meet changing economic needs.

Changes in the curriculum have tended to follow the functionalist principles: there has been more concern about the need for a more vocationally based curriculum. The Technical Vocational Education Initiative (TVEI) was introduced in 1984 to assist in this respect. The Certificate of Prevocational Education (CPVE) was introduced in 1985 for those who after compulsory schooling will benefit from more education as a preparation for adult life, but who do not wish to take A level courses.

In an endeavour to establish greater equality of opportunity some writers have suggested new approaches to the curriculum:

Points of criticism

1. Lawton (*Class, Culture and the Curriculum*) suggests that although there are differences between classes in attitudes and values, there are areas of similarity. Schools should endeavour to impose a common culture curriculum. This could be based on a heritage of knowledge and belief common to all.

1. The fact that there are major class differences in society makes a common culture curriculum impossible. The dominant middle-class value system would inevitably prevail.
It would not be possible to establish a consensus as to the content of a common culture within the existing social system.

2. Torrey (*Illiteracy in the Ghetto*) argues that where necessary lessons should be taught to ethnic minorities in their own speech patterns and they should be tested in the same way.

2. In Britain the ethnic minority consists of less than 4% of the population which makes the culturally differentiated curriculum impractical.

THE HIDDEN CURRICULUM

Whereas the official curriculum is the planned instructional activities in the school, the hidden curriculum is that which is not taught by the teachers.

Head (*Free Way to Learning*) says that the hidden curriculum describes the rules which pupils learn to survive. It is all the other things that are learnt during time in school. Children pick up an approach to living and an attitude to learning. It includes the rules for coping with problems, with delay, with teachers, with routine etc. Children learn how to feign interest, understanding and ability where there may be none.

Meighan (*A Sociology of Educating*) points out, however, that there is a problem with the definition. It is not clear whether the hidden curriculum is a concept with a recognisable content.

The Marxist perspective

1. The hidden curriculum can be seen as a means of achieving additional control of pupils in situations normally considered to be non-academic or informal: showing deference to staff, accepting humiliating references to themselves etc.
2. Children learn to internalise a particular self-image based on the perception of teachers ('non-academic' 'slow' etc.)
3. Children learn about their social-class position and what to expect in life as a result, following their grading and streaming in school.
4. They learn to accept a hierarchy of power and implicit criticism of being working class. They learn how to cope with boredom and repetition which will be valuable when they enter the world of work.

The Functionalist perspective

1. Children learn a great number of valuable rules about social life from contact with peers and teachers in school: to be punctual; to behave in acceptable ways in particular situations; to accept criticism; to aim for a particular occupational status in a realistic way; to be a part of a team; to be competitive; to accept defeat as well as success. Also, to seek appropriate goals; to adopt appropriate roles according to sex, ability, age etc.

EDUCATION AND GENDER

What differences are there between the educational experiences of boys and girls?

Studies suggest that teachers, in the course of their work, come to develop images and stereotypes of their pupils. They then operate with what they consider to be 'professional' knowledge and understanding, based on notions of what is best for a particular type of pupil. They do, however, according to some authorities, evaluate them in terms of 'family background' or 'school record'. They are also influenced by pressures from the local community to produce 'satisfactory pupils', from colleagues and superiors to 'maintain standards' as well as from university department and employers to produce 'the kind of person needed'. The result is that there are processes of selection and stratification operating in schools which may be far more subtle than crude streaming. Pupils can be persuaded to take certain courses of action and drop others because 'they are predicted failures from the start' or 'they are not the type'.

The effect operating on both boys and girls can be significant, but the following research indicates that girls are generally treated in ways that do much to discourage them from taking science subjects, entering technical careers, and, to a smaller extent, entering higher education.

1   Meighan (*A Sociology of Educating*) says that the regular patterns that appear in the educational biographies of girls and boys in Britain include the following:

(*a*)   Boys' and girls' achievements in school are similar up to the age of eleven.

(*b*)   Achievements of both sexes at O level show few differences except that twice as many boys as girls gain passes in science subjects.

(*c*)   For every hundred boys leaving with one A level or more there are ninety girls.

(*d*)   The following ratios exist (1978) between boys and girls:

Subject	Boys	Girls
Physics	6	1
Chemistry	4	1
Biology	9	8
Technical Drawing	200	1
Languages	1	2

(*e*)   More boys than girls achieve entry to university and other forms of higher education.

(*f*)   More girls than boys undertake courses of teacher training, nursing and catering.

2   Spender (*'Don't talk, listen'*: T.E.S.) argues that males dominate conversation, which is a reflection of the domination they have in society as a whole. Those without power are always the most vulnerable and tend to play a more submissive role. Girls learn this attitude in the classroom (it is part of the hidden curriculum). They discover that by avoiding a dominating role and that of the intellectual, they become less of a threat and more acceptable to their male peers. She notes how in one study girls thought it natural that male students should ask the questions and make the protests. The females should 'just get on with it' even though the work was considered tedious or pointless.

3   Nightingale ('What Katy didn't do', *Spare Rib*) found that books speci-

fically for girls showed a preponderance of discussions about 'love, dating, romance, with side-lines in problems like spots, glasses and so on, which interfere with romance . . .' The tom-boy's world is presented as ultimately unsatisfactory, with messages that it is perhaps better to be a girl, after all . . .

4   Grandall et al. (Child Development) noted how girls were brought up to be less competitive; their attitudes towards success are more likely to be mixed with doubts and lack of confidence. Girls tend to take the blame for failures and suggest that success is due to luck. Boys more readily blame others for failure and praise themselves for success.

5   Sharp (Just Like a Girl) notes how girls, particularly from working-class backgrounds, are seen and see themselves as primarily aspiring girl friends, wives and mothers, and at best aspiring typists, nurses or teachers. She argues that it is the comparatively low horizon of expectation that causes girls to do less well in school, especially at A level, than boys. It is her conclusion that as a result of the processes of socialisation in the home, which inculcate feminine attitudes, in school, where girls are given less of the teachers' attention and time and expected to be less able in certain fields, the sexual divison of labour is reinforced and any differences that do exist are greatly exaggerated.

6   Blackstone (New Society, February 1980) also argues that there are so few women scientists and engineers because of the impact of environmental influences on attitudes both in the home and the school. They are seen as 'male subjects' and the acceptable female role is constantly reinforced by the media, advertising and in the course of day-to-day interactions.

POLITICS AND POWER

CONTENTS

Questions on this topic cover the following areas:
1   The nature of politics:
    What is political behaviour?
2   Power
3   Power elites
4   The state
5   Voting behaviour:
    (a)   the significance of social class
    (b)   the political parties and their support

THE NATURE OF POLITICS

We can be said to act politically whenever we exercise constraint on others to behave as we want them to . . . Discuss.

Writers throughout history, from Plato and Aristotle to those of the present day, have speculated and theorised about the nature of politics. Aristotle said 'politics arises in organised states which recognise themselves to be an aggregate of many members, not a single tribe, religion, interest or tradition . . .' Politics is the master-science because it gives some priority and order to rival claims on the scarce resources of society.

Ferns and Watkins (*What Politics is About*) say that 'politics is about much more than government and administration, parties and elections. It embraces education, information, sciences, technology; in short, the totality of the human situation. Further, it is global in character . . .'

A sociological approach adopts a broad view of politics because political behaviour is seen primarily as power behaviour. This is the control exerted by one person or group over another in any social context. A narrower definition of political action would restrict it to the specialised machinery of government together with the administrative bureaucracy of the state. This refers more to 'party politics'.

WHAT CONSTITUTES POLITICAL ACTION?

1   The view that political action is the ability to exercise constraint over others is that of Weber. He said that power is 'the chance of men . . . to realise their own will . . . against the resistance of others who are participating in the action . . .' This view arises from the argument that power must be examined in terms of social relationships. There is only a limited amount available and one person holds power at the expense of others who do not. Therefore, they must be coerced to behave in particular ways.

(b)   From an interactionist perspective power may also be available in more subtle ways. People perceive themselves to be in inferior or superior social positions. Those in inferior situations may expect power to be exerted over them. These political realities are constructed in the process of day-to-day interactions.

2   (a)   From a functionalist perspective, Almond et al. (Civic Culture) suggest that political action occurs when decisions are made to undertake policies which promote integration and adaptation by means of the employment of threat or physical compulsion. Social liberty cannot exist without social restraint. There must be restrictions on some for others to experience freedom.

(b)   From this perspective there are inevitably unequal power relationships in society. This is because the more able are in superior positions. Those in inferior status positions must expect coercion and control so that social order is maintained. A government must have power to enforce its rules.

3   (a)   From a Marxist perspective there are unequal power relationships in society because the economic structure ensures that power is retained in the hands of a ruling elite. Political control is achieved by exerting power through force.

(b)   The constraints imposed by some over the freedom of others is the result of the exploitation of the proletariat by the bourgeoisie. In a truly free society such constraints would be unnecessary since all would be working for the common good without conflict or social divison.

POWER

Compare and contrast two different sociological theories of the nature and distribution of power in western democratic societies.   (AEB)

Power is central to political organisation. Legitimate governments claim power to control, coerce and direct the behaviour of people in order to achieve specific goals.

There is much debate among sociologists about the origin of power and how it is distributed in society. In the seventeenth century, the philosopher Hobbes said that the power which every individual had as a citizen was devolved on the sovereign in exchange for his protection. In the twentieth century the Chinese leader Mao Tse-tung said that 'power grows from the barrel of a gun'. Those who hold illegitimate power must surrender it to those whose rights have been ignored. Leaders must hand it back to the people.

Whereas Hobbes opposed the idea of equality of power among individuals since this would lead to conflict between them, Mao stood for the opposite principle.

The Marxist view

1   The distribution of power in a capitalist society reflects the inequalities that exist within it.
2   The capitalist economic infrastructure produces two main classes: the owners of the means of production and the proletariat.
3   Economic and political power are closely linked. To possess economic power is to possess political power.
4   The state is an agency of class power. There is an illusion of democracy but the reality is different.
5   The ruling elite possess the cultural capital and the ideological power which is imposed on the rest of society.
6   These values are transmitted through such social institutions as the family, education, religion, media etc.

The functionalist view

1   Power is a special resource which enables the holder to organise the means at his disposal to achieve goals for which there is a general commitment. A government promises greater economic growth or improved living standards.
2   Although some may have to suffer in the short term, eventually the majority will benefit, so that power is used for the social good. This will help achieve greater social cohesion and integration.
3   In an efficient social system more power exists in the society because there are constantly more things to be achieved.
4   The greater the chance of cooperation the greater the chance of achieving goals.
5   To achieve goals some people must be given special authority to direct others.
6   People will accept this, so legitimating the government, because it can be seen that there will be wide-ranging benefits in the long term.

POWER ELITES

Are members of power elites also members of a ruling class?

Is the concept of a political elite relevant to understanding contemporary British politics?

Marxists argue that the political structure in Britain (and all capitalist societies) is controlled by a powerful elite who are drawn from a ruling class and who conduct their activities in the interests of their class.

Pluralists claim that those who achieve power are people who have been drawn into the political arena from a variety of backgrounds and exercise their power on behalf of all citizens.

ELITES

1   From a pluralist perspective elites may be benign, having special skills, knowledge and abilities which are highly regarded in the society (e.g. educational or professional elites).
2   They use their abilities on behalf of others.
3   Members of power elites are those who occupy positions of total command in the society. They formulate policy, instigate it and ensure it is carried out. They may achieve their position by merit or sponsorship.
4   In society there are a range of elites (financial, political, etc.) which may compete against each other for influence and whose membership may change frequently.
5   Blondel (*Voters, Parties and Leaders*) says that in Britain political practice is a network of influences, counter-influences and compromises and is open to pressure from many interest groups. The apparent authors of policies may not be their real authors . . .

RULING-CLASS

From a Marxian perspective this implies:
1   There is a small class whose members own the major instruments of economic production.
2   Members perceive themselves to be a cohesive social group.
3   They have interests in common.
4   They are in permanent conflict with the classes they exploit.
5   They also hold positions of political power.

RULING CLASS THEORISTS

1   Miliband (*The Power of Labour and the Capitalist Enterprise*) criticises the pluralist view. He says that capitalist enterprises enjoy a 'strategic position' in their dealings with government because they control economic resources. He argues that the power of labour (working people) is not equal to the power of capital. He sees the growth of trade unions as an essential countervailing elite which is seeking to moderate the power of business owners. This is one reason why unions get so badly attacked in the media.
2   Lupton and Wilson (*The Social Background and Connections of Top Decision-Makers*) examined the findings of the Parker Tribunal (1957). They noted the network of relationships it revealed among top businessmen and politicians of that time. They claim it showed a

shared background, culture and set of customary procedures between powerful banking families and politicians. There was an interconnection between family, school, university, occupation and club.

3 Westergaard (*Power in Britain*) argues that the dominant grouping in Britain is that of a small homogeneous elite based on wealth and property. It is assured of the press support, as well as that of the Conservative Party. Its members have exclusive educational backgrounds and are often united by close ties of kinship. (The kind of evidence that might be used to support this argument would include the fact that, in 1970, of the 339 Conservative MPs 51 were educated at Eton; 152 came from other public schools; 114 went to grammar schools; Mrs Thatcher's 1979 administration included 13 members of the House of Lords, of whom 3 were in the Cabinet. Of the 22 members of the Cabinet only 2 did not go to a public school; 17 were graduates of either Oxford or Cambridge).

One of the problems that arises in accepting this model of social power is what happens when the Labour Party wins an election, since its members tend not to have the same social background as Conservatives? One view is that during such times the ruling class simply maintains its position because it has only to endure small and ineffectual changes. The Labour Party cannot introduce extreme socialist policies because it requires the support of businessmen and the City.

THE PLURALIST VIEW

1 Dahl (*Who Governs*?) argues that the hypothesis of the existence of a ruling class being also a ruling power elite is difficult to test. To do so:

(*a*)   The group would have to be clearly defined.

(*b*)   A situation must be established in which the preferences of the elite are challenged and yet they prevail.

(*c*)   A ruling class must be shown to have members who exhibit group consciousness, coherence and conspiracy.

(*d*)   Who is to decide the number of decisions that constitute 'power'? Who decides what constitutes a decision? Without clarification of these issues it is difficult to evaluate the extent of a group's power.

(*e*)   The whole concept is also ideologically tainted.

2 Wakeford (*Power in Britain*) says that there is much evidence to indicate a substantial degree of the clustering of power in modern Britain. This suggests support for the pluralist perspective:

(*a*)   Power is not located in any single centre or controlled by any specific group.

(*b*)   Although direct democracy is not possible in a large society, there is representative democracy, in which elected representatives may hold power from one election to the next.

(*c*)   Because there is competition for power this ensures that it is not misused and not monopolised.

(*d*)   It is both inevitable and necessary that power elites should exist since a society needs the most able to lead.

THE STATE

How would you account for the development of the modern state?   (Cam)

Sociologists have increasingly focused their attention on the role of the state in modern society. Explain why this is so and examine the major competing views of the role of the state in contemporary society.   (AEB)

Fern and Watkins note that there are 175 nation states in the world. They have three characteristics: a territory, a population and a government. The government is said to possess sovereign authority over the people in the state's territory. Governments differ greatly in their form and organisation. They have one common characteristic: they are all a minority of the population they govern.

An important aspect of the study of the political organisation of society is man's efforts to organise the government of his community. Throughout history there have been debates as to the nature of the legitimate power to rule, as well as the origins and functions of the state.

HISTORICAL PERSPECTIVE

Plato in the fifth century BC said that the state originated as a means of defending the interests of the individual who is helpless and alone. An organised system of authority for promoting and defending the interests of groups and individuals is necessary.

Aristotle in the third century BC said that man was by nature a political animal who desired an organised social life. The city states of Greece had the power to make and enforce decisions. The ability to make laws and exercise power on behalf of citizens of the state is the function of government.

In the bible, St Paul explains why people should obey the state: 'Let every soul be subject unto the higher power. For there is no power but of God . . .'

In medieval times the spiritual base of society was still recognised. Ethical codes were backed by spiritual sanctions. The political system was seen to be divinely ordained; conformity to the rules of the state meant conformity to the rules of God.

In the seventeenth century there was a new sceptical spirit of enquiry. The philosopher Locke explained the origin of the civil state by arguing that there had previously existed a state of nature. This was unsatisfactory because of 'a want of an established, settled known law' as well as a lack of 'an independent and indifferent judge to pronounce on conflicts between men in a state of nature . . ' The resulting chaos led people to realise that there were some advantages in accepting the restraints of civil society in order to preserve life, liberty and property.

In the same period, Hobbes justified the rule of the state by an absolute monarch. People entered a contract with the sovereign who would provide an environment of peace, order and security in return for unquestioning obedience. The aggregate of consenting people united under one sovereign power becomes 'the state'.

In the eighteenth century the Swiss writer Rousseau argued that the surrender of individual rights was not made to the sovereign power but to the whole of society. The contract is between all people who agree to forgo their natural freedom by constituting an organised state which is to act for all its members. People are compelled to obey common laws which make them free (from uncertainty, conflict etc.) Every citizen has a share in the rule-making process to which each is subject.

In the nineteenth century Hegel argued that 'the nation state is the highest form of social organisation. We are born into the state and it is this which gives our lives meaning. People must therefore work in a united way for the benefit of the state.'

In the same period the philosophers Mill and Bentham opposed these views. Mill argued that the aim of the state was to provide the conditions in which individuals could flourish. He was suspicious of a government that increased its range of activities for fear that it suppressed individual liberty. The best government was said to be least government.

Bentham accounted for man's obedience to the authority of the state in terms of the idea that its laws and rules were designed to produce the greatest good for the greatest number.

In contemporary society the heirs of these debates reach some consensus:

THE MODERN STATE

In the modern state:
1 There is centralisation of power.
2 The state is the legitimate source of power.
3 There develops a bureaucracy to administer power.
4 There is increasing unity of language, currency and legal system throughout the territories administered.
5 There is a hierarchial structure of power.
6 The ideal of government should be to promote the good of all its citizens.
7 Subjects, in obeying laws, are seldom conscious of clear rational motives. Political obedience is a form of 'social compliance'.

The Marxist view	The pluralist/functionalist view
1. To control the economy is to control the state. 2. The state organises relationships between different interest groups. It helps maintain power in the hands of the ruling class, which controls the economy. 3. The state is 'the committee of the whole bourgeoisie' in capitalist society. 4. In a truly socialist society there would be the abolition of the state's repressive controls. Then, Lenin said, 'every cook would rule the state'. 5. Later, neo-Marxists have argued that the state is relatively autonomous in that it is not staffed entirely by the bourgeoisie. If it were, it might become divided by sectional interest and open to greater working-class criticism. 6. The concept of democracy is a myth. The benefits of power are too tempting.	1. No single individual or group controls the state in a democratic society. 2. There are many groups competing for power in open elections. Also, the activities of interest groups act as a means of limiting the power of any one. 3. The state takes account of the needs of all its citizens; if it did not there would be constant disruption (as in South Africa). 4. Socialist societies are often noted for use of repressive controls. 5. Access of power and authority in the administrative bureaucracy of the state is open to all on the basis of qualifications. The most able reach the highest positions and obtain the highest rewards. 6. Forms of representative democracy operate fairly effectively.

Conclusions:

Remember that it is important to summarise and reach a conclusion:

1 A major concern of sociology has been who has power and how it is used.
2 The state represents political power: policies can be enforced by law.
3 Sociologists also wish to understand the relationship between economic and political power.
4 The major perspective by which analyses are made are those of Marxism and pluralism: the distinction between a single power elite and many groups who share political and economic power. These may be summarised:

Marxist view	Pluralist view
1. The state serves the interests of the ruling class.	1. The state is impartial. It seeks to maintain order and stability.
2. The state promotes conflict by promoting capitalist values.	2. The state manages conflict by promoting liberal values.
3. Mills (*The Power Elite*) said that in the USA power was in the hands of political, military and business men.	3. The state provides agencies which manage the competing demands of groups.
4. The state promotes the illusion of political and economic freedoms.	4. The state is composed of a plurality of interests; people have many different allegiances so that different groups emerge and disappear according to goals.

5 Some contemporary writers argue that both perspectives contain some truth. Pahl has suggested that more research should be focussed on the power of bureaucracies and the decision-making processes in key state agencies, especially national government.

VOTING BEHAVIOUR

How far does class explain allegiance in modern British society?   (Cam)

Describe the major changes in the relationship between social class and voting behaviour in Britain since the Second World War. Examine the sociological explanations of deviant voting behaviour.   (AEB)

SOCIAL CLASS

Butler and Stokes (*Forces Shaping Electoral Choice*) quote Pulzer, who says 'class is the basis of British party politics, all else is embellishment and detail . . .'

Objective social-class membership has been described by many writers as the most important factor influencing voting behaviour, the traditional alignment being for middle-class groups to vote Conservative and the working-class sector to vote Labour (the party founded by the trade unions in 1906). But since the majority of people in Britain fall into classes 3b, 4 and 5 there must be cross-class voting, otherwise there would not be any Conservative victories.

Table 1: Percentage of each social class by voting intentions, general elections, October 1974.

Party	Class 1	Class 2	Class 3a	Class 3b	Class 4	Class 5
Conservative	68	60	46	30	25	34
Labour	14	20	28	50	59	52
Liberal	19	19	23	18	14	12

Source: Gallup Polls

This suggests a clear line of support for the major parties between manual and non-manual workers who intended to vote. It also indicates that about one third of manual workers intended to vote Conservative.

Table 2: Voting by class in 1983 general election.

Party	Classes 1 & 2	Class 3a	Class 3b	Classes 4 & 5
Conservative	62	55	39	29
Labour	12	21	35	44
Alliance	27	24	27	28

This suggests that the decline in class alignment and voting behaviour continues to change. The Conservatives increased their support among the skilled manual sector (3b).

There has been much research into the behaviour of the working-class Tory: between 1951 and 1964 the Conservatives won three consecutive elections. This led some observers to suggest that there must have been some major change in the class structure in this period:

1 Butler and Rose put forward the embourgeoisement thesis. This stated that the more prosperous sections of the working class (3b) are losing their identity as a social group and are becoming merged into the lower middle-class. This influences their voting behaviour.

2 Lockwood and Goldthorpe (*The Affluent Worker*) tested the thesis and rejected it because they said class is a complex concept and is not determined by income alone. They used four criteria (norms, relationships, economic and political factors) in their study but found that major class differences existed between blue- and white-collar workers with regard to each.

They pointed to the emergence of a new working class whose members shared some of the materialistic aspirations of the middle class but whose values and identity are still with the working class.

3 Nordlinger (*The Working-Class Tory*) found that many working-class voters preferred the candidate who had high ascribed status. Some voted Tory for pragmatic reasons; they believed that their policies offered them more than Labour.

4 McKenzie and Silver (*The Working-Class Tory in England*) reach similar conclusions. They argue that the pragmatic voters (whom they term 'secular') are more concerned about party policy than the deferentials. Such working-class Tories were generally better informed than traditional Labour voters. There were a high proportion of women among the deviant working-class Tories, probably because they had more regard for traditional values, family, religion etc. More recent research suggests that more women are supporting the Labour Party.

5 Crewe (*The Disturbing Truth Behind Labour's Rout 1983*) says that it is not age or sex but class that continues to structure party choice, but this has steadily weakened over the last twenty-five years. Labour remains the party of a segment of the working-class. The implication is that there is much pragmatic voting occurring now which cuts across traditional class lines.

The Labour vote largely remains working-class but the working-class has ceased to be largely Labour (Crewe). Explain and discuss this statement in the light of recent election results.

In his analysis of the loss of the 1979 and 1983 elections Crewe explains how, although the Labour Party continues to rely largely on the working-class vote for its present strength, there is much evidence to show that the working-class is becoming fragmented in its distribution of votes. He argues that in 1983 the Conservative landslide victory (144 majority) was not the result of increasing its own vote (which fell 1.4% from 1979) but to an even split in the non-Conservative vote.

Table showing the distribution of votes in 1979 and 1983 Elections.

Table 3:

Election	Tory %	Labour %	Alliance (Lib/SDP) %
May 1979	43.9	36.9	13.8
June 1983	42.5	27.6	25.4

(*a*)   The Labour Party can no longer rely on a solid working-class vote.

(*b*)   Its share of the working-class electorate is about 27%. It is now increasingly the middle-class whose vote reflects class consciousness and solidarity.

▶ *Factors working against the Labour Party*:

(*a*)   The spread of home ownership.

(*b*)   The contraction of public-sector employment.

(*c*)   The decline of blue-collar trade-union membership. Between 1970 and 1984 there were one million more white-collar trade unionists; one million fewer blue-collar members; 500,000 more women members.

(*d*)   An ageing electorate. The Labour Party has much strength among the over-sixty-fives.

▶ *The consequences*:

(*a*)   In 1959 there was a 40% gap between Labour's share of the non-manual as against the manual vote. In 1979 the gap was 27% and in 1984 21%. Mass unemployment has failed to produce class polarisation.

(*b*)   A large proportion of the Labour vote was lost to the Alliance. For every three switching to the Alliance one vote went to the Conservatives.

(*c*)   More women voters are moving to support the Labour Party (24%), although the Alliance has benefited most (28%).

(*d*)   In 1979 Labour had the support of 55% of voting trade unionists. In 1983 support had fallen to 39%.

(*e*)   Labour did badly in the 1983 election and could fall behind the Alliance.

Conclusions: Crewe argues that the transformation of working-class partisanship over the past twenty-five years must rank as one of the most significant of all post-war changes in the social basis of British politics: 'Labour remains the party of only a segment of the working-class. That is the traditional, semi- and unskilled sector at the bottom of the social scale. It no longer automatically represents the new working-class.' He is referring to those employed in private-sector occupations, who are increasingly affluent, home owning and who are less likely to be protected by a unifying working-class subculture.

It is his view that the division of Britain is no longer between the classes but within the working-class.

The major development affecting political life in recent years has been the changing pattern of support for the main political parties. Discuss.

A political party An organisation of active political agents, who are concerned with the opportunities for gaining power and who compete for popular support with another group which holds different and divergent views. The party operates with an ideology which determines its policies and activities.

Table 5: showing the distribution of skilled voters.

	1970	1974 (Oct)	1979	1983
Labour	55	49	41	35
Con.	35	25	41	41
Lib/SDP	8	20	15	24

Sources: Butler *et al. The British General Elections; Mori*.

1 The Conservative Party
(*a*)   Crewe notes that the party has increased its support from young to old (except among the over-sixty-fives).
(*b*)   It is beginning to lose some of its female support.
(*c*)   In general Conservative support has remained fairly solid among its 1979 supporters.
(*d*)   There has been a growth of 26% in professional occupations between 1971 and 1981 which benefited the Conservatives.
(*e*)   The Conservatives conducted an effective media campaign to attack their opponents in 1983.
(*f*)   Mrs Thatcher maintained her image as a tough leader (Falklands Factor).
(*g*)   Thomas ('The Man Who Put Mrs Thatcher In . . .' *New Society*, May 1983) argues that:
          (i) any party seeking victory must be in tune with the feelings of the skilled workers. They are affluent, potentially socially mobile; car owners; home owners and increasingly have children who enter middle-class occupations.
          (ii) The Conservatives succeeded in capturing 41% of the votes of this sector in 1970 and held it in 1983 (see Table 5).
2 The Labour Party
King ('The People's Flag Turns Deepest Blue', *Observer*, 1979) argues that Labour lost the 1979 election because:
(*a*)   When in power in 1978 they failed to control the level of strikes.
(*b*)   A gap has opened up between the Parliamentary Labour Party

activities and the general public. The electorate prefers moderates whilst the activists prefer radicals.

(c)   Regular opinion polls show that a decreasing number of traditional supporters favour Labour Party policies on defence (unilateralism); home ownership (refusal to sell council houses); trade-union connections.

(d)   People do not favour radical socialist policies which they perceive are part of the Labour Party programme.

Ryan ('The Slow Death of Labour England', *New Society*, June 1983) argues that the traditional social basis of the old Labour Party is now dead:

(a)   The emergence of the Alliance Party has taken many votes from Labour.

(b)   The committed middle-class socialist segment still exists but takes little part in active politics.

(c)   There is no demand for extreme radicalism in contemporary Britain. The Labour Party has lost its 'middle of the road' image to the Alliance.

(d)   Voters are increasingly pragmatic and supporting the party that seems to have most to offer them at the time.

(e)   The Labour Party has not managed to change its appeal. The non-Conservative electorate is a forward-looking one attached to competence, individual freedom and security.

3   Social Democratic Party and Liberal Alliance

The SDP was first mooted in the Dimbleby Lecture on TV in 1979 by Roy Jenkins. The party was duly founded by Jenkins, Shirley Williams, William Rogers and David Owen, all elected Labour MPs who had held Cabinet posts. They were joined by other MPs from Labour and one from the Conservative Party.

(a)   They have adopted the image of 'the party in the middle' by establishing an alliance with the Liberals.

(b)   Owen (*The Future that Will Work*) claimed that it was a right-of-centre party with a social conscience.

(c)   Shirley Williams in a speech said 'A centre party may lack roots and principles but the SDP at least has David Owen . . .'

(d)   It has been criticised as 'a media party', its leaders being well known as a result of wide media coverage.

(e)   The Alliance has won a high proportion of its electoral votes from previous Labour supporters. Crewe has pointed out that to have a serious chance of breaking through and holding the balance of power the Alliance needs to have at least 27% of popular support. In the 1983 election it won twenty-three seats and polled 26% of the vote.

(f)   Crewe has also noted that the electoral system penalises the Alliance for spreading rather than concentrating votes throughout the country. To obtain seats in roughly due proportions the Alliance needs 40% of the vote. To obtain about seventy-five seats it needs about 35%.

(g)   In 1985 the Alliance won the Brecon and Radnorship by-election by 559 votes over Labour. The Conservatives who held the seat came third.

(*h*)   Analysts argue that the best chance of defeating the Conservatives in future elections is an Alliance/Labour Pact in which each withdraws its candidate from a limited number of seats which it knows it cannot win. But there is opposition to the suggestion from activists who argue that parties exist for more than just winning elections.

(*i*)   Field (Labour MP) has advocated the formation of 'A Rainbow Circle' which would describe the pact. It would be an attempt to establish a set of pragmatic policies, avoiding ideological principles, which would attract a wide range of public support in an election.

(*j*)   Dahrendorf (*The Collapse of Class . . .*) argues that the traditional class structure is changing rapidly. One of the results is that the traditional loyalties to political parties are also changing. This has allowed the SDP to emerge as a new and effective third party in British politics in the 1980s.

(*k*)   The SDP and the Liberals split in 1988. The Liberals became the Democrats (or Liberal Democrats/SLD).

4   The 1987 election result.

Crewe (*A New Class of Politics*) presents an analysis.

He argues that:

(*a*)   Media coverage had little effect on voting intentions.

(*b*)   The Alliance maintained its middle class support although it had one fewer seat than in 1983. (23% of the vote).

(*c*)   The Labour Party is representing a declining segment of the working class and gained only 20 seats more than in 1983. (32% of the vote)

(*d*)   The Conservatives maintained widespread support and lost only 15 seats since 1983. The Party held the support of the 'working class Tories'. In the 1980s these are the affluent skilled manual workers (43% of the vote).

He concludes that the Labour Party must break out of the old class fortress and broaden its appeal. It is a view opposed by Heath *et al* (*How Britain Votes*). They argue that the working class has not permanently lost its identity or consciousness. Any de-alignment in voting is temporary.

Voting patterns by social class 1987 election

Social class		Con	Lab	Alliance
middle class	1 professional/ managerial	59	14	27
	2 office/clerical	52	22	26
working class	3 skilled manual	43	34	24
	4 semi/unskilled	31	50	19
	5 unemployed	32	51	17

Quota sample 4886 people June 10/11th 1987

RELIGION

CONTENTS

Among the important topic areas on which questions are based are the following:

1 The secularisation debate:
   (a) The problems of definition.
   (b) The problems of measuring the extent of secularisation.
   (c) The causes of secularisation.
2 Sects, denominations and churches:
   (a) Examples of the typology and its value to sociologists.
   (b) Reasons for the emergence of sects.
3 Theories of religion:
   (a) Functionalist.
   (b) Weberian.
   (c) Marxian.

SECULARISATION

THE PROBLEM OF DEFINITION

The concept of secularisation is used in so many different ways that it now obscures rather than clarifies the debate about the place of religion in contemporary society. Explain and Discuss.   (AEB)

The secularisation debate has focused around the question of whether religion is of increasingly less significance in the day-to-day lives of people in society and whether it is also of less relevance as a social institution.

1 Shiner (*The Concept of Secularisation in Empirical Research*) discusses the range of meanings which writers have adopted in their use of the term 'secularisation' and shows the confusion that has resulted. He endeavours to bring the concept into focus by considering the range of possible definitions:

   (a) It is used to mean *the decline of religion*: previously accepted symbols, doctrines and institutions lose prestige and influence. He points out that the problem is to find the golden age from which the decline started.

   (b) It is used to mean *increasing conformity with this world*. Society becomes absorbed with the pragmatic tasks of the present. He suggests that the difficulty with this view is that there is a problem in measuring 'conformity with this world'.

(c)   It is used to mean *the disengagement of society from religion and religious values*. Religion is more of an inward type with little or no influence on social institutions. There is a separation of religion from political life.

He says that the difficulty with this definition is that it is not easy to know at what point secularisation has occurred. In Britain, for example, religion is still associated with political institutions: the Church of England has been described as the Conservative Party at prayer.

(d)   It is used to mean *the transposition of religious beliefs and institutions*; knowledge and behaviour once understood to be grounded in divine powers are transformed into purely human responsibility. The problem with this view is that it cannot be proved that some secular belief systems contain elements from Judeo-Christian beliefs, such as some Marxist theory; or that the capitalist ethic had religious origins.

(e)   It is used to mean that *the world is deprived of its sacred character*. Man and nature become the object of rational/causal explanation and manipulation. The problem arises that this definition starts from the assumption that man has become largely independent of religion. Some argue that man is 'incurably religious' and that the sacred may/must have been temporarily pushed into the unconscious and that it is finding new forms of expression.

(f)   It is used to mean *a movement from a sacred to a secular society*. All theories of change become grounded in secular rather than sacred explanations. But critics argue that this is a general theory of change and does not relate specifically to religious change.

Shiner's conclusions: (a)   The term has often served the special interests of the users. The result is that it is swollen with overtones and implications, especially those associated with indifference or hostility to whatever is considered 'religious'.

(b)   The appropriate conclusion to draw from the confusing connotations would seem to be that the word should be dropped and replaced with one such as 'differentiation' or 'transposition', which would be neutral.

(c)   If it is used, it must be neutralised to avoid polemical connotations.

2   Martin (*The Religious and the Secular*)

He too argues that the concept of secularisation 'is the tool of counter-religious ideologies'. He rejects the use of the term because:

(a)   There is the unavoidable presence of religious elements in an anti-religious position.

(b)   It is difficult to interpret 'religious decline' and decline in 'religious practices'.

(c)   It is unfair to make comparisons over time because they can be misleading. Attitudes and norms are relative to time and place.

3   Berger (*The Social Reality of Religion*)

He accepts that it has been employed by different writers in both negative and positive ways. In anti-clerical writers secularisation has come to mean the liberation of modern man from religious constraints; whereas some Christian writers (e.g. Bonhoeffer) have used it to argue that secularisation is evidence for the truth of Christianity. It is a part of God's plan that man should become more mature and come of age by acting in Christian ways without recourse to 'belief' in God. However, he says, the term is useful and refers to

(*a*)   'empirically available processes of great importance in modern western history. Whether these are to be deplored or welcomed is irrelevant. . .'

(*b*)   It also has a subjective meaning. There is secularisation of society and consciousness. People create reality and act on the basis of their interpretations.

▶ He describes the impact of secularisation:

(*a*)   It is stronger on men than women.

(*b*)   It affects the middle aged more than the young or old.

(*c*)   It occurs more in the cities than in the country.

(*d*)   It affects classes more directly concerned with modern industrial production than those in more traditional occupations.

(*e*)   Roman Catholics are more immune than Protestants and Jews.

He concludes that there is little doubt that the west has produced an increasing number of individuals who look upon the world and their own lives without reference to religious interpretations. So the concept does have some relevance.

PROBLEMS OF MEASUREMENT

Though there is considerable evidence that participation in institutional religion has declined in Britain there is also considerble disagreement over the sociological interpretation of this evidence. Explain and discuss.

There are some writers who argue that the empirical evidence relating to church participation shows decline in every important aspect. There are others, however, (e.g. Martin) who argue that the same data can be interpreted to show it has the opposite implications. It may even suggest that the orthodox churches become leaner but healthier as they discard peripheral members for a hard core of genuine devotees.

1   Wilson (*Religion in a Secular Society*)

He describes the erosion of the institutional power of the established churches and uses much statistical evidence to support his case. He accepts the problems of measurement but argues that the process is well under way.

2   Wilson ('The Anglican Church and Its Decline', *New Society* 5 December 1974)

He develops his arguments further:

(*a*)   The process of secularisation in Britain (as in other advanced industrial societies) affects the Church of England more acutely than the other denominations.

(*b*)   Statistics indicate that the Church of England faces serious problems:

> 1966–69: a fall of 27% in numbers confirmed.
> 1956–68: a fall of 18% in numbers baptised.
> 1929–73: a fall of 19% in numbers marrying in church.
> 1861: 1 clergy man to 960 people.
> 1971: 1 clergyman to 4,000 people.

(*c*)   The church is regarded increasingly as a welfare service agency, available for use in an emergency. It is used on a regular basis by about 12% of the population.

(*d*)   He concludes that on any range of indicators the facts of decline are evident. There is an increasing disposition by the public to regard Christian belief as incredible and irrelevant.

3   The Paul Report was a fact-finding report suggesting that many of the problems faced by the Church of England related to the payment and deployment of clergy.

The report is criticised by Wilson who says the weakness of the church is the result of many factors including:

(*a*)   The effects of books and TV programmes by theologians (e.g. Cupitt's *The Myth of God Incarnate* and the Bishop of Woolwich's *Honest to God*) which appear to question and doubt fundamental Christian doctrine. These help undermine people's faith.

(*b*)   The emergence of new sectarian movements which attract people away from orthodox Christian churches in large numbers, and which often provide non-Christian belief systems.

4   Paul (*The Church in Daylight*) found that in the 1970s there were just 339 clergy looking after 3,700,000 people in the 97 most densely populated parishes. In 1971, of 10,000 clergy, only 27 were under 30. 51 were aged 80–92 and there was a shortage of about 3,000 clergy.

5   Wilson's view is that the clergy are losing status in modern society because they are largely redundant; the increasing likelihood of the ordination of women is an attempt to make up the shortfall. His general conclusion is that the statistics indicate that secularisation is well advanced so that the Church of England is gradually becoming reduced to the condition of a sect. The first Protestant woman bishop was appointed in the USA in 1988.

▶   Alternative interpretations of the empirical evidence:

1   Martin (*A Sociology of English Religion*) argues that:

(*a*)   It is difficult to locate a golden age when England was totally religious in attitude and behaviour.

(*b*)   Whilst people may not be attending churches in large numbers this does not necessarily indicate that they do not have strong beliefs in Christian doctrines. These are very difficult to measure. Some studies suggest that the numbers identifying with the Church of England amount to as many as two thirds of the population; about two in ten with the Roman Catholic Church and one in ten with the Free Churches.

(c)   Although only 12% may attend every Sunday studies suggest that about 25% attend every other Sunday, 30% each month and 45% once in the year.

(d)   People continue to have a strong sense of the supernatural. Large numbers express belief in 'subterranean theologies', belief in superstition, luck etc. The growth of fringe sects suggests that people are simply expressing their religious needs in different ways.

(e)   Religion still plays an important part in daily life: there are daily services on the radio listened to by millions; the church is still used by most people in times of crisis or celebration by means of ceremonies associated with 'rites of passage'.

2   Statistics indicate that although there has been a decline in the membership of the Church of England the Catholic Church has made some gains:

Table: showing percentage changes 1975–79.

	Membership	Adult attendance	Child attendance
All Protestant churches	−3.6	+ 0.5	−3.9
Roman Catholic	+1.1	+16.7	0.0
All churches	−1.4	− 2.4	−2.5

Also there has been a growth in many sectarian groups, especially those catering for ethnic minorities; the West Indian Pentecostal churches and the Rastafarian movement have increased in numbers.

3   The Ecumenical movement, to unite all the main Christian churches, will greatly increase the strength of Christianity in Britain; as will the ordination of women. Also the clergy are taking a greater lead in social issues. In 1978 a Baptist conference urged members to speak out against apartheid, the National Front and other social evils. In 1982 a conference of Roman Catholic priests voted to support unilateral disarmament.

THE CAUSES

How can the process of secularisation be explained?

There is much debate as to what is meant by secularisation and how it can be measured. But if it is taken to mean a long-term decline in the relevance of religion both as an institution and in the day-to-day lives of people in society, then certain explanations can be put forward to account for the process.

▶   The proponents of the view argue:

1   The impact of science and technology has helped to make religious faith redundant. All apparent mysteries can be viewed as problems for which explanations are possible.

2   Berger (*The Social Reality of Religion*) argues:
     (*a*)   The economic process of industrialisation is a secularising
     force. The development of divergent lifestyles encourages a crisis in
     the credibility of religion.
     (*b*)   This also causes a collapse in the plausibility of traditional
     religious definitions of reality.
     (*c*)   The man in the street is confronted with a wide variety of
     reality-defining agencies that compete for his allegiance. People have
     greater choice as to which belief system to adopt. This helps to
     increase the 'secularisation of consciousness'.

3   *Urbanisation:* with the growth of large towns and cities people are
     attracted away from traditional, stable societies in which social order
     is related to the power of the church. In cities life is more anonymous
     and there are many other activities to compete for their time and
     attention. Wilson sees church-going as a leisure activity in contem-
     porary society.
         Martin has described a loss of community in society which has
     resulted in increasing apathy running through the society. There is a
     loss of membership in a range of voluntary associations including
     trade unions, political parties and churches.

4   *Bureaucratisation:* as societies become more economically developed
     they produce more highly rational bureaucracies. These are the
     means of administering large complex economies. As they become
     institutionalised the previous religious legitimations of the state lose
     their significance. Religion becomes more privatised, a matter of
     choice or preference.

5   *The media:* Crockford's *Clerical Directory* stated that 'one sometimes
     has the impression that control of the press and BBC is in the hands of
     men who are hostile to the Christian religion and mainly to the
     Church of England.' The authors complained of a loss of emphasis on
     moral and ethical values at the expense of trivia and entertainment.

6   Harvey Cox (*Secular City*) argues that secularisation is inevitable and a
     part of God's plan. The book is by a Harvard professor of divinity. He
     describes secularisation as the celebration of the death of religion and
     the birth of a new, true Christianity. Secularisation delivers mankind
     from mystical controls over his destiny. Urban, scientific man repre-
     sents the development of maturity and responsibility. Far from being
     something to oppose, Christians should see it as man's coming of
     age.

7   *Ecclesiastical reforms:* these may have caused many traditional church-
     goers to become more critical of the churches and cause defections
     from them. For Catholics, the reforms of Vatican II which abolished
     the Latin mass and made other changes in dogma and liturgy, and for
     many members of the Church of England the changes in the language
     of the prayer book, destroyed traditional strengths and assets.

Is the sect, denomination, church typology helpful in the study of religious organisations?

Why do sociologists construct typologies of religious organisations?

TYPOLOGIES

The ideal type is intended as a means of clarifying complex concepts by extracting their key characteristics. They should serve to stimulate empirical investigation. A model is constructed against which researchers can compare similar items in the real world to see how far they conform to or deviate from their ideal descriptions.

1   Troeltch (*The Social Teaching of the Christian Churches*) The sociological concept of the sect was first evolved by Troeltch. He tried to give it some precision by making a comparison with the concept of the church. He developed a continuum between the conservative church and the perfectionist sect.

The sect	The church
1. A protest movement	1. A means of social integration
2. Egalitarian	2. Hierarchic.
3. Radical	3. Traditional
4. Appeals to outcasts	4. Appeals to higher classes
5. Opposed to the state	5. Works with the state
6. Members show total commitment	6. Members exercise choice
7. No specialist priests	7. Specialist priests, teachers etc.
8. Emphasis on fellowship	8. Emphasis on relationship between the individual and the institution
9. Status by achievement (members must qualify)	9. Status by ascription (members are born into the church
10. Non-institutionalised	10. Highly institutionalised

Wilson is critical of this typology because he says that the sect should not necessarily be understood in direct contrast with the church. He says the sect may appeal to those opposed to the state secular institutions of society or other groups within it. It is not necessarily just opposed to the established church.

2   Niebuhr (*Social Sources of Denominationalism*) tried to establish how sects became denominations. Later writers have introduced distinctions between a sect, denomination and a church.

Broom and Selznick suggest:

The sect	The denomination	The church
1. Concerned with purity of doctrine	1. Limited membership	1. Highly institutionalised
2. Depth of religious feeling	2. Limited aspirations	2. Offers integration with social and economic order
3. Emphasises active participation	3. Children inducted at a young age	3. Members born into the church
4. Intolerance towards other groups	4. No great demands for high levels of commitment	4. Routinised participation
5. Critical assessment of the secular world	5. Reflects belief in separation of church and state	5. Deepest commitment is provided by specialists

Other distinctions that have been suggested include:

1. Usually of recent appearance (Scientology 1954)	1. Of longer existence (Methodism, 18th century)	1. Very long existence; highly organised structure
2. Represents only a small minority of devout believers	2. National membership with regional differences	2. Represents the majority in society
3. Often advocates unorthodox ideology (salvation only for sect membership)	3. May specify some limitations on behaviour (no alcohol)	3. Salvation is available to all (no sense of exclusiveness)
4. Expulsion is possible	4. Expulsion unusual	4. Expulsion rare
5. Emphasis on charismatic leadership	5. Some charismatic preachers	5. No emphasis on charismatic leadership

3   Yinger (*Types of Religious Organisation*) produced a classification which focuses on the degree of institutionalisation which distinguishes different types of religious organisations. He identifies five categories: cults (religious groups whose main preoccupation is an esoteric belief or form of worship: there is much secrecy and the exclusion of outsiders); sects (of recent origin); established sects; denominations and churches.

Wilson argues that classifications must avoid being culture-bound (e.g. centred on Christian organisations). They must use categories which recognise the similarities of social processes in different contexts and provide methods of analysis which have wide applicability.

4   Wilson (*Patterns of Sectarianism*) argues that it is important to explain the relationship between doctrine, organisation and form of association and action, all of which may change independently of each other. The categories must not be from the Christian tradition alone and from only one historical period. He examines a series of sectarian organisations. He accepts that the elements fused in any sect are always a unique combination of variables which may not be distinctive of one sect alone. For him the principal criterion of classification is 'response to the world', how they resolve the question 'what shall we do to be saved?'

He has analysed a range of sects and noted that different types make a different kind of appeal at different times.

He identifies seven types of sect and the message each offers:

1. **Revolutionist**   God will overturn the world
2. **Introvertionist**   God calls us to abandon the world
3. **Reformist**   God call us to reform the world
4. **Utopian**   God calls us to reconstruct the world
5. **Convertionist**   God will change us
6. **Manipulationist**   God calls us to change our position

7. **Thaumaturgist**   God will grant us powers and will work miracles

He says these represent a complex orientation to the wider society and its cultural values and goals. They all represent ways of attaining salvation.

Why do so many religious sects emerge and flourish in an apparently secular world?

(Cam)

To what extent can the growth of religious sects be seen as a response to conditions of social disorganisation and change?   (AEB)

SECTS IN SOCIETY

Wilson (*Religion in a Secular Society*) says that sects are not static. They undergo change. Some attributes may recede in importance over time. They provide examples of attempts by people to construct their own societies in which they establish new norms and values often in opposition to those of mainstream society. They have a carefully ordered structure of social relationships and patterns of behaviour.

Some examples of recent sects which have emerged:

Year	Sect	Founder	Membership
1949	The Divine Light Mission	Guru Gi	approx. 6,000
1954	The Reunification Church	Mr Moon	2 million
1954	Scientology	L. Ron Hubbard	5 million
1968	Children of God	Moses David	5,000 (GB)
1969	Hare Krishna		1,000 (GB)

▶   Possible explanations for their emergence:

1   They fulfil basic human needs of their members who are:
   (*a*)   given strong group support in crisis
   (*b*)   presented with a sense of enlightenment
   (*c*)   provided with definite answers to problems
   (*d*)   subjected to strict disciplines
   (*e*)   provided with 'a father figure' as leader.

2   Mainstream churches do not meet basic needs. The vacuum is filled by new sects.

3   Yinger (*Sociology Looks at Religion*) argues that sects offer hope, status and understanding for the disprivileged members of society whom they frequently attract. They enable those who wish to express their opposition to the social structure to 'orient them to the new order in a way that helps individuals and groups to maintain in a sense of control and dignity. . .' In the USA the Black Muslim sects developed in the 1960s as protest movements for improved rights. The sects offered a means of providing solutions to problems of disprivilege.

4   They are likely to attract those of low status or who feel they have little access to the scarce resources of the society. The sect provides ways of coping as well as explanations, with the promise that one day things will be different for those who are marginal in society. The Rastafarian movement arose in the slums of Jamaica out of unemployment and social disadvantage. Members believe that one day they will return to Africa; the promised land is Ethiopia and the late Haille Selassie is the Messiah. They believe that the Bible contains the truth about their future but that its message has been distorted by the white man to conceal the truth that they are in reality the true children of Israel and God's chosen people.

5   Some sects also attract more middle-class membership (e.g. Christian Science). These may include some who are intellectually dissatisfied with orthodox ideologies and others who feel relatively disprivileged.

6   Sects provide a universe of meaning. People may turn to sects at times of social change and upheaval. Pentecostal sects provide a strong appeal for West Indians. They provide a meeting place for those recently arrived from other societies; they are a source of group support and integration and stability.

7   The rapid growth in the number of new cult and sectarian movements in recent years, which include Pyramidology, the Emin, the Avatar, the Axminster Light Centre, the Aetherius Society, the Dartington Solar Quest, suggest that people continue to have a need for the mysterious and the supernatural in a scientific age. This interest in bizarre movements has been criticised by the Committee for the Scientific Investigation of the Paranormal in the USA. They warn that the increasing acceptance of reports of the paranormal 'fosters anti-scientific sentiment' and leads to support of 'the dangerous doctrines and virulent programmes of such sects'.

THEORIES OF RELIGION

THE FUNCTIONALIST VIEW

What are the major social functions of religion?

Examine the view that religion is necessarily a conservative force in society.

(AEB)

Religion There is a problem in defining the term. Beliefs in forms of supernatural powers seem present in every society. Some definitions are so broad that they take account of any strong belief system. However, more useful definitions include:

Some pattern of belief and action by means of which certain vital social functions are performed. It is a group-supported road to salvation . . .' (Yinger).

'The belief in the existence of supernatural beings which have a governing effect on life . . .' (Robertson).

1 Durkheim (*The Elementary Forms of Religious Life*) as a functionalist is interested in the sources of order and stability in society. He argues that religion is a major source of integration. All religious activity has one major function, the celebration of the social group. Religious activity draws people together. There is value consensus in that they share common beliefs. This increases the sense of community. He concludes from his analysis of aboriginal society that religious worship is in reality the worship of society itself.

2 Parsons (*Religious Perspectives in Sociology*) argues that human behaviour is shaped by pressures of social norms. These are built into the social culture. Religion is a central part of the culture and religious values are transmitted to each new generation. These provide guidelines for acceptable patterns of behaviour. In this way consensus is maintained, and stability and order ensured.

3 O'Dea (*The Sociology of Religion*) argues that religion also functions to provide answers to questions which science cannot explain; it satisfies emotional needs in times of crisis; it provides an ethical code as guide to conduct; prayer and sacrifice may have a cathartic value for people.

Points of criticism: The theory neglects:

1 the ways that religion can cause conflict
2 the increase in secularisation and loss of belief
3 religion as a source of change (Weber's view).

Why did Weber attach importance to the role of religion in society?

WEBERIAN VIEW

Weber was interested in the effects on society of the interaction between people and the social institutions of society. He argued that religion can be seen as a source of social change. He shows, for example, how when new charismatic leaders appear they advocate change. These have a wide-ranging effect over time. He suggests that most of the radical changes which occurred in Britain in the nineteenth century were instigated by religious groups.

The Protestant ethic and the spirit of capitalism

Capitalism: 'The pursuit of profit forever renewed profit.'
'Rational business transactions.'

The spirit of capitalism is epitomised in the writings of Benjamin Franklin in the eighteenth century: 'Time is money. Time wasting, idleness and diversion lose money. . .'

Weber argued that the sixteenth-century theologian, Calvin, established an ethic which is a way of life which provided duties and obligations.

Weber wished to see to what extent religious values influenced the development of the spirit of capitalism.

Calvin's teaching emphasised abstinence, self-discipline and austerity. Weber says that Protestant sects were based on these principles of good conduct:

(*a*)   a man must have a well-defined career
(*b*)   this must be pursued in a single-minded way
(*c*)   God commands man to work for His glory
(*d*)   success in one's calling means God has helped
(*e*)   making money is a concrete sign of success.

Weber's argument is that this teaching was a vital influence in the creation of the capitalist ethic. It attacked laziness and time wasting. Making money became a religious and a business ethic which justified improved methods of production and the division of labour.

In this way religious beliefs influenced and changed social attitudes in the west. Capitalism did not emerge in the east because the religious teachings and ethics were different.

Points of criticism:

1   Many places in Europe have had a strong Calvinistic tradition but have not been prominent in developing capitalistic attitudes or structures in the ways predicted (e.g. Scotland).
2   Many places had strong capitalist ethics and structures before Calvin developed his teachings. Some of these are in Catholic countries of which Weber's theory would not take account (e.g. Florence.)
3   The success of the development of capitalism could be accounted for by other factors: e.g. imperialism. Some of the most successful early capitalists may have been non-religious people, as are many of the contemporary rich.

Assess the view that 'religion is a kind of mystified reflection of relations of economic dominance in society'.

MARXIAN VIEW

Marxists argue that religious institutions and organisations are a part of the social superstructure. This operates in the interests of the ruling class who thereby use religion as a means of social control:

1   Religion serves to legitimate power which is held by the ruling elite.
2   Rulers promote the myth that their position is divinely ordained (the monarch is crowned in a cathedral and the anthem says 'God save the Queen').
3   Religion serves the function of justifying the exploitation of the proletariat and the *status quo*.
4   People are blinded to reality; they are alienated and deluded by religious indoctrination.
5   In that religion is an illusion which eases the pain caused by exploitation it is 'an opiate of the people'.
6   'Religion is the sign of the oppressed creature, the sentiment of a heartless world. . .' The reality is that God did not create man, rather man created God.

7   Religion promises heaven to those who have nothing on earth, it makes poverty more tolerable by offering long-term rewards in heaven. It deters people from seeking changes which would destroy the stability of society (Blessed are the poor . . .').

8   Religion is an essentially conservative force which inhibits social change. It is an effective source of social control.

Points of criticism:

1   Kibbutz societies are both religious organisations and adopt socialist principles. The two do not appear to conflict.

2   Some Roman Catholic priests in South America adopt Marxist principles in their support for social change.

3   Some powerful leaders do not appear to make particular use of religious organisations as a means of support or legitimation [e.g. Hitler].

CRIME AND DEVIANCE

CONTENTS

The questions on this topic tend to fall into the following broad areas:

1 The criminal statistics: problems of interpretation.
2 The age and sex of offenders.
3 Theories of crime:
   (a)   Functionalist.
   (b)   Marxist.
4 White-collar crime.
5 Theories of deviance:
   (a)   Interactionist perspective: distinctions between crime and deviance.
   (b)   Labelling theory.

CRIMINAL STATISTICS

What problems are there in the use of official criminal statistics for sociological research?

(Cam)

Crime has a specific legal meaning. It includes both indictable (serious notifiable offences) and non-indictable, less serious offences, normally tried in a magistrates' court.

Positivists make use of the statistics as social facts about the extent of social problems and disorder. Phenomenologists argue that sociologists must do more than describe social facts. They must take care over their use and interpretation. They emphasise the need to explain how people become criminals; they ask who collects the statistics and why and how they are interpreted in particular ways.

Indictable (notifiable) offences recorded by the police (England and Wales) 1951–82 (in 1000s)

Total recorded	1951	1961	1971	1981	1982
Total	525	807	1646	2900	3262
No. proceeded against	144	193	351	523	539
No. found guilty	133	182	322	480	486

Source: Social Trends

Comments: 1   The number of recorded offences has increased from half a million in 1951 to over 3 million in 1982.

2　The number proceeded against is less than one fifth of the total.

3　In 1982 theft and handling stolen goods accounted for about 50% of all serious offences; burglary accounted for about 25%. One in twenty of all recorded offences were violence against the person.

4　The clear-up rate fluctuates between 35%–45%: 1971, 45%; 1981, 38%; 1982, 37%.

PROBLEMS OF INTERPRETATION

Wiles (*Criminal Statistics and Sociological Explanations of Crime*) argues that statistics of crime may be imperfect as instruments from which to draw definite conclusions about the state of a society. There are major problems in their interpretation. He disputes the idea that they indicate that there is an increasing crime wave.

The 'dark figure' of crime

This refers to criminal acts which are not reported. They are known to exist as a result of admissions from both observers and victims.

The British Crime Survey (1982) found that:

(*a*)　　　There may be as many as fifteen or twenty times as many crimes committed as are recorded.

(*b*)　　　Most of the unreported offences are less serious types.

(*c*)　　　Crime may not be reported where the observer does not perceive the act to be an offence; where the observer has a close relationship with the offender; where the observer justifies non-reporting on the grounds that 'it's nothing to do with me. . .'

(*d*)　　　There are anomolies in the recording procedures: e.g. if five bottles of milk are stolen five offences are recorded. If a cheque book is stolen and fifty thefts occur, only one offence is recorded.

The authors conclude that the crime that is recorded is only the tip of an iceberg. We do not know with any precision how much goes unrecorded.

Apparent increases may be the result of the following factors:

(*a*)　　　Changes in reporting behaviour.

(*b*)　　　More policemen being asked to police areas suspected of having high rates of crime. The result is more arrests.

(*c*)　　　Most serious offences are committed by young men aged 17–20. There has been an increase of 400,000 in this age group in the years 1960–80.

(*d*)　　　It has become easier to report offences as the number of telephones has increased. There are also more policemen.

(*e*)　　　There is more opportunity to commit offences (e.g. super-markets).

(*f*)　　　The police are more efficient in recording offences (com-puters).

(*g*)　　　The statistics do not take account of the 'meaning' of the offence to the offenders. Many people may offend by chance. Increases in crime may represent more of the iceberg being revealed.

THE AGE AND SEX OF OFFENDERS

Account for the differences in the rate of male and female delinquency.   (Ox)

Cowie *et al.* (*Delinquency in Girls*) make the point that the literature on the subject of delinquency in girls is not more than a small fraction of that relating to offences committed by males.

They suggest that the reasons are:

(*a*)   The delinquent girl is a rarity.

(*b*)   She is criminologically much less interesting. The offences for which she is likely to be charged are shoplifting and sexual misdemeanours. Delinquency in the male is more varied, dangerous and dramatic.

Comment:

1   The highest rate for offending is by males 14–16.
2   The offence rate for females is much lower, but is increasing.
3   In 1975 there were six men for each woman cautioned or found guilty. In 1982 there were five.
4   In 1977 there were less than 200 girls in Borstals. In 1982 there were about 250.
5   The number of girls aged 15–20 sent to penal institutions increased by 20% from 715 to 860 in the first year of the 1982 Criminal Justice Act.
6   The peak age for delinquency in males is 15 and for females 14.

▶   Studies:

1   Belson (*Juvenile Theft*) found in his 1975 study that by the time the average boy in London leaves school he will have committed a hundred thefts. Only 13% had been caught.
2   Cambell (*New Society* January 1977) found evidence that adolescent girls admitted to nearly as much deviance as males.
3   Mayhew (*New Society*, June 1977) says:

(*a*)   Little attempt has been made to see how the social patterning of women's lives determines the chances they have of committing crime.

(*b*)   There are few situations in which males and females have equal opportunity to offend and it is difficult to measure these in a simple and reliable way.

(*c*)   In the case of shoplifting he found that there was no difference in the proportion of men and women who shoplifted which was statistically significant. Men and women appeared, on the basis of the results of three studies, to be equally likely to commit this offence.

4   Cowie *et al.* suggest that the factors associated with higher rates of

delinquency in girls were: low-income family; large family; parents having low levels of intelligence and also having a criminal record. (These were similar to the findings of West (*Delinquency, Its Roots, Causes and Prospects*) who studied 400 delinquent males aged 8–24).

5 Wilkinson in a study in the USA (1983) found in California a 'near epidemic' of cases which involved women in embezzlement. Of one hundred cases, eighty were women. He suggests that this is because more women are engaged in those high occupational positions where they are able to control a company's finances.

6 Research and Planning Unit Bulletin (1985). This report outlined the factors which related to levels in delinquency among boys and girls:

Boys	Girls
1. Having delinquent friends	1. Having delinquent friends
2. Not feeling guilty about stealing	2. Poor parental supervision
3. Going out a lot	3. Not regarding stealing as serious
4. Not having a close relationship with his father	4. Not having a close relationship with her father
	5. Having friends who would not be worried about stealing

▶ Possible explanations for the increase in female offenders:

1 With more mothers at work there is less supervision of children in the home.

2 With more marriages ending in divorce there is more disruption to family life and less opportunity to develop a close relationship with the father, for security and discipline.

3 One-parent families are likely to face more financial hardship.

4 The feminist movement has encouraged women to become more autonomous and to seek wider goals (see Merton's Theory page 209).

5 Girls may be more likely to become attached to youth cultures which tolerate and encourage deviant behaviour.

6 It may be that there is not necessarily an increase in female deviance but that there is a dark figure of which more is being uncovered.

▶ Possible explanations of why females offend less than males:

1 Girls are socialised into roles which promote conformist attitudes.

2 They are less motivated to commit serious crime.

3 They are less often in situations which are conducive to crime (e.g. less likely to fight; to get drunk).

4 Church attendance: although evidence is very limited there seems to be some (Wootton: *Social Science and Social Pathology*) suggesting that regular church attendance is relatively uncommon among offenders. Girls are more likely to attend than boys.

5 Truancy from school is also associated with delinquent behaviour. (One third of juvenile offences are committed in school hours). Girls are better attenders than boys.

THEORIES OF CRIME

**THE FUNCTIONALIST
VIEW**

Examine the view that crime occurs as a result of the discrepancy between aspirations which society has socialised into its members and the ways their society provides for realising such aspirations.

Is crime normal? Discuss.

Functionalists look for the source of deviance in the culture and structure of society and examine the agencies of socialisation. Writers such as Durkheim argue that crime is normal and helps to sustain conformity and stability. Crime is inevitable because many people are badly socialised.

Durkheim (*The Division of Labour*) says 'crime brings together upright conscience. . .' He notes how 'when some moral scandal has been committed . . . people stop each other on the street . . . they talk of the event and wax indignant. . .' The effect is to develop a sense of solidarity among people as they become sensitised to a social problem, which they are agreed requires a solution. The identification and punishment of a deviant helps to unify the community.

Other functions include:

(*a*)   The social rules of the society are made clear when someone can be identified as having broken them.

(*b*)   By uncovering deviance and establishing why it is 'a crime', undesirable behaviour can be identified and the young socialised to perceive it as such.

(*c*)   Undesirable types of people ('criminals') can also be identified.

(*d*)   Social rules can be clarified, maintained and if necessary modified. (Some may be dysfunctional in that they increase the number of law-breakers because the law is badly drafted.)

(*e*)   There is justification for sanctions and punishments imposed on deviants. They are potentially disruptive and socially irresponsible. Moral values can be established and upheld.

It is in ways such as these that the collective sentiments of society are maintained at a strong level.

▶   Theorists who emphasise structural and cultural factors:

1   Merton (*Social Theory and Social Structure*)

He argues that deviance arises from the way society is structured.

(*a*)   The majority of people share similar values as to what are the most important goals in social life.

(*b*)   Unfortunately, there are differences in the opportunities available to people to achieve them.

(*c*)   In the USA the 'American dream' is to attain material success. This includes getting a good job, owning a house and having all the material goods needed for a successful life.

(*d*)   Those who cannot attain these may suffer anomie. To resolve this their response may be one of the following:

1   Conformity: they will seek success through orthodox channels.
2   Ritualism: they seek more modest goals.
3   Retreatism: they are resigned to failure.
4   Rebellion: they advocate a re-modelled society.
5   Innovation: they turn to deviant means to achieve the goals.

(*e*)   Merton concludes that it is more likely to be members of the lower social classes who will innovate.

2   Cohen (*Deviance and Control*)
He opposes Merton's view that the motivation for deviant behaviour arises out of the frustrations of failing to achieve success by legitimate means. He discusses the subcultural values of deviants.

(*a*)   He notes that delinquent acts are not always undertaken as an individual response to frustration.

(*b*)   Many delinquent acts are not undertaken for financial gain, but are 'non-ultilitarian and malicious. . .'

(*c*)   He sees the cause of much delinquency as status frustration. Success goals are replaced with an alternative set which provide a means of gaining prestige in the eyes of their peers. These are the values of a lower working-class, delinquent subculture into which such boys are socialised.

Points of Criticism: 1   Merton's theory does not take account of non-financial acts of deviance of working-class offenders.
2   Cohen's theory does not account for middle-class offences and for only a small minority of working-class crimes.
3   Cohen's theory may overemphasise the extent to which deviants belong to 'delinquent gangs'.
4   There must come a point when too much crime is dysfunctional and causes social disharmony.

MARXIAN PERSPECTIVE

Discuss the contention that most crime is committed by members of the working class.
                                                                    (Cam)

Discuss critically any theory of juvenile delinquency.

1   The Marxian analysis of crime is based on the view that:
(*a*)   it arises because of the private ownership of property and the exploitation of one group by another.
(*b*)   the high rate of crime in western capitalist societies represents a protest against alienation and powerlessness.
(*c*)   capitalism is a competitive ideology; people are encouraged to become aggressive and hostile. In such a society, criminal behaviour is understandable.

(*d*)   Chambliss and Mankoff (*Whose Law? What Order?*) examine laws from a colonial and historical perspective. Acts are defined as criminal which serve the interests of the colonial rulers. The law is always used to control the work force and to maximise profits.

2   Young (*Mass Media, Drugs and Deviance*) argues that the mass media are always supportive of the *status quo*. Although the only concessions to working-class people in legal rights have been gained by united labour movements, such as trade unions, these come to be seen in a negative light. Strikers are portrayed as deviants. He also notes a different level of social reaction to the use of drugs: 72 million tablets are used each year legally; but there is a widespread sense of condemnation about the use of certain drugs by teenagers, hippies etc. In *The Drug Takers* he suggests that they come under police surveillance because those who reject the values of capitalist society are seen as a potential threat.

3   Pearce (*Crimes of the Powerful*) sees organised crime as a tool of the ruling class. Gangsters have been known to assassinate political opponents, break strikes etc. He also argues that there are few prosecutions of powerful companies and very rich people because they have the power to control the legal processes. Yet there are major infringements by them (e.g. tax evasion) which are often regarded as legitimate. This also creates the impression that such activities are minimal.

▶   *The merits of this approach:*

(*a*)   It provides an explanation for why so much crime is related to the desire for material goods (most serious crime is theft).

(*b*)   it provides an explanation for the fact that most offenders who are prosecuted come from the lowest social classes, although studies suggest crime is committed by all classes.

(*c*)   The prison population exceeds 47,000 in 1985, the majority of whom may be described as 'the poor and the powerless'.

▶   *The weaknesses of the approach:*

(*a*)   It is based on a specific ideology. Marxists are committed to major social changes. They see the law as instrument of class control.

(*b*)   The theory doesn't explain the presence of crime in socialist societies in which there is no private property and the ownership of the means of production is communal.

(*c*)   The theory doesn't easily explain the fact that there are middle-class offenders who are prosecuted.

Conclusion: The Marxist sees crime as an inevitable feature of a capitalist economic system which promotes self-interest and greed. Emphasising the more sensational crimes usually committed by working-class people helps maintain ruling-class ideology and power. The view that the most serious offences are committed by the working class is promoted through media reports. Law enforcement agencies are said by Marxists to be employed not to reduce crime but to manage it.

WHITE-COLLAR CRIME

What is white-collar crime? What is its significance for the sociology of crime?

Definition: Sutherland (*The Professional Thief*) says that white-collar crimes are those 'committed by persons of respectability and high social status in the course of their occupations'. Although these can include clear breaches of the law, such as tax evasion, breach of factory and company Acts, there are some actions which may be interpreted as bribery or as 'extravagant gifts'. Taking a broad view of such activities in the world of business and company transactions, Sutherland suggests that such practices are widespread in this and political life (e.g. Poulson).

Mays (*Crime and the Social Structure*) says that 'some of the so-called perks which businessmen enjoy are legalised forms of theft'.

Carson (*The Sociology of Crime*) argues that the study of white-collar crime raises crucial questions about how and why certain kinds of laws are enacted, confronting the investigator with the need 'to cast his analysis not only in the framework of those who break laws, but in the context of those who make laws as well. . ...'

▶ Research findings:

1   Carson (*White-Collar Crime*) sampled 200 firms in the south east of England. He found that every firm had committed some violation in the four and a half years studied, but the offences were rarely prosecuted. Official warnings were the most usual means of dealing with infringements.

2   Sutherland sampled seventy large corporations in the USA and found many types of violation were accepted practice. They were successful because:

(*a*)   they were hard to detect

(*b*)   there were seldom any victims

(*c*)   they were often seen and justified as 'normal business practice'

(*d*)   the public was seldom aware that an offence had been committed

(*e*)   even when detected there was seldom a prosecution, which may have encouraged others.

He concludes that there is a constant bias involved in the administration of criminal justice under laws which apply to business and the professions and which therefore benefits the upper socio-economic group.

3   Mars (*Cheats at Work*) describes the 'normal crimes of normal people in the normal circumstances of their work'. He suggests that the nature of 'fiddling' varies with the nature of occupations. In jobs in which people's activities are highly controlled by management and in which they are often isolated from each other by noise or by distance, then their work fiddles may involve a single type of offence, e.g.

checkout staff over-charging customers. In fact these may even have arisen because of managers attempting to set the books right by encouraging fiddles at times of stocktaking. However, in jobs where the individual has more freedom to apply different levels of skills, fiddles cover a wider spectrum and involve a more complex range of illegal activities.

4   Pearce (*Crimes of the Powerful*) examined the criminal activities of large US business corporations and says that in monetary terms the activities of working-class offenders are a drop in the ocean. A more recent study in Sheffield (Levy) points out that middle-class crime is often more difficult to detect because it is more sophisticated. Middle-class offences such as tax evasion have been estimated to cost ten times more in losses than social security fraud by working-class people.

Some conclusions: Carsons raises some of the issues relating to white-collar crime:
(*a*)   Why do the infringements by companies appear to enjoy substantial immunity from the legal process?
(*b*)   Is there legislative bias in dealing with such irregularities?
(*c*)   Studies indicate it is widespread and should undermine the myth that law-breaking is primarily a working-class phenomenon.
(*d*)   How and under what circumstances can the law deal with such crime and so function as an instrument of social change? 'The efficiency of repressive criminal law in this respect is an issue on which sociologists, like contemporary politicians, are by no means agreed. . .'

DEVIANCE

Distinguish between crime and deviance. Why are some deviant acts classified as criminal and others not?

Crime A crime is a breach of the criminal law. There are two main types: indictable (notifiable) which are serious offences normally tried in a Crown Court and punishable by imprisonment or fine. A non-indictable offence is a less serious breach (e.g. motoring) and is normally tried in a magistrates' court.
(*a*)   Many acts defined as crimes are related to the social culture (what is regarded as a crime in one society may not be in another). In Eskimo society the ritual killing of the elderly was socially and morally acceptable, since food supplies were precious.
(*b*)   There is little evidence that there is much behaviour which is universally condemned in every society.
(*c*)   The concept of the meaning and significance of punishment also varies between cultures.

Deviance This is a more relative term which avoids the legal meaning attached to the term crime. Deviance has both a legal and a non-legal usage. There is no absolute way of defining behaviour as deviant in a society, whereas it is possible to define an act as criminal.

(*a*)   It implies behaviour which incurs public disapproval.

(*b*)   It is behaviour which departs from the norms of a group.

(*c*)   Whether an act is deviant depends on who commits it and who sees it and what action they take about it. The same act may be considered deviant when committed by one person, but not by another. One observer may define it as 'deviant' to cause trouble in a football ground; the troublemakers may regard it as 'normal'.

(*d*)   Erikson (*Notes on the Sociology of Deviance*) says that deviance is not a property inherent in certain forms of behaviour; it is a property conferred upon these by the audiences which witness them. 'The critical variable in the study of deviance is the social audience rather than the individual actor.'

(*e*)   Taylor (*Deviance*) says that the explanations for deviant behaviour are to be found 'inscribed on the cultural map which belongs to the actor and his community'. The key concepts for interpreting this are those of 'role', 'interest' and 'expectations'. These change over time and help to shape behaviour.

IDENTIFYING DEVIANTS: LABELLING

What are the strengths and weaknesses of the labelling approach to social deviance?

Becker (*Outsiders*) has said that deviance is rule-breaking behaviour in which someone is labelled as 'deviant'. Deviance is not a quality that lies in the behaviour itself, but in the interaction between the person who commits an act and those who respond to it.

The process of labelling:

(*a*)   To be successful there must be an audience or group who perceive others as being in some way different from themselves.

(*b*)   There must be a group or an individual to receive the label.

(*c*)   The label affects the status of both groups; the differences between them are made clear. The label 'deviant' produces a negative image of those labelled ('football hooligans') and develops a negative self-image in those labelled ('non-academic').

(*d*)   Once the label is confirmed, either by someone of high status (the headmaster) or by further observations, then it becomes more firmly fixed.

(*e*)   The effect is to establish stereotyped images which reduce uncertainty about those observed; the label makes the world more consistent. It makes predictions about future behaviour easier. (He's always been a troublemaker. . .')

▶   Research findings:

1   Cohen and Short (*Juvenile Delinquency*) note that middle-class offen-

ders do not get as far as lower working-class boys in the legal process when apprehended. Even though the offence is similar, they are less likely to be charged or convicted and sentenced. This is because the label 'deviant' is less likely to be effectively attached to boys in the upper middle class. Therefore, there are different expectations about them.

2 Vincent (*Unmarried Mothers*) notes that the reaction of the local community to 'illicit pregnancy' is likely to be much more severe as far as the mother is concerned, whereas the unmarried father tends to escape much censure.

3 Hall (*Policing the Crisis*); his work (as well as that of the authors who follow) illustrates how the enforcement agencies operate with pre-existing conceptions of what criminals and deviants are like.

The selective discrimination arises from the expectations that the police, lawyers and court officials have, which arise from the labels attached to certain types of people. Hall argues that this is why young black males are perceived to be deviant and treated accordingly. They have become the archetypical 'mugger'. This was a term imported from the USA in 1972. Its use in the media sensitised the public to a new problem: the headline 'Must Harlem Come to Handsworth?' appeared in a paper which warned that 'mugging' was starting in Britain (there were no cases described as mugging before 1972). This helped to establish a 'self-fulfilling prophecy'. It anticipated a problem, described the typical offender and shortly after, the first offenders were located. The problem became amplified as more black youths were arrested and there was more publicity in the press. Their own sense of alienation and anomie was increased.

4 Cohen (*Folk Devils and Moral Panics*) also shows how the label 'deviant' became attached to mods and rockers in the 1960s as a result of the publicity they gained in the popular press. He notes how some of this was manufactured by journalists. But the effect was to polarise the youth and the police and the public. The deviants developed a self-image and many behaved in accordance with it, causing further problems in more seaside resorts.

5 Cicourel (*The Social Organisation of Juvenile Justice*) shows how in the course of exercising discretion about their treatment of offenders, the enforcement agencies can produce delinquents.

(*a*)   The police stop and question someone.

(*b*)   This is based on their interpretation of 'suspicious character' and the fact that some areas are perceived as worse than others.

(*c*)   The interrogation may lead to arrest depending on the appearance and manner of the person questioned.

(*d*)   If arrested, further action may depend on the details learned about home background, school record etc.

(*e*)   If charged and prosecuted the outcome may also rest on such factors. In Britain the majority found guilty of an offence between the age of 10–17 and therefore designated 'juvenile delinquents' come from Classes 4 and 5.

Cicourel concludes that what ends up as justice is the result of negotiations in the interaction process.

▶ The merits of the interactionist labelling perspective:

1 It presents an alternative to the positive approach which assumes that the 'facts' of crime are found in an analysis of the statistics.

2 The labelling theorists argue that deviant behaviour is the result of meanings derived from interaction.

3 The view argues that criminals are not different from non-criminals in that they are necessarily imbued with a criminal culture. There is unlikely to be any adult who has not committed a crime at some time in their lives.

4 Instead of searching for final causes the interactionist analyses the processes whereby behaviour comes to be defined as 'deviant'.

5 Interactionists do not adopt an absolute view of crime but present a position of moral relativism (attitudes change over time and place as to what is considered deviant).

6 There does seem to be much evidence that people develop stereotypes of others and respond to them.

▶ Some criticisms of the interactionist view:

1 It may appear that there is too much concern for the offender.

2 It may be argued that there is too much concern for those in the most marginal areas of deviance (social deviance, drug-takers etc.).

3 They do not explain the origin of deviance, but imply that it only arises after the label has been attached. It seems strange to suggest that deviance does not occur unless there is someone to observe it.

4 The role of the deviants is underplayed. They appear as rather passive victims of the observers of their actions.

5 The theory suggests that the deviants act without gaining pleasure or satisfaction from their behaviour. (It may be that there are some who deliberately cause trouble in football grounds for the 'excitement', 'status' etc. that it brings.)

6 It may be that observers of deviant acts actually help to cause a decrease in such behaviour (by expression of disgust etc.).

7 Some people may deliberately seek the label 'outsider' to distinguish themselves from other groups or generations.

YOUTH AND AGE

CONTENTS

There are questions on this topic which relate to:

1 The social construction of age:
   (a) Childhood.
   (b) Adolescence.
   (c) Old age.
2 Youth cultures:
   (a) Functionalist perspective.
   (b) Structuralist explanations: working class subcultures.
   (c) Interactionist perspective.
   (d) Middle-class youth cultures.
3 Soccer hooliganism

THE SOCIAL CONSTRUCTION OF AGE

What comparative evidence is there to suggest that the terms such as childhood, adulthood and elderly refer to expectations about how individuals should act rather than the number of years they have lived? (Lon)

Societies vary in their expectations of children, adolescents and old people. Does evidence from both pre-industrial and industrial societies support the claim that the various stages of the family cycle are a matter of social definition?

Sociologists are interested to study the way that people are treated in terms of their age in society. Although ageing is a biological process there is evidence to show that cultural interpretations of its significance and meaning are relevant and important.

There is evidence, too, to suggest that in pre-industrial societies the terms childhood, adulthood and the elderly do tend to refer to expectations about how people should act, rather than the number of years they have lived. In western industrial societies the terms have meaning in both respects.

CHILDHOOD

1 Aries (*Centuries of Childhood*) says that this is a phenomenon of the twentieth century. In medieval times, the idea of childhood did not exist. Children became the companions of adults as soon as they were

considered capable of doing so without mothers or nannies. This could have been as early as the age of seven.

2 Musgrove (*Youth and the Social Order*) says that in the late eighteenth and early nineteenth centuries parents began to value children largely because they became an economic asset. The new industries were heavily dependent on the skills and ability of the young. They presented an insurance against misfortune in later life and old age. The birth rate after 1870 slumped with the first Education Act. 'By the early part of the twentieth century children were no longer central to the economy; they were moving to the periphery, into marginal and relatively trivial occupations. . .'

3 Malinowski, Meade, Maddock and other anthropologists have shown how transitions from one age group to another in pre-industrial societies are usually marked by initiation rites and ceremonies. The traditions and customs of the society are transmitted from one generation to the next and their new roles made clear.

4 Barnouw (*Anthropology*) says that 'different societies hold up contrasting ideas of the growing child, ranging from the proud self-assertive warrior to the mild, self-effacing citizen.'

5 The problems facing children in contemporary Britain are highlighted in a report published in 1983 (*Children Today*). This stated that there are:
(*a*)   more than 100,000 children in care
(*b*)   about 2 million in low-income families
(*c*)   1.5 milllion in one-parent families
(*d*)   25,000 homeless families with children
(*e*)   20,000 children in care awaiting adoption

ADULTHOOD

Whilst childhood and old age are clearly differentiated, it is more difficult to clarify the specific features of adulthood.

Rosser and Harris (*The Family and Social Change*) have described the family cycle in contemporary Britain:

Family Phase	Definition
1. Home-making	From marriage to the birth of the first child
2. Procreation	From the birth of the first child to the marriage of the first child
3. Dispersion	From the marriage of the first child to the marriage of the last child
4. Final phase	From the marriage of the last child to the death of the original partners

They accept that these do not represent clear and distinct milestones in the progress of an individual family through the typical cycle. But they are able to identify particular patterns of family behaviour with each phase.

The period of adulthood might be taken to be the time between phases 1 and 3, from twenty-five to forty-five, before the time of the onset of 'middle age'.

In the west it is a time when careers are established; children are produced; marriage relationships are established and the family becomes more privatised. It may also be a time of increasing frustrations if careers or marriages fail and new relationships form. Children may come to be seen as 'problems'.

In simple societies there are initiations into adulthood. For boys this may involve separation from their mothers and closer association with adult men. The rites help to celebrate and reinforce the bonds of male and tribal solidarity. Boys may be given a new name, new privileges and new status in society.

Brown (*A Cross-Cultural Study of Female Initiation Rites*) found that no initiation ceremony takes place for girls in societies where they leave home upon marriage since the act of leaving marks that change. But in societies where the girl remains in the same social setting after marriage, a ceremony may be performed to mark her change of status, especially in societies in which women make a notable contribution to subsistence.

There are many cross-cultural anthropological studies which emphasise the significance of socialisation and training for adult roles rather than the influence of biological factors.

OLD AGE

Old age can also be said to be socially constructed in the sense that in western societies we tend to treat people differently when they reach 'old age'. They are perceived as 'pensioners' or 'senior citizens'.

This perception affects our treatment of them:

(*a*)   Their roles change when they are no longer economically active.

(*b*)   Their income falls on retirement.

(*c*)   They are seen to be less active.

(*d*)   They are believed to be out of touch with the values of a younger generation.

(*e*)   Their status tends to fall.

(*f*)   The family remains the chief source of support for the elderly. About 6% of those over sixty are in residential homes, hospitals etc. One of the chief roles undertaken by the elderly is that of 'grandparent' whereby they may regain some status in the family.

(*g*)   For Marxists, old age is structured by capitalism: the consequences of economic crisis are most detrimental to the old on fixed incomes. They are affected too by cuts in health-service arrangements and by problems of inner-city deprivations where many live in poor housing conditions. The plight of the elderly is not vote catching.

In simple societies people are also classified as old and receive different treatment as a result. But they may increase status if they take on positions of advisers, guardians of secret knowledge, tribal customs etc. The old may also be very important members of extended family structures in such societies. Generally, there appears to be less disengagement from society than is the case in western industrial societies.

YOUTH CULTURES

The term culture accurately reflects neither youth-adult relationships nor the diversity of youth subcultures. Explain and discuss this view.   (AEB)

The concept of youth culture is a relatively recent one in the analysis of patterns of behaviour of young people in western industrial societies. It has been used particularly in the years since 1945.

Functionalists emphasise changing patterns of social life to explain the emergence of a distinct culture of youth: particularly the effects of affluence, following pre-war and wartime austerity; the expansion of education and the effects of the mass media which helped to spread a mass culture. They focus on the positive values of a youth culture. Some suggest that youth tends to share a general culture, almost as a classless tribe, members passing through a peer group holding stage before entering the serious phase of adulthood.

More recently, Marxist researchers have placed emphasis on the significance of class differences among youth which affect the form the cultures take. Explanations have emphasised the need to 'read' the signs and symbols of youth cultures in relation to that of competing cultures. Particular attention has been paid to lower working-class subcultures which are seen as attempts to cope with the deprivations of an exploitative society.

Interactionists have examined the way youth cultures are manufactured by the media reports which help to bind the participants into an amplification spiral. This serves to promote the values of the culture and to polarise its members from others in society.

THE FUNCTIONALIST VIEW

1   Parsons (*Essays in Sociological Theory*) explains the emergence of modern youth culture in terms of the impact of changes which occur in modern industrial societies. There is more self-interested action and there is less concern for the individual as bureaucratic institutions develop and social roles become more specific. Membership of youth peer groups in which there is a shared culture may be seen as a useful period of transition and as a means of coping with the marginal status of adolescence.

2   Martin (*A Sociology of Contemporary Cultural Change*) examines the possible dysfunctions of youth cultures. She describes the development of a 'counter culture' (a culture of opposition) which developed in the 1960s as 'a cultural revolution among a small minority of crusading radicals'. This culminated in 'altering some of our deepest

and therefore most customary and commonplace habits and assumptions'. She says it was a search for 'liminality'. This represented an attempt by young people to counter the restrictions of social life by moving to the thresholds of 'no-man's land', the edge of the 'abyss' and to embrace a state of anomie for the sake of creative possibilities that it offered.

She is critical of the movement because:

(*a*)   It was based on romantic values which emphasised the needs for self-fulfilment and experiential richness at the expense of the individual's commitments to wider society.

(*b*)   The search led people awayfrom a sense of social integration.

(*c*)   It was excessively individualistic, which countered the traditional values of social solidarity.

(*d*)   The group that acted as the main carrier of these expressive values was a cultural elite, namely middle-class radicals.

(*e*)   The movement could only prosper as a result of the freedom and affluence of western societies and yet it was critical of it.

(*f*)   The quest for a boundary- and rule-free utopia is a fruitless one.

(*g*)   The need for rules and order is deeply rooted in mankind.

(*h*)   The expressive youth culture has had a dangerous effect in wider society because others have inadvertently been infected by them. The boundaries of good taste, moral values etc. have all been pushed back. It was an attempt to make all life 'an evening of freedom' in which rules, roles and conventions were abandoned.

However, she notes that there have been some attempts to counter the counter culture with the regeneration of religious values.

Can any significant distinctions be drawn between working-class and middle-class youth cultures?

Theories of working-class subcultures

1   Miller (*Lower-Class Culture*) writing in 1962 described a distinctive cultural system associated with lower working-class youth. These values include 'toughness', being 'smart' and seeking 'excitement'. There is also concern for 'masculinity' in the face of physical threat. To be smart means being able to outwit, dupe or 'con' others. Excitement involves the search for thrills and is found in gambling, the use of alcohol etc. All of these can be obtained by being out with the peer group. Miller argues that the concern is to find enjoyment outside the dull routine of work as a compensation. These cultural values are always likely to lead a working-class youth into acts of deviance.

2   Clarke (*Resistance Through Rituals*) argues that skinhead culture represents an attempt to recreate the working-class culture of the East End which has been lost.

The emergence of the culture can be seen in terms of the skinheads' exclusion from existing subcultures and because they perceived themselves to be under attack and subject to the authority of others.

(*a*)　　Their need for solidarity derived from the solidarity of their working-class community.

(*b*)　　This had been lost as a result of slum clearance etc.

(*c*)　　The result has been an exaggerated 'style'.

(*d*)　　Support for local football teams helped emphasise the importance of 'territory' and provided a sense of identity.

(*e*)　　He concludes that territoriality, solidarity and masculinity are all ways of re-creating a sense of community and become significant aspects of the culture of the East End Youth.

3　Hall, Jefferson and Cohen (*Resistance Through Ritual*) argue that working-class subcultural activities are an attempt to resist middle-class values being imposed on them. This is achieved by developing a pattern of behaviour and a cultural style that distinguishes them from those they oppose.

(*a*)　　The style is evident in the clothes they wear, the music they listen to and the language they use.

(*b*)　　Such styles carry the youth culture to which they adhere.

(*c*)　　The culture often encourages ritualistic behaviour especially at football matches.

(*d*)　　Aggressive behaviour is interpreted as a means of compensating for loss of status and power.

(*e*)　　In some cases aspects of the culture have been incorporated by the media into the mainstream of society (e.g. punk dress becoming 'fashionable').

4　Corrigan (*Schooling the Smash Street Kids*) argues that working-class youth seek to construct and control their own activities and avoid or oppose anyone who threatens to stop them doing so. This is why much time is spent 'hanging around' street corners, which in effect offers the possibility of making something happen. They reject the idea of conformity to school norms and the idea of obtaining qualifications.

5　McRobbie and Garber (*Working-Class Girls and the Culture of Femininity*) argue that girls are subject to the subordination of both their class and their gender.

(*a*)　　Their destiny as adults is to do low-status work since they are discouraged from achieving high qualifications.

(*b*)　　They share an anti-school culture and may gain status from deviant activities.

6　Willis (*How Working-Class Kids Get Working-Class Jobs*) showed how anti-school subcultures are carried over into the work place. He noted how 'the boy's culture provided criteria for the kind of work the lad is destined for, basically manual and semi-skilled work. Because these criteria arise from a culture, and because the school-based culture also has profound similarities and continuities with the work place . . . once the kids get onto the factory floor . . . they feel at home. . .'

7　Cashmore (*Rastaman*) discusses the significance of youth cultures for black youth, especially involvement in the Rastafarian movement.

One of the most important factors relating to every example of youth culture is music (jazz; rock; new wave) and for black youth in particular, it is reggae music. This stems from the subculture of Jamaica and is a product of deprivation and poverty. The music grew out of a specific context of slavery and colonialisation. The music makes constant reference to these roots, together with biblical sources. The slave-owners had used Christianity as a method of control.

Rastafarianism, founded by Marcus Garvey, uses biblical prophecy to show that when the millenium comes there will be peace and brotherhood among blacks and whites. The saviour is the late Haile Selassie of Ethiopia and the promise is that the Rastas will one day return to their cultural home in Africa.

These ideals are expressed through reggae music.

(a) Both the music and religion are important for black youth because they provide a source of popular nationalism, an identity with Jamaica.

(b) It is a source of black consciousness and relates them back to their African roots.

(c) It has a social significance in that it is the religion and the music of poor blacks.

The music therefore has a strong ideological content, although it has developed into a highly commercial sound which nevertheless reaffirms and resurrects the culture of Jamaica for the audience. It has been described as a dialogue between Black Africans and dispossessed Jamaicans.

Theories of middle-class youth cultures

Functionalist theorists have been criticised for presenting too generalised an account of youth culture and for failing to consider the significance of class and gender differences.

Theorists of working-class subcultures have been criticised for concentrating on a small section of working-class youth whose behaviour is atypical of the majority.

Less attention has been paid to middle-class subcultures. (Marxists would argue that this is because it is not the middle-class radicals who will be the agencies of revolutionary change.)

1 Marcuse (*One-Dimensional Man*) argued that society is a confidence trick offering high standards of material comfort in exchange for slavery to the industrial machine. The only people likely to rebel against this are the unbribed poor, racial minorities and the young. Marcuse argues that violence lurks behind the liberal façade. He provided intellectual justification for student movements which advocated revolutionary change. His appeal was to the radical university students of the 1960s who staged major demonstrations to try to raise people's level of political consciousness.

2 Touraine (*The French Student Movement May 1968*) argues that the world-wide student movement arose from symptoms of post-war confusion. It reflected crises within the capitalist states in which grievances had to be aired by those with access to the greatest privileges in it, young middle-class students. He claims that its signifi-

cance in France was that it presented a challenge to the ruling classes since there was no longer a consensus about the future.

3   Frith (The Punk Bohemians', *New Society*, 9 March 1978) argues that punk culture was the product of middle-class art students, not working-class dole queues. It was not a product of simple commercial manipulation; rather it has a firm place in the history of radical British Art. He says that art schools have always been the basic source of British youth cultural symbols. They played their part in punk, providing key musicians, gigs, audience and fashion. They have always encouraged students to question and innovate.

4   Wilson (*Youth Culture and the Universities*) argues that the hippy culture of the 1960s was a revolution by urbanites who were clearer about what they were against than what they were for. He says their lifestyle was a reaction against middle-aged and middle-class values. They were largely apolitical personal revolutionaries. They provided the literary aspects of the culture.

5   A survey in 1988 by Ann Holt sampled 1400 young people. She found that there was emphasis on industrial enterprise and high reward in work, among both boys and girls. She concludes that the entrepreneurial urge is not particularly middle class or overwhelmingly masculine. It appeals to a section of both sexes hoping to enter skilled manual jobs.

What part do the mass media play in the development of youth cultures?

THE INTERACTIONIST VIEW

This view is based on the arugment that behaviour is not determined by environmental factors, but is shaped by people's response to events as they occur. Laws explaining the causes of behaviour cannot be found because behaviour is not determined. It is shaped by people's interpretations of the meanings that events have for them.

(*a*)   Cohen (*Folk Devils and Moral Pauics*).

(*b*)   Hargreaves (*Deviance in Classrooms*).

Such studies suggest that cultures grow out of an interaction between individuals as well as a set of events which frequently gain wide media publicity.

(*a*)   Labelling theory shows how labels precede deviant behaviour, by sensitising the public.

(*b*)   The media both transmit and perpetuate the bourgeois culture to which many working-class youth are opposed and it transmits the culture to others.

(*c*)   Shared patterns of behaviour have meanings, however bizarre the behaviour may appear to 'outsiders'.

(*d*)   Young people seldom see their youth culture as one of conscious opposition. It is therefore necessary to take account of their views and to produce explanations which make sense to those who participate in the cultures shared by young people.

(*e*)   Ryan (writing on the last day of the UN's International Youth year, 1985) said 'the press view of the young as collectively yobbos and scroungers with an occasional look-in for the exceptional achiever, has remained largely unchanged. . . .' He complains of the effect the media stereotyping has in alienating young people.

Summary points: 1 For the functionalists it is a culture of the badly socialised but it may function as a useful period of transition between adolescence and adulthood (Parsons; Martin).

2 For the subcultural theorists it is a culture of opposition (Clarke).
It is a process of socialisation into the demands of the capitalistic work order (Willis; McRobbie).
It is a culture of resistance to middle-class values (Hall and Jefferson).

3 It is a culture that advocates musculine values (Miller).

4 For interactionists it is a culture which derives from the responses and perceptions of young people to particular problems and needs that confront them, so that allegiances can change rapidly. It may also be manufactured by the media (Cohen; Becker).
Proponents of the various explanations need to consider some points of criticism of their explanations:

FUNCTIONALISTS

(a) Some explanations focus on youth as a classless group, all sharing a 'culture' of youth by virtue of their age. They will generally pass through this unscathed, ready for the embrace of the affluent society. But class differences may be very significant.

(b) Others emphasise the dangers and dysfunctions of youth cultures, resulting from the social experimentation of youth in flouting social conventions. But it may be argued that many adults flout convention in their lifestyles without causing social disorder and without having been influenced by attitudes of youth.

(c) Youth cultures tend to be group activities rather than excessively individualistic.

MARXISTS

The Marxist structuralists may be criticised for being too deterministic in their interpretations:

(a) Subcultures are seen to arise from environmental pressures and the form youth cultures take represents deliberate opposition to mainstream middle-class values. But it may be argued that radical pop lyrics advocating anarchy etc. may not be well-thought-out philosophies of the group.

(b) It does not explain the origin of middle-class youth cultures.

(c) If working-class youth opposes middle-class values why do many working-class cultures emerge in opposition to each other?

(d) If punk culture was one of opposition to the conventions of middle-class society and musical forms etc. why does it also appear in the USSR?

INTERACTIONISTS

Interactionists are frequently criticised because they:

(*a*) Fail to take account of the class background of the actors. It may be unusual for middle-class youth to adopt working-class cultures.

(*b*) There may be too much emphasis on the power of the media to mould attitudes and behaviour rather than reinforce already existing beliefs. Values are promoted by group contact.

(*c*) Some writers (e.g. Becker) argue that cultures arise quickly in response to the needs of the group to cope with specific problems of the moment and dissolve as quickly. But many cultures have a permanence and importance in the lives of members and do not seem necessarily to be mere coping mechanisms.

A criticism which all the theorists face is that there is little attention paid to the youth who do not appear to identify with any specific youth culture and regard themselves as 'conformist youth'.

SOCCER HOOLIGANISM

Give a sociological account of soccer hooliganism.   (Ox)

---

1 Marsh, Rosser and Harre (*Rules of Disorder*)
They applied a range of techniques, including observation and interviews, in their analysis of violence in football grounds. They say that 'we have come to see it through the eyes of the people who take part in it'. They conclude that by sharing the excitement of the fans they are able to feel what it is like to be in that situation. The day-to-day existence of the fans is generally dull; the football match provides an experience worth talking about. It becomes a part of the group culture. Saturday becomes an important day of the week. There is a build-up of group activity and excitement. The crowd develops particular norms and rules of behaviour. To be a fan serves an important function. It provides an identity and dictates the rules governing forms of aggression. Ritualising aggression becomes a way of channelling it in a comparatively safe way. They do not excuse the behaviour but show how events can be construed in other ways. There are rules of disorder.

2 Robbins argues that by the mid 1960s the first generation of ex-urban youth were expressing dissatisfaction with the shortage of public leisure amenities and were seeking ways of achieving the kind of group solidarity they had known as children. Communities and neighbourhoods were lost in processes of re-development. One of the strongest ways of achieving solidarity was in support for football teams. These became the focal points for exiled teenagers. Around spectacular match-day activities a whole under life grew up, involving group allegiances and territorial alliances. He suggests that 'if

you are out of work, a student failure with little to do and nowhere to go, there is a great appeal in joining up in a supra-local army with a national reputation. . .'

3 Seabrook (*Landscapes of Poverty*) says that soccer hooliganism may be a rather tormented reassertion of needs that may have found an earlier outlet in a sense of class identity, which on the whole has always been very temperate in Britain, with its reasonable labour movement, its readiness to compromise and its modest claims to a share in the country's riches.

4 Dahrendorf (in a letter to *The Times*, 1985) says that in some places soccer has turned from a working-class game into an under-class game. This is a group which combines desolate living conditions and lack of traditional bonds, even of class, with low skills and hopeless employment prospects. The result is cynicism towards the official values of a society bent on work and order.

5 Pearson (*A History of Respectable Fears*) has said that because we are frightened of violence we find it hard to comprehend. We are prone to the idea that violence is some kind of epidemic sweeping the country like a pestilence. 'We imagine some earlier golden age in which the streets were safe and a Dixon of Dock Green pounded every beat . . . In fact the belief that we live in a mounting crime wave is likely to do with the changes in the reporting of crime and the attitudes of the courts.'

6 Redhead and McLaughlin ('Soccer's Style Wars', *New Society*, 16 August 1985) describe how contemporary troublemakers at football grounds have been increasingly concerned about group style and structure. They dress in expensive clothes and travel to matches in luxury coaches or by inter-city express trains. They adopt such names as Inter-City Firm, Anti-personnel Firm, Main Line Crew. They have no visible club identification or chant which makes them difficult to identify or detect. These regional style wars have resulted in increasing levels of organised violence both inside and outside the ground. They become a more serious problem since the groups are not subject to the 'the rules of disorder' described by Marsh. As a result there could be more serious injuries in less ritualistic patterns of behaviour.

THE COMMUNITY

CONTENTS

The questions which arise on this topic include the following areas:

1 The community:
   (a)   Problems of definition
   (b)   Loss of community
2 The urban-rural continuum debate:
   (a)   The types of distinctions that have been suggested.
   (b)   Their validity.
3 The suburbs:
4 The distribution of population in cities:
   (a)   The social factors. Ecological models.
   (b)   The processes that sustain segregation.

COMMUNITY

Assess the notion that community has become too much of an overworked and value-laden term to be of any objective social scientific use.   (Lon)

A spirit of community depends on shared values and interests. As cities become socially mixed, maintenance of community spirit becomes impossible. Discuss.   (Ox)

Sociologists have been interested in the concept of community since the discipline was established in the 1830s. This is because the earliest writers were concerned about the nature and effect of social change; in particular what happened when a society changed from rural to urban in structure.

Subsequently, many sociologists have developed typologies to illustrate the differences between types of societies, and theories to explain the processes of change. The result has been a range of definitions and models which some critics complain has caused more confusion than clarification.

1 Tonnies (*Gemeinschaft und Gesellschaft 1887*). He used an ideal type based on Gemeinschaft (community) and Gesellschaft (association) and said that the trend in human history was a movement from community to association. He described typical relationships related to each:

Gemeinschaft	Gesellschaft
1. Intimate 2. Enduring 3. Personal 4. Based on ascribed status 5. Based in a homogeneous culture 6. Enforced by moral custodians (e.g. church; family) 7. Upheld by traditional values	1. Few important primary relationships 2. Contractual and calculative 3. Impersonal 4. Based on achieved status 5. Based in heterogeneous culture 6. There is no widely agreed source of moral values 7. There are no sustaining traditional values
The result is a strong sense of territoriality; a sentimental attachment to a beloved place.	The result is no sense of attachment to place; increased isolation; anonymity and alienation.

He sees the loss of community resulting from the effects of industrialisation, urbanisation and the growth of capitalism.

2   Durkheim (*The Social Division of Labour*) also discussed this issue but used different concepts. He described a move from simple mechanical society to complex organic types. He was concerned with the question of social order in times of change: how can social solidarity be maintained where the pattern of life is subject to rapid change? His answer was the social division of labour. This helps to bind people more closely into their society since it increases their dependence on each other.

Mechanical	Organic
1. Simple, traditional society 2. Rural 3. Little division of labour 4. Homogeneous culture, population 5. Cohesion based on shared norms 6. Law based on repression	1. Complex, modern, industrial 2. Urban 3. High degree of division of labour 4. Heterogeneous culture and population 5. Cohesion based on contract 6. Law based more on restitution

Later research, especially in the USA, revealed the problems of clearly defining the concept of community. Debate centred on the question of whether community implies the existence of a basic unit or structure which can be objectively defined and located. Some believed that it did, others, more recently, see it as a more flexible and less easily defined concept.

Community as a basic unit

1   Redfield (*The Little Community*) describes community as having four key qualities:
   (*a*)   Distinctiveness
   (*b*)   Small size
   (*c*)   Self-sufficient economy
   (*d*)   Homogeneity of inhabitants.

This has been criticised because such places are impossible to find in the real world. If communities are identifiable units then everyone ought to know to which community they belong. In fact most people can identify several, which may overlap.

2   McIver and Page (*Society, an Introductory Analysis*) define community as a term we apply to a pioneer settlement, a village, a city, a tribe or a nation. 'Wherever the members of any group, small or large, live together in such a way that they share . . . the basic conditions of a common life, we call that group a community.' The problem with this definition is that it also emphasises a limiting boundary within which a community is formed whereas other writers prefer a wider interpretation.

3   Wirth (*Urbanism as a Way of Life*) argues that historically community has been an expression that emphasised the unity of common life of a people or of mankind; and that community must have a territorial base. It must be possible to locate the centre and boundaries of community. The loss of community has resulted from the rapid growth of urban life which introduces qualitatively new forms of social existence.

Community as a more flexible concept

1   Arensberg and Kimball (*Family and Community in Ireland*) say that in Ireland the rural community is not defined by a geographical area. 'Kin are scattered . . . the farmer attends church in one parish and sends his children to school in another . . . They have a variety of interests or sets of interests and they are liable to pursue them within a series of different communities which do not necessarily add up to a clearly defined whole . . .'

2   Seeley *et al.* (*Crestwood Heights*) describe a prosperous upper- middle-class suburb of Toronto. The adult male population spends little time in the area since they work in the city. Yet they describe the area as their community, 'because of the relationships that exist between people . . . revealed in the functioning of the institutions they have created . . .' Participation in the community is largely related to the central life interest of child-rearing.

3   Durant (*Watling; A survey of a New Housing Estate*) points out that community life flourished while new residents fought against external authority, 'but might perish when the battles for gardens, tarmacadam and street lights had been won.' Conflict acted 'as a stimulus for establishing new rules, norms and institutions . . .'

Comment:

(*a*)   Such studies suggest that communities are not necessarily 'basic units', but consist of overlapping groups.

(*b*)   They involve social relationships and these can change according to the factors giving rise to the sense of community.

(*c*)   The source of community may not be harmony, but conflict.

(*d*)   Redfield, Wirth etc. said that communities could not exist in amorphous urban and suburban areas.

(*e*)   Pahl (*Patterns of Urban Life*) argues that the meaningful social area which people inhabit depends on class, life-cycle characteristics, length of residence, career pattern etc.

Conclusions:

There is no doubt that the word community has been subject to a vast range of definitions and interpretations:

1 Hillery reviewed ninety-four definitions and stated 'beyond the recognition that people are involved in community, there is little agreement about the usage of the term.'

2 Wirth (*Towards a Definition* . . .) has said 'community . . . has been used with an abandon reminiscent of poetic licence . . .'

3 Dennis (*The Popularity of the Neighbourhood Community Idea*) said 'in the vocabulary of the social scientist there must be few words used with either the frequency or looseness of "the community".'

4 Pahl (*Patterns of Urban Life*) says that 'the word community serves more to confuse than illuminate the situation in Britain today . . .' He suggests a solution to the problem is to use the phrase 'a locality social system'. This is related to the local distribution of power, status and facilities. These are open to empirical investigation and would allow more specific statements about patterns of social relations to be made and more useful conclusions to be drawn.

THE RURAL-URBAN CONTINUUM DEBATE

What contrasts have been drawn by sociologists between urban and rural societies?

In their attempts to understand how patterns of behaviour change in different social situations, sociologists have endeavoured to construct systems of classification. Some of the early writers developed ideal type models (e.g. Tonnies and Durkheim). These theories of contrast led to the view that where people live influences how they live. The work of a number of American sociologists starting in the 1920s developed the concept of rural-urban distinctions. Empirical studies were undertaken to show that these existed and significantly affected patterns of life.

More recently attempts have been made to construct a continuum to show the different stages in social life between rural at one end and urban at the other. The continuum is used to show the differences in social life as rural areas become infected with urban values.

Criticisms have been made of both approaches by sociologists in recent years.

Theories of contrast: polar types

1 Redfield (*The Little Community; Folk Society*) claimed that there are clear-cut differences between urban and rural societies. Community is an identifiable unit found only at the rural end.

2 Wirth (*Urbanism as a Way of Life*) claimed that:
   (*a*)   Urbanism characterises modern society.
   (*b*)   Urbanism is unnatural and breaks with tradition.
   (*c*)   Modern culture is urban culture.

(d)   The city is the centre of innovation.

(e)   Urbanism has changed every aspect of social life.

(f)   The city and the country are two opposite poles.

He said that urbanism has distinctive characteristics:

A   The size of population:

(a)   There is more differentiation by class and social area.

(b)   Utilitarian relationships prevail based on contract.

(c)   Anomie develops.

B   Increased density of population:

(a)   Social and economic differences between people are accentuated.

(b)   There is greater competition for scarce resources.

(c)   There is more social friction, overcrowding and crime.

(d)   There is the 'lonely crowd' effect in which people feel isolated and alone in a crowded city.

C   Heterogeneity of population:

(a)   It is more varied because of the increasing division of labour.

(b)   There is a more complex class structure.

(c)   There is a fluid mass society in which there is more mobility.

His conclusions are that urban life has many negative qualities which can be contrasted with the more positive features of rural life.

Points of criticism: 2   Many empirical studies indicate that theories of contrast are mistaken because there are many examples which do not fit the predictions.

Examples of urban studies	Examples of rural studies
1. Seeley *et al.* (*Crestwood Heights*). This study shows how an 'interest' community existed in a suburb. 2. Willmott and Young (*Family and Kinship*). They found Gemeinschaft relationships existing in an urban area. 3. Gans (*The Levittowners*) found people living on housing estates experiencing a sense of community which they found satisfying.	1. Lewis (*Life in a Mexican Village*) went back to Tepoztlan, a village studied by Redfield, on which he based his findings. Lewis found class conflict, anomie and tension where Redfield found the opposite. 2. Littlejohn (*Westrigg*) found social disharmony and class divisions in a remote Cheviot village. 3. Weightman (Small-Town Life, *New Society*, 3 October 1974) says that Lewes is not one community, but several mutually exclusive social groups.

2   Pahl (*Readings in Urban Sociology*) says 'for a long time polar typologies . . . served as justification for . . . the uncritical glorifying of old-fashioned rural life . . .' He questions whether there are fundamental differences between urban and rural.

Some sociologists have constructed a continuum based on various characteristics of urban and rural life: how useful is this concept?

1   Frankenberg (*Communities in Britain*) says 'towns and cities make more sense if they are seen as part of an evolutionary process in which the progression from a simple to a diversified technology is accompanied by certain sociological changes . . .'

He reviews studies of communities in a rough order of increasing economic complexity:

(a)   truly rural
(b)   the village in the country
(c)   the town that is a village
(d)   small town communities in cities
(e)   urban housing estates.

From his analysis he ends with a typology based on some of the key differences between the polar extremes. Some of these include:

Urban (less rural)	Rural
1. Association	1. Community
2. Overlapping role relationships	2. Multiple role relationships
3. Diverse economy	3. Simple economy
4. Organic solidarity	4. Mechanical solidarity
5. Loose-knit networks	5. Close-knit networks

2   Southall (*An Operational Theory of Role*) suggests a continuum could be based on social role differentiation:

(a)   Number of persons in a particular area.
(b)   Type of role played.
(c)   Inequalities in role distribution.
(d)   Number of roles played over a period of time.
(e)   Number of roles an individual perceives as being open to him.

Points of criticism: 1   Benet (*The Ideology of the Urban-Rural Continuum*) says that this continuum was a figment of the imagination, but it helped to develop an anti-urban mentality.

2   Pahl (*Patterns of Urban Life*) says of Frankenburg that 'he asserts rather than explains by convincing argument'.

3   Pahl (*Urbs in Rure*) says that his study of commuter villages indicates that they do not fit easily into the urban-rural continuum. The commuters were frequently the source of resentment by local manual workers and caused a breach in community feeling.

Conclusions: 1   Studies from other areas of the world cast doubt on the usefulness of the concept of the continuum. African studies referred to by Pahl indicate that tribal and urban can exist side by side, with migrant workers moving between the two worlds. In the city they wear western clothes and work as clerks; in the village they change into traditional clothes and behave as villagers.

2   Banton (*Social Alignment and Identity in a West African City*) argues that there are 'urban villages' in Africa where urban values have permeated the countryside. He says that the rural-urban continuum must remain open to empirical investigation.

3   Pahl concludes that 'I find little evidence of a rural-urban continuum. More important is a distinction between the "local" and "the

national"; the "large-scale" and the "small-scale" society.' He suggests that both the theories of contrast and the theories of a continuum are no longer fruitful. He suggests they can be largely abandoned in favour of concentration on the processes of change; more comparative work on patterns of community leadership and further analysis of the concepts of role and social networks.

SUBURBS

Examine the sociological contribution to our understanding of suburbs.

Although doubts have been cast on the view that there is a clear distinction between urban and rural lifestyles and relationships, some writers continue to search for a particular way of life associated with a specific type of social environment, especially in the suburbs.

1 People are initially attracted into cities because there are better opportunities for work, housing, welfare, entertainments etc. Wirth argued that as the city develops and expands, the population becomes more socially segregated.

2 Burgess (*The Growth of the City*) helped to develop the Ecology School of analysis. He argued that population in a city is distributed according to particular factors, in particular 'the struggle for space'. There was competition for the scarce resources available. As a result new suburbs became attractive to particular social groups. They were able to leave behind the poorest section in the zone of transition.

3 The suburbs also offered improved facilities: better living environments; new housing; better leisure opportunities etc.

4 In recent years there has been an attempt to encourage industrial re-location in suburban areas, in special industrial estates. The effect has been to encourage the growth of the suburbs with new housing and shopping areas.

5 To try to counteract the decline of the city and especially the decline of the inner-city areas which have fallen into decay, governments have made more money available for re-development (e.g. in 1984 Liverpool with 20% unemployment received £140 million under an urban aid programme, £110 million from the Department of Trade and £134 million from the Docks and Harbour Board and £96 million from MSC).

6 Wirth predicted the major problems and dissatisfactions with urban life in his writings between 1928 and 1938. He argued that in urban areas people become increasingly depersonalised, alienated and isolated. Primary group relationships are replaced by impersonal secondary relations. He described the city as the prototype of mass society.

(*a*) The crowding of different types of people into small areas led to the development of separate neighbourhoods.

(b)   Lack of physical distance between people led to the 'melting-pot' effect. This would lead to a breakdown of primary relationships.

7   Later, these ideas were taken up by Whyte (*The Organisation Man*). He believed that the suburbs attracted a particular type of person who would quickly adapt to the new suburban lifestyle. This was likely to be the upwardly mobile white-collar worker. This was now seen to be the home of the modern alienated man.

Points of criticism: 1   Berger (*Working-Class Suburb*) argues that a myth of suburbia has developed in the USA. This relates to the social and cultural ramifications that are believed to have been present in the exodus, often depicted as presenting 'a new way of life'. It is assumed:

(a)   The suburbanites are the upwardly mobile.
(b)   They are predominantly young.
(c)   They are well educated.
(d)   They will lead a hyperactive social life.
(e)   They have a maximum of similar interests.
(f)   They are increasingly 'classless'.
(g)   The central interest is child-rearing.
(h)   They are primarily commuters to work in cities.
(i)   There is a voting shift to the right.

He argues that if any of these are true they relate only to the middle-class suburbs. The reports on which they are based are highly selective. Large numbers of blue-collar workers are moving away from inner-city areas and on to estates and there is no evidence to show that a shift in location is causing them to adopt a new way of life.

2   Gans (*Urbanism and Suburbanism as Ways of Life*) produces a severe critique of the views of Wirth. Among the points he makes are:

(a)   People do not necessarily adopt new ways of life in their move from city to suburb. The range of house prices attracts a range of different social types with different cultural values.
(b)   Ways of life are not the result of living in a particular area but of economic factors; cultural values; stage of the life cycle and social class. The latter two are particularly important.
(c)   People's behaviour relates to the choices they have and the roles they play according to occupation etc.
(d)   He rejects the ecological model and emphasises the cultural factors. A young married couple are directed to modern suburban estates because they have little capital and high incomes. Therefore, they can obtain a mortgage more easily.

THE DISTRIBUTION OF POPULATION IN CITIES

What factors determine the pattern of residential segregation in cities?   (Ox)

Sociologists have examined the spatial distribution of population in terms of the determining social factors and also the social processes which are inherent in the patterns. These two approaches are closely interrelated.

THE SOCIAL FACTORS **A** The Ecological School of sociology was established in Chicago in the 1920s. This describes the relationship between people and their environment. Burgess described Chicago in terms of five zones, each of which had distinctive social and physical characteristics. There were particular subcultural values dominant in each. They concluded that the main factor which helped the appropriate people select to live in their appropriate areas was competition based on the struggle for space. (Those in the most powerful economic position controlled the most valuable parts of the city).

B Collison and Mogey (*Residence and Social Class in Oxford*) made use of three zones in their analysis. They described how the pattern of residential development spread out in wedges from the centre for historical and social reasons.

(i) Classes 1 and 2 were mainly represented in the northern wedge and also close to the city centre, where the university is situated.

(ii) Class 3's numbers increased in moving from the centre, especially in the east where they were attracted by the chance of cheaper homes and easier access to the industrial areas on the outskirts of the city.

(iii) Classes 4 and 5 were also concentrated close to the centre but in the southern sector. This was because the poorest housing was in an area known as St Ebbs.

C Chombart de Lauwe (*Paris et l'agglomeration parisienne*) described seven concentric zones in his analysis, similar to those of Burgess. He notes the significance of class differences in areas of residence. There is a contrast between the bourgeois west with its broad streets and open spaces and the proletarian east. This has narrower streets, less regular patterns, much industry and poorer quality housing.

SEGREGATION IN CITIES Some sociologists have examined the ways in which patterns of social relations within the different zones of the city are sustained in daily life.

Pahl makes the point that people are distributed more as a result of the constraints that operate on them in the choices they make rather than being distributed according to chance.

Economic constraints The rich can exercise more choice than the poor; the employed more than the unemployed.

Social constraints People tend to seek a home according to their income, occupation and stage in the family cycle. Gans makes the point that young couples with high incomes but small amounts of capital and with young children, are forced into housing estates where mortgages are available.

Racial constraints Rex and Moore (*Race, Community and Conflict*). Their aim was to contribute to an understanding of race relations in Birmingham. They examined the factors affecting the distribution of population in the area known as Sparkbrook. They divided the area into three zones.

Zone 1: Originally an affluent middle-class area, but which had fallen into a state of decay. From the 1930s onwards the middle-classes began to move out into more desirable suburbs. The large houses were divided into lodging houses which attracted Irish and black immigrants in the 1950s.

Zone 2: An area first developed in the 1830s which came to house the working class 'but not rough labourers'. The authors suggest it is an area similar to Bethnal Green. There was a gradual increase in levels of black immigration since property was cheap, although much was awaiting demolition and redevelopment.

Zone 3: Most of the property was built in the 1890s by the Barber Trust. It was good quality and attracted the respectable working class. Much of the housing remained in good order and was still occupied by mainly white residents.

They note how a class struggle arises where people in a market situation enjoy differential access to property. The immigrant population having lowest status and least power were forced into the poorest quality housing in Sparkbrook. The zone of transition is characterised by overcrowding, high rents and lack of privacy. 'The immigrant, the discharged prisoner, the deserted wife have little in common except their housing conditions . . .'

POPULATION

CONTENTS

Questions on this topic include the following areas:

1 Factors affecting the birth rate.
2 Factors affecting the death rate.
3 Factors affecting population trends:
   (a)   Social factors.
   (b)   Comparative data.
4 Class differentials:
   (a)   Mortality
   (b)   Fertility
5 Immigration and emigration.

FACTORS AFFECTING BIRTH RATE

What factors would you take into account in explaining the long-term decline of the birth rate in Britain?

Describe and account for patterns of fertility in any one society in the last thirty years.

Birth rate The number of live births in one year per 1000 people. It is an important determinant of population growth.

Fertility rate The number of live births in one year per 1000 of women of child bearing age (15–45). Age-specific rates would be the number of children born each year per 1000 women in age groups: 15–19; 20–24; 24–29; 30–34; 35–39; 40–45.

Useful statistics:

Crude birth rate 1841–81

1841–50	32.5
1861–70	35.2
1881–90	32.8
1901–10	27.2
1921–30	18.3
1941–50	18.0
1961–70	17.4
1971–80	13.1

Source: RG's *Statistical Review of England and Wales and Social Trends 14.*

Live births: totals and rates

Year	Total live births	Crude birth rate	General fertility rate	Total period fertility rate
1951	768,000	15.7	72.5	2.16
1956	796,000	16.0	78.2	2.38
1961	912,000	17.8	90.0	2.78
1966	946,000	17.8	91.1	2.78
1971	870,000	16.1	84.2	2.40
1976	649,000	11.9	61.0	1.72
1981	704,000	12.9	61.5	1.79
1982	692,000	12.6	59.9	1.75

Source: *Social Trends*

Factors affecting a decline in the birth rate	Factors affecting an increase in the birth rate

1. Economic
  a. High cost of housing.
  b. Lack of job opportunities.
  c. Children not economic assets.
2. Normative
  a. Where class norm is for small family.
  b. Childlessness is socially acceptable.
  c. Large families socially unacceptable.
  d. Rising age of marriage.
  e. Increasing frequency of cohabitation.
3. Social and Medical
  a. War or other major social crisis.
  b. New efficient methods of contraception.
  c. Abortion Act (1967).
  d. Improved education (especially for women, offering better career chances).
  e. More women in paid employment. In 1900 25% of women were in childbirth every year. In 1930 it was 10%. In 1980 a woman aged 20 will spend 7% of her remaining years child bearing.
  f. Improved medicine, welfare and childcare limit need for large family as survival rates increase.
4. Immigration, Emigration
Since 1965 there has been a net loss of population.
	1. Economic
	  a. Economic boom: more houses available.
	  b. More jobs available.
	  c. Children are an economic asset.
	2. Normative
	  a. Class norms encourage large families.
	  b. Childlessness carries stigma.
	  c. Large families provide high status.
	  d. Falling age of marriage.
	  e. Delayed family building brings later increases in birth rates.
	3. Social and Medical
	  a. End of war or other social crisis.
	  b. Changes in attitude towards family planning (e.g. scares about the pill).
	  c. Growing religious opposition to family planning.
	  d. Decline in number of women in paid employment.
	  e. Having gained qualifications and career more women may increase family size.
	  f. New medical techniques may enable more women to have children who previously could not do so.
	4. Immigration
	Because the ages of a high proportion of women in ethnic minorities is young their birth rates are initially high.

Points to note:

1 Forecasters have found predictions as to future trends very difficult:

(*a*) They base estimates of future fertility rates on events that have occurred before. These may not have the same effect in the future.

(*b*) It is difficult to predict when trends have or have not peaked. For example, in 1949 the Royal Commission on Population asserted that there would be a substantial decline in the annual number of births lasting until the mid 1960s because there were fewer women of child-rearing age in the population. In fact birth rate rose during the 1950s and early 1960s. In 1965, new predictions were made suggesting that the fertility rate would rise until 1975 and continue into the early years of the next century. It now appears that the peak was reached in the early 1960s and some decline has followed.

2 The number of births in 1982 was almost 10% more than the low point of 1977, but this was about 30% fewer than that of the highest (1966). The links between fertility and socio-economic factors are complex.

3 The crude birth rate from the highest point of 1966 to the lowest point in 1977. It has subsequently fluctuated but is still higher than in 1977.

4 The total period fertility rate (which is the average number of live births to women having passed through a given set of age-specific fertility rates throughout their lifetime) has fallen from the highest rate of 2.78 in 1966 to the lowest in 1977. In 1982 the rate had fallen from the slightly higher 1980 figure.

Concluding points:

(*a*) There appears to be a cyclical element in fertility rates.

(*b*) Population does not increase by regular and unvarying amounts each year, which would make predictions easy.

(c)   There appears to be a tendency to defer having children until later in marriages in the 1980s.

(d)   There is no clear explanation of why patterns of family building change.

(e)   Projections into the future are always suspect because it is so difficult to identify trends. Should a fall over a few years be considered or an overall rise over a longer period?

In 1970 the government's Actuary Department said:

'a large element of personal judgement has to be exercised in projections . . . and it seems doubtful whether the prospects for predictive accuracy are improving . . .'

(f)   In the mid-1800s the number of live births per 1000 of the population was about 35. In the mid 1900s it was 12.5. In 1985 it was 11.5. In 1885 a smaller proportion of women were producing more children.

(g)   From 1970 to 1976 the population of the UK grew about half a million. Most of this took place before 1974. Between 1975 and 1985 it was stable.

5   In 1987 the over 60s (27%) outnumbered the under 30s (25%) for the first time. In 1991 there will be 600,000 fewer 18–24 year olds and 200,000 more over 60s.

FACTORS AFFECTING THE DEATH RATE

What have been the major changes that have occurred in mortality rates in Britain since 1900? How would you account for the changes?

Crude death rate is the number of deaths per year per 1000 people.

Infant mortality rate is the annual deaths of infants aged 0–12 months per 1000 live births in the same year.

Mortality patterns show the trends in deaths. In Britain the mortality rates for all age groups has declined. Although the number of infant mortalities has declined for all social classes there are still differentials between those in the highest and lowest classes. Health still appears to be related to family environment.

Table 1: Death rate and life expectation 1870–1980 (England and Wales).

Year	Death rate	Life expectation Males	Females
1870	23.0	41	45
1890	19.5	43	48
1910	13.5	52	55
1930	11.4	59	63
1950	11.8	66	72
1970	11.8	69	76
1980	11.7	71	77

Source: *Annual Abstract*

Table 2: Death rates for males and females 1961–81 (UK).

Year	Death rate Males	Females	Average	Total deaths Males	Total Females	(1000s)
1961	12.6	11.4	12.0	322.0	309.8	631.8
1971	12.2	11.1	11.6	328.5	316.5	645.0
1981	12.1	11.4	11.7	329.1	328.8	657.9

Comment:

The crude death rate has remained fairly stable since the turn of the century. Men tend to have higher mortality rates than women. Birth rates are usually higher than death rates, which accounts for the steady growth in population, even though birth rates are falling. Population has grown more slowly in recent years as birth and death rates have become more finely balanced. The only year in which there were more deaths than births was 1977.

Research (1985) by the Royal College of Physicians stated that the number of centenarians in Britain has increased at least ten-fold between 1955 and 1985. This has been the result of such factors as clean air legislation, use of antibiotics and improved standards of care for the elderly. The chance of a woman reaching 100 is nine times better than that of a man.

Table 3: Infant mortality rates 1850–1980.

1850	162
1870	160
1890	151
1910	105
1930	60
1950	30
1970	17
1980	16

Although infant mortality rates have fallen it is important to note that death rates still vary between classes at all ages. These relate to income differentials, nutrition, occupation and educational levels.

Table 4: Comparative death rates (1975 in 6 industrialised societies.

UK	11.8
Denmark	10.1
France	10.6
Netherlands	8.3
West Germany	12.1
Belgium	12.1

Source: *Annual Abstract*

The effects of a switch to stable population growth is difficult to predict with accuracy. But policy-makers have to plan for the future: the number of schools and hospitals needed; numbers entering and leaving the work force and the services needed for the young and old.

DECREASE IN DEATH RATES

1 Economic
(a)   Greater economic prosperity, resulting in more affluence; better homes, improved nutrition.
(b)   Improved conditions of work, shorter hours, more safety-conscious employers etc.

2 Social

(*a*)   Improved living standards, better amenities etc., which make life more healthy and satisfying.

(*b*)   Increased state provision of welfare, town planning etc.

3 Medicine

(*a*)   Improved medicine has helped reduce disease and infection.

(*b*)   The advance of medical science, vaccination, sanitation, pure water supply, midwifery etc.

4 Education

(*a*)   This produced a better informed public who pressed for reforms in welfare, hygiene etc.

(*b*)   Parents became better informed in child care, diet etc.

POPULATION TRENDS

Are human population trends socially determined ?   (Cam)

The question is asking you to discuss the social factors which might operate in a society to help control the growth of population. If population size is related to changing social norms, then are specific population policies necessary?

A report of the Select Committee on Population (1971) argued that the government ought to act to prevent the consequences of population growth becoming intolerable for the everyday conditions of life. It was pointed out that although Britain had a slow-growing population, if the rate of growth continued the population would reach 980 millions in the year 2500. To stabilise the growth the report said that every three families needed to have one less child between them.

► Among the consequences of overpopulation were:

(*a*)   Pressure for accommodation.

(*b*)   Demand for greater employment opportunities.

(*c*)   Pressure on education services.

(*d*)   Pressure on medical and health and social services.

(*e*)   Increased environmental problems.

► Among the suggested means of stabilising population were:

(*a*)   Improved methods of birth control.

(*b*)   The government should talk, tax or legislate the average family down from 2.5 children to 2.1.

(*c*)   Removal from the welfare system of any features which appear to encourage families increasing.

(*d*)   Encourage more women to go out to work.

(*e*)   Provide benefits for those who don't marry or who don't have families.

▶ *Research findings*:

1 Turnbull (*The Demography of Small-Scale Societies*). He examined the ways in which small-scale societies manage to control their levels of population and suggests that large-scale societies (complex industrial) may have similar methods of control based on social factors.

He accepts that many of his points are speculative since non-literate societies have no specific records or data to which to refer. Anthropologists rely mainly on observation and discussion.

Population control operated on the following bases:

1 Marriage of young girls to much older men.
2 Ritual taboos prevented sexual relations between partners after the birth of a child for up to three years.
3 There was wide-ranging acceptance of homosexuality.
4 Ritual groupings between members of the same sex made contact between men and women less frequent.
5 There were powerful stipulations as to possible marriage partners (often exogamy was encouraged: marriage outside the tribal group).
6 Infanticide may be acceptable where a child is deformed etc.
7 Twins are often unacceptable and one child may be abandoned.
8 There are high mortality rates among infants.

He suggests that a complex industrial society is also quite sensitive in its adjustment to environment demands to maintain levels of stability and equilibrium. This hypothesis does seem to be supported to some extent by the fact that population increase has slowed in recent years, making many of the suggestions of the Select Committee of 1971 unnecessary.

2 Gilje and Gould (*Population Growth or Decline?*) Writing in 1973 they noted the continued fall in fertility rates since 1964 and argued that a decreasing population ('or at least one that's not growing') was a possibility for the future.

They examined the difference between the government's Actuary Department projections (GAD) and Greater London Council (GLC) projections as to future population trends.

The GAD projections did not assume that reproduction rates would fall below replacement levels for the next forty years. GLC projections assumed a falling rate which would result in a stable replacement level within a few years.

▶ Fertility patterns are the product of several factors:

(*a*) The number of women in the fertile age groups (15–49).
(*b*) Current norms about ideal family size.
(*c*) Actual family size (the extent to which the ideal is realised).
(*d*) Rate of family formation (birth spacing between children).
(*e*) Changes in marriage patterns (whether people tend to delay age of marriage; 97% of births are to women under thirty).
(*f*) The number of marriage eligibles (the higher birth rate in the late 1950s and early 60s was a product of the population bulge after the war ended).

▶ Factors affecting the size of families:

(*a*)   Changing norms as to ideal family size.

(*b*)   The couple's estimate of their ability to maintain a family of a particular size.

(*c*)   GAD suggested that there was a trend towards deferred child bearing until later in marriage. GLC argued that fertility rates were declining, not just being deferred.

(*d*)   Spacing between children increased.

(*e*)   Improved contraception made family planning more accurate.

(*f*)   More women continued to enter the work force.

(*g*)   More emphasis on companionship in marriage.

(*h*)   More emphasis on higher living standards in preference to larger family.

Conclusion: These research studies provide support for the view that social norms and pressures do help to control 'automatically' population size in accordance with Turnbull's thesis based on small-scale societies, suggesting they are socially determined to some extent.

HEALTH

CONTENTS

The questions which appear on this topic include the following:

1 Key concepts (definitions and explanations of terms: health; illness etc.)
2 Theories of health:
   (*a*) Marxist (structuralist)   (*b*) Functionalist   (*c*) Interactionist.
3 Inequalities in the distribution of health and medical care.
4 Class differences in mortality rate.

KEY CONCEPTS

Cross-culturally, health and disease have different meanings. Compare these between at least two different types of society and show their implications for what is done to cure people.   (Lon)

There is no general agreement as to what is meant by health and illness. Explain with examples why this is so.

To answer such questions you must be able to define and explain the significance of the key concepts referred to in them.

CROSS-CULTURAL DEFINITIONS

Different societies place different meanings on terminology. Words like 'health', 'illness', 'disease', may have different meanings within different cultures. It is important to recognise the conceptual differences in order to make sense of different approaches to health and illness that can be identified. Without such awareness there can be a danger of an ethnocentric bias, assuming that one's own cultural definition is somehow superior to that of others.

1 In the west medicine operates in a tradition which stresses scientific methods of analysis. The patient is viewed as an isolated object. There is a tendency to ignore different levels of experience. The aim is to isolate the cause of a specific physical illness and produce a cure. If there is uncertainty each new hypothesis is tested in turn until a solution is reached.

2 Wilson (*Magic and the Millennium*) notes how in societies where medical practice has been intimately involved with religious ritual and

where modern medical services are scarce, then religious cults have been concerned with healing as well as death.

3   Other observers have noted how in such societies the 'shaman' (medicine man, witch doctor) combines the roles of what in western society would be described as 'priest' and 'psychotherapist'.

4   He operates with a detailed knowledge of the healing properties of plants as well as 'tribal psychology'.

5   Patients are treated in terms of their spiritual and their psychological needs as well as in terms of their physical illness.

6   The shaman works with traditional beliefs about the world and its creation as well as with knowledge of how breaches of morality can cause illness.

7   The causes of illness are therefore seen to be associated with a complex pattern of relationships which exist between the patient's personal, social and moral life and his relationship with the well-being of the tribe itself.

8   Illness is seen as the possible result of witchcraft or a spiritual failing as much as a physical or biological problem.

9   Recovery relies on antidotes which involve a complex set of ceremonies which may last many days. The problem of recovery relies on overcoming the spiritual and social dysfunctions and by seeking a means of reintegrating the patient into society.

10 Such ceremonies may serve important cathartic functions. Not only may they cure the patient but in providing remedies for social reintegration (assuring him of the affection of friends and family) they help to increase tribal solidarity and cohesion.

Outline and evaluate the sociological insights provided by viewing health as a *social construct.*

Traditionally, in Britain, it has been assumed that 'good' or 'bad' health was an objective physical characteristic. However, some sociologists have raised questions as to the validity of this view. How is good health to be measured? (Most people complain of some ailment from time to time without visiting a doctor.)

What is 'illness'? At what point does it start and finish?

Two people may suffer the same ailments. One claims to be ill and is off work, the other does not and continues to work.

1   Gomm (*Social Science and Medicine*) argues that illness and disease, as well as health, are social products. The processes that distribute health chances are social processes. Definitions of terms, their diagnoses and treatment vary from place to place and time to time.

2   The process of becoming defined as 'ill' is a complex one. People have their own self-perceptions and can make decisions about what to do about them. Others, in the family, may seek to impose the role of invalid on an individual, in order to care for them, protect them etc. In the case of mental illness, some writers such as Laing and Cooper suggest that this can have disastrous consequences (see page 103).

3   There is a range of culturally derived knowledge about illness and health and how to respond to it. In Britain it may be 'having a temperature' and 'going to bed and calling a doctor'. In a tribal society it may be the failure of crops and the death of animals.

4   In western societies the process of acquiring a label which defines the individual as ill is complex. It is not necessarily a matter of objective facts, but more a social process by which a person claims illness, is diagnosed and treated by a professional (or family amateur) and then comes to adopt the characteristics of illness (lethargy, distress etc.). The work of Roth and Goffman (see page 260) illustrates how patients in hospitals learn their roles and appropriate patterns of behaviour.

5   Some Marxist theorists have argued that the organisation of medicine is related to the economic structure of society and the interests of a ruling elite. Other functionalists have argued that there is a functional aspect to the organisation of medicine. Weberians focus on the interactional processes by which people are labelled as 'sick' or 'ill'.

THEORIES OF HEALTH

Social work and medicine are best described as part of the apparatus of state control, a means of making individuals conform to society. Discuss.

THE MARXIST PERSPECTIVE

This is based on the view that people's lives are shaped by the economic infrastructure of their society. In a capitalist society illness is defined as the inability to work.

1   Definitions of illness are in the hands of middle-class professional medical workers. They diagnose and establish who is and who is not ill. Working-class people are more likely to be perceived as malingerers. Their opportunities to receive time off through illness with pay are less than those of middle-class workers.

2   The state has taken an interest in the health of workers to ensure a healthy work force.

3   High levels of illness among working-class people is a reflection of their poor working conditions, stress and alienation.

4   For the same reasons there are higher levels of mental illness among working-class people. Working-class women are particularly prone to psychiatric illness as a result of their exploitation as workers and housewives.

5   Because profits come before health consumption patterns among working-class people are determined by capitalist exploitation: (white bread, cigarettes, alcohol etc.; the diseases of affluence).

6   Unemployment rates are highest among those in Classes 4 and 5. Studies indicate that there is more ill health among the long-term

unemployed. They have higher mortality rates, suicide rates as well as higher divorce rates. This is also related to stress and discontentment.

7 By encouraging the assumption that ill health is an objective physical ailment which strikes the population at random, this diverts attention from the class-based inequalities of illness and disease. They claim that their health is not under their own control.

Points of criticism:

1 The state is constantly seeking to improve health care. The fact that working-class people appear to be less healthy may be because they fail to make use of the facilities available.

2 As soon as an industry is regarded as hazardous it is subject to stringent health laws.

3 Capitalism has assisted the poorest sectors of society to improve their living conditions.

4 High rates of mental illness among women may be the result of their spending more time in the home, isolated from wider society and with more limited opportunities for careers.

5 The capitalist market doesn't determine what people buy; it provides opportunities for choice. It is not just working-class people who suffer from diseases of affluence.

6 There is some statistical evidence that suggests that unemployed women have longer life expectations than those who are employed full time. It may be that the unemployed subjectively feel more ill because they have more time to ponder ill health and to visit doctors.

7 People's health could be improved by better education so that they become better informed about how to lead healthier lives.

Patterns of health and illness can be understood only in the context of the social and economic system. Examine this view.   (AEB)

THE FUNCTIONALIST PERSPECTIVE

This is based on the view that every institution in a society serves a function. Among the most important are those which help maintain stability and the integration of the individual in society. The state must provide a means of welfare to ensure that people can obtain the necessary care and advice when they are ill. Medicine is therefore seen as a device to ensure the adequate performance of important social roles.

▶ *Main points:*

1 Since it would be dysfunctional to allow everyone to be absent from work simply because they 'felt ill', it is necessary to have an organised system of diagnosis and control. Doctors serve this important function. They can issue certificates to those they regard as genuinely ill. This system must operate in all societies whether capitalist or socialist.

2 The role of the doctor is a highly professional one. It is subject to

training, qualification and control by a professional organisation. It is a position achieved on merit. This is an example of the need for a hierarchical social system in which the most able reach the top and the least able remain at the bottom. (About 75% of doctors come from Classes 1 and 2.)

3 The claim that medicine does and should have scientific status is justified.

4 As far as the patient is concerned one function of illness is to allow the individual to escape activities which are stressful or unpleasant for a period of time.

5 Vogel and Bell (*The Emotionally Disturbed Child as the Family Scapegoat*) argue that it may be functional for parents to have a disturbed child in the household since it enables them to release their tensions and draws them closer together. This helps to stabilise the family unit by enabling the parents to perform their roles in society more effectively.

6 Health care and health chances are distributed in a rational way in contemporary society. People have a choice as to which services to use and when to use them. Private medicine increases this choice. If there appears to be inequality in distribution it is only because some people make better use of the facilities than others.

7 The groups in poor health are declining as medical welfare improves.

8 Upward social mobility ensures that more people are leaving the dangerous, unhealthy jobs. New technologies will eventually see their eradication.

Points of criticism:

1 The organisation of occupations into professions is a way in which particular groups maintain their privileges and power. Gomm points out how doctors often develop 'deterrent strategies' to cope with what they consider to be abuse. They may keep lists of suspect patients or 'shelter behind a fierce receptionist, refuse home visits or adopt a cold attitude. . .'

2 The professionalisation of medicine is an example of capitalist self-interest in which power is passed on from one generation to the next. Those at the bottom have no real chance of reaching top professional positions.

3 Illich (*Medical Nemesis*) attacks the view that the medical profession confers scientific benefits on society. New drugs are introduced but they have harmful side effects. Their increasing use means that people are less likely to face pain which gives strength to them and to the whole culture. Medicine engenders drug addiction and ill health which produces a weaker society. He concludes that the medical establishment has become a major threat to health. Health has improved as a result of better diet not drugs. Medical treatment is a means of convincing those who are subject to poverty and hardship that it is they who are ill rather than allowing them to see that their society is sick.

4 There can be dangers in allowing a person to accept the label 'invalid' about themselves since this can lead to negative patterns of behaviour.

5 The views of Vogel and Bell place the interests of the family as a whole over that of the individual child whose chances of becoming an adequate parent in the future may be limited as a result.

6 Programmes to improve people's awareness of their rights with regard to health will have little effect because they do not affect the fundamental economic inequalities in society. The Court Report (see below) suggests that those parts of the country with greatest need get the worst provision of welfare services.

7 Prosser and Wedge (*Born To Fail*) showed that there remain an increasing number of disadvantaged children suffering major health problems, especially in Classes 4 and 5.

8 High rates of unemployment inhibit upward mobility. Most mobility from Class 5 is into Class 4 and mortality rates have not improved in this class relative to others.

At first sight 'health' and 'illness' appear to be simply medical issues. In what ways have sociologists contributed to an understanding of these aspects of human behaviour?

(JMB)

THE INTERACTIONIST PERSPECTIVE

This view is based on the idea that action develops from negotiated meanings which are constructed in the course of social interaction. People derive meanings from events and act on their interpretations.

1 Roth (*The Treatment of TB as a Bargaining Process*).

He wrote his findings based on field notes, kept while he was a patient, an attendant and as a social observer. He spent time 'hanging around' the hospital wards and offices, attending conferences, making rounds and listening to doctors discussing their 'problems' with one another.

He argues that the treatment relationship may be conceived of as a conflict for control of the patient's behaviour, a conflict usually resolved by bargaining. Through their observations and pooling of information, patients learn appropriate behaviour patterns.

Roth is arguing that what happens to patients in a hospital is not a matter of objective fact relating to illness, but more a matter of subjective interpretation on the part of patient, nurse and a doctor.

2 Goffman (*The Effects of Inmate Status*)

He used similar observational methods to describe how a mental patient starts by clinging to his memories and knowledge of his past. He gradually gives up this effort at anonymity and enters the hospital community. This is regarded as 'settling down' by the staff. He then undergoes further 'humbling moral experiences' as he becomes socialised into the patterns of hospital life and he accepts his new persona as 'mental patient'. He is presented with new models of behaviour, both by the staff and other patients. He comes to accept the reasons for his hospitalisation.

Points of criticism: 1 This perspective focuses on the micro-level of analysis. It does not take much account of the individual in relation to wider class or cultural values.

2 Staff would no doubt be surprised to be informed that they were teaching someone to become a 'mental' or a 'hospital' patient. They would have a different interpretation.

3 The views are also open to the criticism of all interactionist research, that it relies on the skills and accuracy of the observer, who draws on his own observations and interpretations of events, rather than on 'objective' scientific data.

INEQUALITIES IN THE DISTRIBUTION OF HEALTH AND MEDICAL CARE

The social distribution of good health closely reflects the social distribution of wealth and income. Discuss.

The availability of good medical care tends to vary inversely with the needs of the population served. Discuss.

There is much debate as to the extent of inequalities in the distribution of wealth and income in Britain. The Low Pay Unit reports that some workers earn less than £1 per hour (1985) whilst the *Sunday Times* (1983) reports that the Duke of Westminster has an income estimated to be around £10,800 per hour! Inland Revenue Statistics (1982) indicated that the gap between the wealth of the rich and the poor was no longer narrowing, as it had been in the years 1945–79. However, in 1985 *Social Trends 15* suggested that there may be a change in this position. The top 1% owning most marketable wealth, plus occupational and state pensions, was declining (from 21% in 1971 to about 11% in 1984). However, there remains evidence for inequalities among the poorest 50% and the most wealthy 10% of the population. In 1985 the Bishop of Southwark warned that the gap between the rich and poor could create increasing conflict in the near future. This was a particular problem of increasing unemployment.

There is evidence from research which suggests that the poorest sector suffers more ill health and has least good access to welfare facilities.

1 The Court Report

This was set up in 1973 by Sir Keith Joseph to examine the health services for children. This stated that the parts of the country with greatest need get the lowest provision of these services. The authors state that there is little evidence that in regions of high need the provision is increased. Indeed, the reverse is true. In regions with a high birth rate, a high proportion of children in the population, or high infant mortality, the numbers of GPs and local authority medical staff are low. Poverty and ill health are fellow travellers, particularly in childhood. The provision of health services has moved in the opposite direction. The pattern that emerges is that in areas with high living standards, health is better and more is spent on medical facilities.

2   Prosser and Wedge (*Born to Fail*)

This 1973 publication showed that nearly 900,000 children were growing up disadvantaged and faced an accumulation of adversities. (They were considered disadvantaged if growing up in a large family or with only one parent, with low income and poor housing.) Such children were found to suffer more health problems; were less likely to be immunised against serious illness; 1:3 never attended a welfare clinic; there was a great prevalence of infection and their general physical development was less good by the age of eleven than those not disadvantaged, in the sample.

3   The Black Report (1980) (Inequalities in Health) also pointed out the major inequalities in health and health services. Death rates vary between social classes suggesting that it may be desirable to reallocate resources and provide more for those in greatest need. The recommendations are set out in The Black Report edited by Townsend and Davidson.

4   Fox (*Unemployment and Mortality*)

He found that in 1981 the unemployed men (compared with others in the sample of the same age) were more than twice as likely to have committed suicide; 80% more likely to have had a fatal accident and 75% more likely to have died from lung cancer.

The death rate was 36% higher among such men than it should have been.

5   Platt (*Leeds University Report 1984*)

He said that the evidence of an association between unemployment and suicide was overwhelming. He concluded that health and social policy should be devised on the assumption that unemployment endangers health. Present policies are based on the opposite assumptions. Unemployment tends to be concentrated in large families where the parents are unskilled. In 1982 96% of professional husbands had a job whereas only 67% unskilled workers were employed.

CLASS DIFFERENCES IN MORTALITY RATES

Discuss and account for the persistence of class differentials in mortality rates in Britain.

Gomm points out that there is evidence to show that differences in premature mortality rates for males and to a lesser extent females, of different classes, have not narrowed but widened. This suggests that despite the provision of the welfare state and all the advances in medicine over the past century there is still some inequality in the distribution and use of resources. It also implies that mortality rates are related to a range of influences; those in the least pleasant jobs having the poorest life chances.

Table 1: Mean annual death rate per 100,000 men by age group and social class.

Age Group	Class 1	Class 2	Class 3	Class 4	Class 5 (1959–63)
15–19	67	99	90	110	132
20–24	67	97	103	114	170
25–34	82	81	100	119	202
35–44	166	177	234	251	436
45–54	535	545	708	734	1119
55–64	1699	1820	2218	2202	2919
65–74	4666	5100	6347	5702	6715

Source: *Quoted in Reid*

Comment:

1 The mortality rates are higher for Classes 4 and 5.
2 In all age groups the death rate of Class 1 is approximately half that of Class 5.
3 Life expectation is related to class membership.
4 The class chances of surviving adulthood into old age are similar to those of surviving birth (see page 264).
   The overall rate of infant mortality remains greatest in Class 5, and least in Class 1. In 1977 there was, on average, one still birth in Class 1 to every 150 births and one in Class 5 to every 80 live births.

Table 2: Mortality of men 15–64 by social class 1910–72.

Year	Class 1	Class 2	Class 3	Class 4	Class 5
1910–12	88	94	96	93	142
1930–32	90	94	97	102	111
1970–72	77	81	104	114	137

Source: OPCS.

Comment:

1 It is difficult to make direct comparisons between class groups because definitions of class in terms of different occupational groups may have changed over the years.
2 Although mortality rates appear to have fallen for Classes 1, 2 and 5 they have not done so for Classes 3 and 4.
3 The 1961 Registrar General's report (*Occupational Mortality*) compared the health and mortality rates of the unskilled with those in the other classes. It found:
   (*a*) A deterioration among the unskilled in life chances.
   (*b*) Mortality rates fell for all men in 1961 (except 70–74) but unskilled men had not benefited from major social changes which had benefited their compatriots.
4 The 1971 report also analysed life chances. It found:
   (*a*) those in Class 5 had 2½ times more chance of dying before retirement age than those in Class 1.
   (*b*) For men there was greater inequality in mortality between Classes 1 and 5 in 1961 and 1971 than 1947 and 1953.
   The same is true when comparisons are made in the above table. In 1970–72 the gap between deaths in Class 1 and Class 5 was wider than in 1910–12. It was narrower in 1930–32.

Year	Class 1	Class 2	Class 3	Class 4	Class 5
1921	38	55	76	89	97
1950	17	22	28	33	40
1970	12	14	16	20	31
1980	9	9	10	13	16

Table 3: Infant mortality rates by social class 1921–80.

Source: OPCS.

Comment:

1　Morris and Heady
They analysed 80,000 stillbirths (death in the first week of life), neonatal deaths (death in the first four weeks) and post-natal deaths (death in the first year of life) between 1949 and 1950 and compared the results with data for 1911. They found:
(*a*)　There was a reduction in infant mortality rates in all social classes, but differences remained between each one.
(*b*)　Rates for infants born into the homes of unskilled workers were about forty years behind those whose fathers were in Class 1. This has now fallen to about thirty years.

2　House of Commons Social Services Committee (1985)
Their report revealed the following:
(*a*)　Babies born into unskilled working-class homes are almost twice as likely to die in the first week of life as those from Classes 1 and 2.
(*b*)　Class differences widened in the years 1978–82, as a result of: the economic recession; poor nutrition among lower working-class mothers; inadequate health care in inner-city areas; the failure of GPs to encourage their patients to check into ante-natal clinics early in pregnancy.

▶　Some possible explanations:

1　Functionalists, who emphasise the operation of market forces in providing what people need according to their demands, argue that apparent inequalities will disappear as numbers in lower class groups diminish and better use is made of facilities. Therefore, there is no need to focus special attention on this sector.

2　Cultural explanations focus on poor diet, poor leisure activities, excessive use of cigarettes and alcohol. Those at the bottom of the social hierarchy do less well in the search for jobs which would raise their living and health standards because they are often ill.

3　Interactionists stress the way that perception of events can influence attitudes to health. Long-term unemployment may result in negative attitudes and values which lead to the greater sense of illness. There are more unemployed people in Classes 4 and 5.

4　Structuralists focus on the weaknesses of the social and economic structure to provide equal opportunities in health care. Class differences in health are inevitable because people in Classes 4 and 5 are employed in more dangerous and stressful work. There is overcrowding in homes, the use of cheap and often dangerous equipment, leading to higher rates of accidents in the home etc. The social distribution of good health is seen to be as unequal as that of wealth and income.

DEVELOPMENT

CONTENTS

Questions on this topic appear most frequently on AEB, Cambridge, London and Welsh Boards. They cover the following areas:

1   Key concepts
    (a)   The meaning, definition and problems associated with terminology; e.g. development; underdeveloped; third world; modern; modernisation; traditional societies.
    (b)   The sociology of modernisation.
    (c)   The sociology of underdevelopment.
    (d)   Possible measures of development.
2   Theories of development
    (a)   Functionalist views: modernisation theory.
    (b)   Marxist views: underdevelopment: dependency theory.
    (c)   Weberian views: diffusion theory.

KEY CONCEPTS

Some societies are described as *developed* and others as *underdeveloped*. Explain what these terms mean and why they are of interest to sociologists.

What are the main differences between modern *industrial* societies and *third-world* countries.

How far is a distinction beteen *traditional* and *modern* valid and useful in classifying societies?

Distinguish between a sociology of *underdevelopment* and *modernisation*.

What is meant by *development*? How can it be measured?

To answer any of these questions you must be clear as to the possible definitions of terms and some of their implications.

1   'Development' may be used to describe:
    (a)   changes within specific institutional forms, e.g. 'the development of capitalist society';
    (b)   the move from one type of social structure to another e.g. 'the development of capitalism from feudalism'.

NB There is a danger in assuming that some form of development is necessarily beneficial for a society and that all societies should aspire to 'development'.

2   Developed, industrialised, modern 'First-world societies':
they have well-organised, long-standing industrial bases, which are the source of wealth and high living standards (e.g. USA; Britain).

3   Second-world countries: those subject to effective industrialisation; but the term is generally used to describe the communist countries in the Eastern bloc. The distinction between First and Second worlds is primarily a political one.

4   Third-world countries are characterised by a low per capita income, an abundance of unskilled workers, a lack of investment capital and an economy which relies on a few main crops which may fail, causing great hardship.

5   The sociology of modernisation:
The process of modernisation from underdeveloped to developed is advocated by many writers (especially in the functionalist school). Such sociologists as Parsons and Moselitz have been interested in the debate as to the processes involved in a society becoming developed and modernised. They have been concerned with the:

(*a*)   speed of social development
(*b*)   ways that development can be encouraged
(*c*)   factors which inhibit development.

For such writers, development implies the following:

(*a*)   The ability to sustain increased population, in providing sufficient food, housing and work.

(*b*)   A more complex social life emerges which provides a hierarchy of power and authority.

(*c*)   Industrialisation reaches 'take-off' point. Machine-based production replaces agriculture as the major source of the production of wealth in society.

(*d*)   Living standards are raised.

(*e*)   Urbanisation occurs in a planned and organised way.

(*f*)   There is division of labour producing more goods more cheaply for wider markets.

(*g*)   There is the development of specialist institutions for education, welfare, leisure etc.

(*h*)   There are more complex forms of bureaucracy for purposes of government and administration, which ensure greater efficiency in all aspects of society.

6   Underdeveloped societies:
There is no general agreement as to how societies develop and change; whether there are developmental stages or what precisely constitutes an underdeveloped society.

(*a*)   One feature they may share in common is a colonial past.

(*b*)   There is an implication that such societies are economically 'backward'. They are sometimes described as 'Third-World' countries, such as those of South America, parts of Africa and Asia. They have some potential for growth and change but have not yet achieved the point of 'take-off'.

(c)   The term 'Fourth World' has also been introduced by some writers to describe those which are even further behind in economic development and which appear to be stagnating (e.g. Haiti; Ethiopia).

(d)   Modernisation theorists suggest that such underdeveloped societies can be assisted towards development and modernisation by specific policies, and by becoming more exposed to the values and ideologies of advanced western societies.

Notes: there are equally difficult problems in the use of this terminology. The use of the term 'a developing society' may convey a sense of optimism that the society is progressing towards an idealised western model. In fact, for many such societies their internal problems may be increasing and any economic benefits may be reaching only a small elite.

2   The sociology of underdevelopment:

(a)   This has tended to be the area of interest of Marxist (or materialist) sociologists and economists. Marxist writers have examined the cause of underdevelopment in terms of the exploitation of western capitalist societies.

(b)   Marxists argue in their analysis of underdevelopment that obstacles to development are externally created by the exploiting powers.

(c)   They see change resulting not from increased aid but from internal class struggle, leading to the overthrow of repressive elites.

Possible measures of development:

Measurement is obviously difficult since there is no precise agreement as to what constitutes an underdeveloped or developed society. However, the following factors could be considered:

Economic   It should be possible to calculate the levels of national and personal wealth in a society. These could be used to establish minimum levels below which a society could be described as underdeveloped. However, it is difficult to make such international and cross-cultural comparisons.

Political   It may be possible to establish levels of development on the basis of answers to such questions as:
Is there a democratic form of government?
Is there an organised bureaucratic administrative structure?

Social   Living standards could be assessed: opportunities to obtain housing, its quality, running water, electricity etc. Also life expectation, average family size, opportunities for education, levels of literacy, etc.

Legal   The legal system in a developed society may be based on a long-standing accepted structure which offers justice, opportunity for appeal etc.

By comparing levels of development and underdevelopment according to some criteria it may be possible to make judgements about standards in and between societies. Where there are deficiencies then policies could be directed to those problem areas.

Points of criticism:

1   There is no universal agreement about what constitutes development or underdevelopment.
2   There is no consensus about how it can be measured.
3   There is also no agreement about how it occurs or what forms are most desirable.
4   Terms like these can be misleading since they tend to divide the world into two or three camps which appear to be independent of each other and which may be ranked in terms of inferior and superior positions. In fact most societies of the world are interlinked in a variety of ways.

Comment:

1   The idea that underdeveloped societies can and ought to be modernised is part of the 'modernisation theory' favoured by functionalist writers.
2   The view that they can become modern (but not that they necessarily will) but they may be held up by lack of necessary leadership or social institutions, fits into a Weberian perspective on development.
3   The view that such societies ought not to follow the western capitalistic pattern of growth is the view of the Marxist writers on the subject.
4   It is easy to adopt an ethnocentric position and view other societies in comparison with one's own.
5   Whilst different schools of sociology tend to focus on different aspects of questions about development and underdevelopment, there are some divisions within each school, differing in their views of the major forces of social change.
6   A major difference between the theorists is that the Marxists tend to make use of mono-causal theory (based on economic factors) whereas others prefer multi-causal explanations.

THEORIES OF DEVELOPMENT

MODERNISATION THEORY

Associated mainly with functionalists.

Examine the view that modernisation theory offers too simple a model for understanding the problems of development.   (AEB)

What are the major obstacles to modernisation in underdeveloped societies today?   (Cam)

Can societies be said to have evolved over time?

Main points:

1   Underdeveloped societies are said to be economically backward. They have the characteristics of Gemeinschaft societies: there is emphasis on ascribed status, primary relationships, and attachment to a locality. There is little social mobility.

2   Development and modernisation are based on a series of changes leading from one type of society to another higher form, which is more complex and economically sophisticated.

3   Any obstacles to development are the result of the maintenance of traditional elements in the society which hinder rationalisation.

4   Development, which is to be encouraged, involves changes in the economic, political, family and religious institutions of society. These are a major part of the social system. To induce development it is necessary to obtain changes in the structure of society.

EVOLUTIONARY THEORY

Early functionalist perspectives

1   Comte and Spencer said that societies developed from simple to complex structures.

2   The evolutionary principles of the natural world could be applied to the social world.

3   The assumption was that societies developed in a fixed way, following the path of those already more advanced.

Points of criticism:

1   It is not possible to generalise from the pattern of the development of one society to that of another.

2   Every society is faced with specific problems in the course of change and the solutions adopted by one may not be appropriate to those of another.

More recent Functionalist views:

1   There is a rejection of traditional evolutionary theory.

2   It is accepted that not all societies have an equal potential for development.

3   It is agreed that developmental change can take many forms. That which appears in western Europe is only one type.

4   Since obstacles to development vary from one society to another, major radical change may be necessary (rather than evolutionary change) to achieve modernisation.

5   Also major structural changes may be necessary. For example, the abolition of primitive religions; the introduction of efficient schools and universities; the encouragement of the nuclear family; the imposition of more democratic political structures; more capital investment; improved transport and communication systems; more financial aid from rich western societies.

Points of criticism:

1   Such views tend to ignore the effects of the colonial past and the effects of the negative attitudes which may have been imbued (e.g. the effects of slavery).

2   Societies which have long-standing social structures based on traditional values, customs and beliefs cannot be 'reformed' in a simple way.

3   There is an assumption that 'the west is best' (i.e. that the social and

economic structure of developed societies is an ideal model for all underdeveloped societies to follow).

4   There is evidence that programmes for modernisation have not been successful. Forster (*The Vocational School Fallacy in Development Planning*) argues that to provide technical, vocational and agricultural instruction in schools has often failed because such experts cannot be absorbed into the economy. He says there is always the problem of 'generalised unemployment'.

DEPENDENCY THEORY

Mainly associated with Marxists.

We should be less concerned with the sociology of development and much more with the sociology of underdevelopment.

Underdeveloped societies remain poor as a result of long-term exploitation in international relations (especially through colonialism and imperialism). It is capitalism which has produced the dependency of the poor societies on the rich industrialised countries.

Early Marxist views

1   There are laws of social development which could be scientifically established to show that all societies move through a series of stages. These are: simple; primitive; ancient; feudal; capitalist; socialist and communist.

2   Social development is related to economic factors. As the economic infrastructure changes so societies develop and new forms emerge. The highest form of social life is the final stage of communistic society in which there are no contradictions or inner weaknesses.

More recent neo-Marxist views

1   The rich western societies have increased their wealth by exploiting and controlling the poor countries.

2   This has continued into the twentieth century. The power elites in these poor societies have aligned themselves with the interests of the west.

3   The result will be internal conflict as class divisions emerge and ultimately revolutionary changes will occur to promote the interests of the proletariat.

Points of criticism:

1   Not all underdeveloped societies can be explained in terms of capitalist exploitation. Many are underdeveloped and have no contact with the west.

2   Some societies remain underdeveloped even though there is aid from the west and it would seem in the interest of the industrialised societies that they should develop rapidly (e.g. Mexico and Turkey).

3   The wealth of the advanced societies comes from advanced methods

of technology and trade. It may also come from investment in other rich societies.

4 Rich countries with interests in poor ones do not necessarily have power over them.

DIFFUSION THEORY

Mainly associated with Weberians.

Examine the major competing explanations for some societies remaining underdeveloped. (AEB)

Critically examine a theory which explains how a society may change from being underdeveloped to developed.

▶ Main points

1 Underdeveloped societies remain poor until the values of a particular group, an innovationg elite, usually inspired by a charismatic individual, predominate in the society.

2 For change to occur it is necessary for a rationalisation process to develop. Bureaucratic organisation is the predominant characteristic of modern industrial society.

3 Affective and traditional action indicates that individuals have no real understanding of why they act as they do. They are guided by emotion and custom. These are the characteristics of underdeveloped societies.

4 Rational action involves clear knowledge of specific goals; it involves assessing a situation and following logical means to attain them. This is the dominant mode of procedure in industrial society.

Progress towards development:

1 The main ways of achieving development are to encourage access to developed societies so their values and ideas are absorbed.

2 Obstacles to development are lack of contact with developed models as well as lack of appropriate progressive institutions.

3 The progress of social development can never be foreseen or predicted in the way that Marxists claim is possible. This is because development is largely the product of processes of interaction which cannot be prophesied.

4 Patterns of social change are in the hands of individuals whose ideas, beliefs and actions can influence events.

Points of criticism:

1 This view argues that a new religious creed or particular type of family structure could cause the development of a new economic system, which could result in developmental changes.

However, some critics have asked whether the economic system creates the conditions for the new religious creed or for changes in the family structure. (In Britain, did the Protestant Ethic help develop capitalism or vice versa?)

2   The view is thought by some to overemphasise the significance of powerful leaders to impose new values on a large, traditionally minded population. Once they have disappeared it is likely that the society will revert to its traditional form.

3   To maintain change the society also requires a rapid growth in disciples of the leader, raw materials, fuels, markets and a political structure which is viewed favourably by western societies who provide other aid. Shared values may not be enough.

4   Many underdeveloped societies have had access to western models as a result of colonial influence but they have not necessarily adopted western values because they are not appropriate. They may also have rejected the values as unacceptable. Charismatic leaders may take the society in different directions and in some cases back to more traditional roots (e.g. Iran).

Contrast different sociological theories to explain the problems facing third world countries

	Underdevelopment theorists (primarily Marxist)	Modernisation theorists (primarily functionalists)	Modernisation theorists (primarily Weberian)
Explanations for why the Third World remains poor	The exploitation of the rich colonial powers	1. Lack of capital investment 2. Failure to develop products for export. 3. Lack of stable political structures. 4. Failure to reform traditional social structures.	1. Lack of an ideology of social and economic progress. 2. Lack of trained, literate administrators. 3. Lack of an ethic of rationality.
Factors affecting the process of development	Failure to escape the influences of western exploiters will inhibit change.	1. The ability of developed societies to exert influence. 2. The acceptance of highly developed western societies as appropriate models for change.	1. The introduction of well-organised educational structures. 2. The presence of an educated modernising elite to impose new values on the society. 3. Charismatic leadership.
Attitudes towards the development of Third-World countries	Whilst the capitalist societies continue to exert influence on them there is little chance of social change.	1. The influence of western developed societies can only be beneficial. 2. The technology and ideology of free enterprise will speed development.	The chances of introducing progressive ideologies is good because the benefits can be seen through the media (e.g. Live Aid Concert to raise funds for famine relief was viewed by 1,500 million people in 140 countries in July 1985).

POVERTY

CONTENTS

Most of the questions on this topic relate to the following areas:

1   Problems of defining poverty.
2   Who are the poor?
3   Theories to explain the causes and persistence of poverty. Analysis in terms of functionalist, Marxist and Weberian theories.
4   The contribution of sociology to the analysis of poverty.

PROBLEMS OF DEFINITION

'Defining and measuring the extent of poverty in Britain is inevitably a value-laden exercise.' Discuss and explain.   (AEB)

To answer the question:
1   You must know at least three different ways of defining poverty.
    (a)   *Absolute or subsistence poverty*:
    This is measured by estimating a list of the basic necessities of life. They may include number of calories and proteins to sustain life; quality of accommodation; availability of medical facilities to maintain good health and even the availability of educational, leisure and cultural facilities.
    (b)   *Relative poverty*:
    This is measured in terms of assessments by people in society as to what is considered to be an acceptable standard of living at a particular time. Lafitte says it must be assessed in the context of the community's prevailing standards.
        Townsend says a person could be poor where their resources are so seriously below those commanded by the average person that they are excluded from ordinary living patterns. Holman (*Poverty*) says it is concerned with the lowest incomes being too far removed from the rest of the community.
    (c)   *Subjective poverty*:
    This refers to the subjective attitudes of people with regard to poverty. Do they feel themselves to be poor? How do they perceive themselves in relation to others in the society and how do their patterns of behaviour relate to their sense of being poor?
2   You need to know the details from studies or results from research

which have produced some measurements of poverty using these definitions:

(*a*)   Rowntree used an absolute method of analysis and found in 1901 15% of people in York had an income insufficient for them to achieve the minimum necessary for the maintenance of life. His last study in 1950 suggested that this had fallen to about 1.5%.

(*b*)   Townsend (*Poverty in the UK*) using a relative concept says that over 50% of the population of Britain are likely to experience poverty at some stage of their lives as a result of failure to enjoy the normal expectations of modern society.

(*c*)   Using a subjective analysis of poverty MORI researchers found between 5 and 12 million people were living in poverty in 1983. More than 5 million said they considered themselves to be poor all the time and nearly 12 million said they were poor some of the time.

3   You must consider the meaning of 'inevitably value laden'. This implies that some or all of the following points are true:

(*a*)   The choice of definition is related to the values of the researcher.

(*b*)   The results produced may be biased by the values of the researcher.

(*c*)   The interpretation of the results may be biased.

(*d*)   The word *inevitably* suggests that it is impossible to conduct research into the topic without this occurring.

You must decide your views on the issue before entering the exam room.

It would be possible to argue, for example, that sociologists who choose a relative definition of poverty are likely to be committed to liberal or radical views and a concern about the least well-off in the society. Whilst this may not in any way cause them to be less than careful in the collection of their statistics, they may interpret their results to emphasise the extent of the problem.

Assess the merits of different definitions of poverty.

You are being asked to state the strengths of the three ways of defining poverty. (It would be reasonable in such a question to include some of the disadvantages, since this will help you to reach a conclusion.)

Some of the merits

1. Absolute poverty
a. This helps to present a clear line between those who are and those who are not in poverty.
b. It is possible by using this definition to show that poverty is being defeated as standards improve in the society.

2. Relative poverty
a. It presents a picture of a society as having serious problems which may help to keep policy-makers more alert to deprivation.
b. It is helpful in that it presents a comparison between people in the same society at the same time period.
c. Townsend says that only by deciding on accepted living standards and lifestyles can we decide on the extent of poverty. Any definition must be related to the needs and demands of a changing society.

3. Subjective poverty
a. It is important to know what people believe, subjectively, about themselves and their relationships to others. This helps us to understand their behaviour.
b. It is also a way of assessing general attitudes at a particular time. If an increasing number of people feel themselves to be in poverty they may become more active in seeking to change their environment.

Some of the weaknesses

1. Absolute poverty.
a. Even within an absolute definition the numbers in poverty will vary according to which 'necessaries' are included.
b. In showing that poverty is disappearing because living standards are improving this may disguise the existence of other forms of deprivation.

2. Relative poverty
This definition may be thought to overstate the extent of the problem and cause some to become more critical of those who complain.
b. This definition makes it hard to see how poverty can ever be defeated since there is always going to be someone who is poor in relation to others.
c. It is difficult to decide what an acceptable living standard is. Mencher says 'standards become so fluid that no definition of need satisfies the ever-changing expectations of modern life.'

3. Subjective poverty
a. Some people may be objectively in very deprived circumstances but they may not perceive themselves to be 'poor'.
b. The failure of some to recognise their poor situation in relation to others may prevent them from applying for all the benefits to which they are entitled.
c. Others may claim that they are poor when objectively they do not seem to be so.

WHO ARE THE POOR?

The official government definition of poverty is the need to claim Supplementary Benefits (SB). These are available for people who are not in full-time work and whose income from pensions etc. is not enough to meet the basic necessities of life. It does not depend on having paid contributions into the scheme. The SB Commission makes allowances for married people, each child and for rent. The total becomes the poverty line for the family concerned. It represents the level below which the state believes that income should not fall. In the 1950s and 60s surveys indicted that between 4% and 12% of the population were below SB levels. In 1965 Townsend and Abel Smith advocated the use of the assessment of poverty on the basis of SB scales plus 40%. In 1979 this indicated that there were about 14 million people within this definition. In 1984 it was estimated that the number was 18 million.

Consider the following questions:

Discuss the view that the major cause of poverty is illness, handicap and old age.

Unemployment has replaced old age as the major cause of poverty. Discuss. (Ox)

The poor are always with us because there are always low-paid and disadvantaged families in society. Discuss.

Questions such as these embrace the main categories of people whom research has suggested are the most likely to fall into poverty (either from a subjective or objective point of view.)

Questions may ask you to assess which of the factors:

(a)   old age
(b)   handicap and disablement
(c)   one-parent families
(d)   unemployment
(e)   low pay

is the major cause of poverty. To answer such questions you must be able to suggest reasons to support and sustain a particular view.

▶ *Examples:*

Old age

1   People over retirement age lose their economic power. Most have to rely on state benefits for survival. Since these are fixed pensioners face particular difficulties in times of high inflation. Numbers in the category have steadily increased:

Numbers of people aged over 60 1951–85

1951	1961	1971	1981	1985
6.6m	7.5m	8.8m	9.6m	9.7m

Source: *Social Trends*

The numbers claiming SB

1975	1985
1.7m	3.0m

2   Many old people fail to claim benefits to which they are entitled, making their economic position more serious:
It is estimated that in 1985 this was between three quarters of a million and one million.

3   The state pension is less than one third of the national average wage for a married couple.

The handicapped and disabled

1   Those in this category have lost economic status and power. They rely on benefits which may often be inadequate.

2   1974: 570,000 were living within the range of SB plus 20%.
1975: 225,000 received SB.
1981: 3.5 million were estimated to be handicapped or disabled.
1982: 29% of households in Britain were thought to be effected in some way by such disadvantage.
1984: 1.25 million were registered as disabled.
1985: 5.5. million were estimated to be qualified to claim for various benefits.
(Source: Royal Association for Disability and Rehabilitation Survey).

3   A 1988 study (Prevalence of Disability among Adults, OPCS) found that there are 6.2 million disabled adults in Britain. The largest group (1.2 million) have locomotion problems.

One-parent families

1 These include families broken by divorce, separation, death, imprisonment etc.
2 They are often headed by a woman who is faced with the problem of raising a family and holding a job. Poverty may be particularly severe for children of an unmarried mother without work and from a low socio-economic background.
3 Numbers in the category are increasing:
1965: it was estimated that they constituted 9.3% of all families.
1985: it was estimated that they constituted 12.5% of all families.
4 No benefit can be claimed if the parent is already getting a child's special allowance; an industrial death benefit; the child is in local authority care for more than eight weeks or if the husband or wife is in legal custody.

The unemployed

1 This group has increased most rapidly since 1965.

1965	1972	1975	1978	1982	1985	1987
.5m	.7m	.8m	1.3m	2.7m	3.1m	2.9m

2 The unemployed have no economic status or power. They rely on benefits. The numbers claiming have steadily increased. Some may also have been poor whilst in work as a result of low income.
3 The number of long-term unemployed (more than twelve months) has also increased from about 150,000 in 1973 to 1 million in 1985.
4 Daniel (*New Society*, 1981) suggested that the types of workers most likely to become unemployed include: (*a*) the low skilled (*b*) the low paid (*c*) black workers (*d*) women (*e*) older and less fit workers.

The low paid

1 Low pay is usually defined as approximately two thirds of the national average wage.
2 1973 n.a.w. was £50 p.w. 2 million adults earned less than £25 p.w.
1977 n.a.w. was £82 p.w. 3.8 million adults earned less than £50 p.w.
1985 n.a.w. was £175 p.w. 1:10 males and 4:10 women earn less that £100 p.w. (TUC's definition of low pay).
3 The National Earnings Survey (1984) showed that women manual workers and the low paid generally received smaller pay rises than the average.

Year	Claimed
1971	82,000
1979	80,000
1984	173,000

4 The low paid can claim Family Income Supplement (introduced in 1970), the level of which depends on the number of children in the family.
5 The Low Pay Unit monitors the wages of those in the lowest paid groups and in 1980 stated that the relative pay of the poorest 10% of manual workers had hardly changed since records began in 1886.
6 Pond 'Too Rich Too Poor' (*New Society* 1984) stated that over the last

five years the proportion of the average adult wage earned by the lowest tenth of men had fallen from 66% to 62% but that of the best-paid tenth had risen from 57% to 72%.

7 Many women workers fall into the category of low paid. Among the lowest paid jobs are nurses, clerical workers, bank workers, catering workers and hairdressers.

8 Among predominantly male workers the lower-paid jobs include farm workers, caretakers, road sweepers.

9 The problems faced by low-paid workers may get worse according to critics when the government abolishes the twenty-six wages councils which set minimum rates of pay in certain jobs. They were set up in 1909 and cover 2.7 million people (11% of the work force). Government ministers argue that they may inhibit employment growth.

THEORIES OF THE CAUSES AND PERSISTENCE OF POVERTY

Examine the implication of the statement that 'poverty is a class phenomena, the direct product of the social pattern of class inequality.' How does this view compare with other sociological explanations of poverty?   (JMB)

It is useful to approach these types of questions by reference to the major theoretical perspective adopted by sociologists:

The Functionalist view

1. The function of inequality is to enable the most able to achieve their full potential in the competitive social world.
2. Poverty persists because only a few can achieve success. The less able are left behind and fill the bottom ranks of the hierarchy. It is amongst this group that the poor are found.
3. Inequalities in society also act as incentives. Those at the bottom should seek to improve their position. But they should never be given more than the minimum in case they lose their will to improve themselves.
4. The welfare state can be justified as a safety net to catch those unable to look after themselves. It serves the function of maintaining stability when people may otherwise become dissatisfied or totally dejected.
5. Poverty thereby helps create jobs for those who serve the poor.

The Weberian/Liberal view

1. A person's class position depends on their market situation: i.e. on the amount of power held by them to influence the chances of obtaining scarce resources. Also on the rewards that the person's skills and expertise can command in the competitive market place. From this point of view groups such as the old, the disabled, one-parent families, the low paid and unemployed have little or no economic power. Therefore, they receive little economic reward. This is why they remain poor.
2. The poor are also among the weakest groups because they lack access to power. They are often non-union, low-paid workers and without the sympathy of the community.
3. The welfare state is important for them as a source of protection. It may also serve as a platform from which to improve their status.

The Marxist view

1. Poverty is an inevitable characteristic of a capitalist society. Wealth is concentrated in few hands (those who won the forces and means of production).
2. Capitalism requires a motivated work force. This is achieved through inequalities and differentials in pay and conditions of work.
3. Poverty continues because it is in the interests of the ruling elite which requires a submissive work force at all times.
4. To abolish poverty by increasing the real wages of the low paid and all the benefits to those who cannot work and by ensuring full employment would, on this view, undermine and destabilise the whole of the capitalist economic structure.
5. The welfare state, although necessary, may generate false class consciousness by deluding people about the level of equality in society.

What explanations can sociologists offer for the persistence of poverty in the 1980s? How adequate are these explanations?   (JMB)

A   Functionalists see the persistence of poverty in the failure of people to recognise that opportunities exist to climb the ladder of success. They may see themselves as trapped in a network of deprivation. In fact many people do achieve success from an impoverished background.

Its origin is in the inevitability of social inequality.

B   Marxists and Weberians would agree to some extent that poverty can be explained in terms of the low status and class position of the poor resulting from economic factors. As a result a culture of poverty develops which enables it to persist. This refers to the cultural values which those in poverty absorb and which leads to similar attitudes and patterns of behaviour. This culture is transmitted from one generation to the next. It causes strong feelings of marginality, dependence on others and a sense of fatality. As a result the poor are more likely to become criminals, or be perceived as deviants. They do not participate much in the community and have no access to power groups to improve their situation. This ensures that the class structure remains largely unchanged. It encourages passive attitudes with high tolerance of boredom which is required from those in low skilled work. For the Marxist the situation is inevitable in a capitalist society; for the Weberian a change in status can bring a change in economic position.

It is for policy-makers and not sociologists to decide what should be done about the evidence uncovered in research.

THE CONTRIBUTION OF SOCIOLOGY TO THE ANALYSIS OF POVERTY

What light has sociology thrown on our understanding of poverty in contemporary Britain?

1   Sociologists have clarified the range of possible definitions of poverty.
2   Much research has indicated the extent of poverty and how its range varies according to the definition used:

1965   Townsend and Abel Smith indicated that the poor consisted of:
(a)   the unemployed (7%)
(b)   the low paid (40%)
(c)   the elderly (33%)
(d)   the disabled (10%)
(e)   one-parent families (10%).

1967   *Circumstances of families* showed that about 500,000 families (including 1 million children) were living below SB level: about 10% of parents were in low-paid jobs.

1976   SB Commission found that about 5 million people were dependent wholly or partly on SB.

1983   MORI Poll found that 7.5 million people could be said to be living in poverty from a relative and subjective point of view. People were asked what they considered to be necessary for a decent life from a list of thirty-three items. Two thirds saw such things as heating for living areas, indoor lavatory, a damp-free home, a bath, enough bedrooms for children, money for public transport and three meals a day for children as essential. The poll found that 3 million people cannot afford to heat their homes and 4 million live in damp homes. They conclude that at least three quarters of a million people are living in intense poverty.

3 Such research has also focused on the problems facing the poor:

(*a*)   The poor are often housed a long way from the city centre on estates. This can result in high travelling costs.

(*b*)   Housing may be of poor quality.

(*c*)   They have poor job opportunities and generally lack skills and qualifications.

(*d*)   High levels of stress may result in poor health.

(*e*)   They lack good-quality clothes and they are frequently in debt.

(*f*)   They have poor life chances and lifestyle.

ORGANISATIONS AND BUREAUCRACY

CONTENTS

Areas on which questions are asked include the following:

1 Why do bureaucracies develop?
  How can they be analysed?
2 The process of bureaucratisation.
  Types of organisation: formal and informal.
3 Weber's analysis.
4 Advantages and disadvantages of bureaucratic organisations.
5 Organisations and level of democracy.
6 Total institutions.

What explanations have been put forward to show why bureaucracies develop and how they can be analysed?

Every society requires some form of efficient administration. Even in pre-industrial societies there are many examples of organisations designed to provide systems of irrigation, the collection of taxes etc. As societies become more complex and industrialised then their size and scope grow.

In contemporary Britain everyone has contact with some type of organisation in the course of their lives. People spend some time in those which are concerned with education, religion, medicine, work (both paid and voluntary), political, legal and in some unfortunate cases those which deprive them of their liberty.

In an industrial society the division of labour becomes a dominant feature in every aspect of work. Each person who is employed in an organisation does a different specialist job which contributes to the success of the whole enterprise. One result is that the organisation becomes carefully structured.

REASONS FOR THE PROCESS OF BUREAUCRATISATION

1 With the emergence of new democratic institutions in industrial societies there was a need to replace old aristocratic traditional institutions of administration. These relied on patronage and wealth for membership and control.

2 Such old traditional institutions were inefficient and contained incompetent people.
3 As societies developed and changed there was a need for efficient organisation to administer the economic and social policies of the government.
4 In business new professional managers emerged to reorganise their companies to increase their profits.
5 New techniques were introduced by social scientists to improve managerial and organisational efficiency.

(*a*)   The scientific school of management advocated providing special tools and techniques for employees to increase their output, to meet the growing needs of their customers and the profits of the organisation.

Also new models of efficiency were advocated, such as the effectiveness of the Army as a hierarchical organisation making use of specialist staff and strict rules.

(*b*)   The Human Relations School of Management, which emerged in the USA in the 1920s and 30s, was the first to modify the views of the scientific managers by emphasising the need to understand and make use of the informal norms of behaviour which developed among staff at various levels. Efficiency and effectiveness in work could be improved by taking account of the aims and goals of work groups. The Hawthorn Plant studies illustrated this view.

6 It was Weber's view that all workers (especially those at the bottom of the hierarchy) would work more efficiently in a well-organised rational organisation.

Weber's contribution has been to establish an ideal type of bureaucratic organisation against which different types of organisation can be assessed to see how far they are similar to or are different from the ideal form. His work has been influential as a source of research and for promoting new theories and explanations about organisations. He drew attention to different types that existed and to their various advantages and disadvantages.

Two analytical approaches:

Analysis of the formal structure and function of the organisation
Among those who adopt this approach are:
Weber, Michels, Lipset *et al.*, Selznick, Gouldner.
Such writers use a 'systems' approach which is based on the idea that an organisation can be viewed rather like a machine which has evolved from a simple to a complex form over time. It will produce satisfactory end results so long as it is maintained and serviced.

Analysis of the interactions of the members of the organisation
Among those who adopt this approach are:
Goffman, Roth.
This approach starts from the view that the organisation consists of groups of people who interact with each other. Consequently, aims,

methods and goals will fluctuate and change according to the relationships of those who are involved in it and who come into contact with it.

The organisation doesn't necessarily 'control' the individual, there can be a two-way effect.

SUMMARY

Large-scale organisations predominate in modern industrial societies. They are important as administrative systems for dealing with large numbers of people in terms of their health, education and other needs. Weber was the first writer to present a careful analysis of organisations. He used a system analysis. This means that he examined how the needs of the system were always paramount and he showed how they moulded the actions and behaviour of people as a result. Some critics have subsequently argued that if looked at from another point of view, based on the interactions of their members, then it is possible to argue that they may not have this moulding effect.

What is meant by the process of bureaucratisation? Illustrate your answer with reference to industrial organisations.   (Cam)

Large-scale organisations tend to be bureaucratic. Illustrate with reference to an example.   (Ox)

TYPES OF ORGANISATION

Formal organisation

A formal organisation is called a bureaucracy.

Weber was the first writer to conduct a major analysis of such organisations. He identified specific characteristics in his ideal type. (For discussion of ideal types see page 292.)

Characteristics	Example
1. It has specific goals to achieve. 2. The rights and duties of all are specified in written regulations. 3. Members must have the appropriate qualifications. 4. Positions of authority are ordered systematically. 5. Those with more power supervise those lower in the hierarchy. 6. Office holding is based on training. 7. Promotions are regulated and based on contractual agreement. 8. There are fixed monetary salaries. 9. There is separation between the employee's official work and private life. The employee cannot own the 'means of administration' nor appropriate the position.	An organisation is set up by the government to administer benefits to those in need. Those who apply for benefits must meet the special rules of the organisation. The rules must be administered according to the written regulations. The staff are qualified and are part of a hierarchy of power, each member being subject to the authority of the Head of Department. The staff are also trained and may achieve promotion over time. A bureaucratic organisation of this type is concerned with administering policies of the government and cannot be held in private hands and employees cannot buy their position. They must achieve any success they obtain through their own efforts. Relationships between staff and clients must always remain impersonal.

Informal organisation

Characteristics	Example
1. Usually created by those working within the formal organisation to cope with particular problems (e.g. unpleasant boss; strict teacher; boring work etc.).	In a school children may develop strong friendship groups.
2. There may be no direct planning in their creation; they arise to meet specific needs.	Some may become a major problem in the classroom especially where their values oppose those of the teacher.
3. Control of such informal organisations is not based on written rules but more on social norms.	Particular children may become labelled as 'troublemakers' and acquire status in the eyes of their peers. These may become 'stars of attraction' whom other children admire and follow.
4. There will be no elected power-holders but some in the group will become opinion leaders.	Children who adopt the values of the group may then behave in accordance with the expectations of its members who share the culture.
5. The power of such informal organisations can be difficult to defeat where it is perceived by the formal organisation as a threat since it may be sustained by a shared group culture.	

▶ *Studies*

Elton Mayo, *Human Problems of Industrial Civilization* (1933) describes studies carried out in the USA between 1927 and 1932 which were intended to inform management about sources of employee satisfaction and dissatisfaction at work. His team looked at the informal processes.

Roethlisberger and Dickenson, *Management and the Worker* (1939). They found that informal norms developed which established what was considered to be a reasonable day's output among work groups. This may not have coincided with the views or desires of management. But the solidarity of the group in the Hawthorne Plant was maintained so long as they all agreed on levels of production. When management tried to introduce scientific methods to increase output (by improving lighting, ventilation etc.) they were unsuccessful. They could not defeat the norms of the group. The conclusion for the management of the formal organisation was that it needed to become more 'employee centred' and to listen more to the needs and problems of the work force.

WEBER'S ANALYSIS OF BUREAUCRACIES

His theory　Bureaucracies are necessary in modern societies to help establish control over economic resources of the society by means of rationally organised administrations. The main features of a bureaucracy are:

(*a*)　specialisation of role by ability
(*b*)　rational decentralised rule
(*c*)　efficient implementation of rules to achieve goals.

His Theory of Social Action　All human behaviour is directed by meanings drawn from social situations. To understand action it is therefore necessary to understand the meanings which underlie them.

(*a*)　Rational Action is goal directed.
(*b*)　Affective Action is based on emotional responses.

(c)   Traditional Action is based on custom.

For Weber, the bureaucratic organisation is the perfect example of rationality. Rationality is the decisive feature of modern social life. It is the 'attainment of an end . . . by means of precise calculation'.

Key concepts   Bureaucratic organisations are systems of control. In order that the control is effective it must be regarded as *legitimate*. Different types of *authority* give rise to different types of legitimacy.

Type of action	Based on	Type of authority	Example	Source of legitimacy
Traditional	Custom ingrained habit	Traditional and customary loyalty	Power of kings in feudal Europe	Inherited status and personal affection
Emotional	Loss of temper. Appeal by an orator	Charismatic: followers devoted to a leader	Jesus; Napoleon Mohammed	Special qualities of the leader
Rational	Agreed goals: Control Profit Advice	Bureaucratic	Civil Servants Managers Administrators	Professional qualifications

---

Bureaucracy is the most efficient type of administrative system. In what circumstances is this true and when is it false?   (Ox)

The main advantage of large-scale bureaucratic organisations is their insistence on rules. Discuss.   (Ox)

To answer such questions you must be familiar with some of the important advantages and disadvantages of bureaucracies as well as some studies in which these are discussed.

Advantages	Disadvantages
1. Weber said that 'the decisive reason for the advance of bureaucratic organisation has always been its purely technical supremacy over other forms of organisation. The fully developed bureaucratic mechanism compares with other organisations exactly as does the machine with non-mechanical modes of production.' (*From Max Weber*: Essays in Sociology, Gerth and Mills). 2. It employs trained specialists. 3. It operates on a rational not a traditional or emotional level. 4. It is normally successful in achieving long-term goals. 5. The hierarchy of officials ensures efficiency, order and discipline. Weber said 'more and more the specialised knowledge of the expert became the foundation for the power of the officeholder'. 6. The growth of many bureaucracies should help to decentralise power. 'The monarch is powerless against the bureaucracy.'	1. Bureaucracies are rule-bound and treat people in impersonal ways. If a claimant does not meet the specifications laid down in the rules then benefit will not be available. 2. Because officials are employed to perform specific tasks their opportunities to develop wider skills may be limited. 3. It is not easy to change the goals of a bureaucracy to meet short-term needs (e.g. the education system is difficult to change to increase the chances of working-class children to reach higher education). 4. Since membership of a bureaucracy requires qualifications this gives rise to status and class differences and possible conflict and disharmony.

Conclusion: Weber saw both advantages and disadvantages in bureaucracies. The benefits were its technical superiority; lack of equivocation; written rules; continuity; sense of discretion; uniformity of operations; the concentration of the means of administration; and the fact that it established a rational-legal type of organisation which provided a set of authority relationships which became permanent and indispensable.

He was critical in that people were likely to become trapped in their impersonal specialist roles; such people would become small cogs in a giant machine; the bureaucratic machine was in the process of destroying all the traditional values and methods of the society by its power and ruthless efficiency. He was also concerned that a bureaucratic state would control every aspect of a citizen's life and reduce levels of freedom and choice; even the elected leaders may become the servants of bureaucrats. (In a speech in 1985 Mr Enoch Powell said that the programme 'Yes, Minister' was an accurate and unexaggerated guide to the way the British government worked).

Weber's concept of bureaucracy is important as an example of an ideal type, not because it tells us of reality. Discuss with reference to an example. (Ox)

Weber attempted to define a 'pure type' of bureaucratic organisation by building a model or 'ideal type' specifying its key characteristics. This was to act as a measure against which different types of organisation could be compared and assessed. He was producing an abstract conceptual scheme rather than a concrete description. His model has subsequently been used by writers as the basis for research into organisations. In the debate some have tended to stress the positive aspects of his ideas, others the negative.

Oligarchy is inevitable in any large-scale organisation. Discuss. Why is it difficult for large organisations to be democratic?

Michels (1876–1936) *Political Parties* (1911) was concerned to show how democracy (the opportunity that people have for electing and dismissing leaders, expressing views freely and of implementing majority decisions) is inconceivable in a large modern state without effective organisations. But the irony is that as soon as people join such organisations as political parties, pressure groups etc. the result is a hierarchical bureaucracy and the chances of achieving true democratic procedures is lost. Direct democracy, in which everyone is consulted, is impracticable. The only possibility is representational democracy.

Delegates represent the masses.

Michels examines the deficiences of such organisations which employ full-time officials and experts. There are more rules to be followed and there is increasing inflexibility. Decisions are taken by executive committees and the masses are excluded from decision-making processes. He concludes that 'bureaucracy is the sworn enemy of individual liberty . . .' Organisations inevitably produce oligarchy, rule by a minority or a small elite. This is the 'iron law of oligarchy'.

Selznick, *TVA and the Grass Roots* (1966) showed in his study how even an organisation introduced by the American government in 1933 to combat poverty in seven southern states lost its democratic principles in order to achieve specific goals. He argued from a functionalist perspective that organisations have needs, especially for survival. Anything which threatens the central goal (even the need for democratic procedures) will be displaced. Hence he concludes 'ideals go by the board when competing realities of organisational life are permitted to run their course . . .' He says that the scheme ended up serving the interests of the farm leadership rather than the general public.

A study which opposes the view that bureaucracies cannot be democratic is that by Lipset, Trow and Coleman entitled *Union Democracy*.

They examined a craft printers' union in the USA and found the following:

1 The union contained a structure which enabled a careful system of checks and balances on power and power-holders.
2 There were frequent elections for national and local officials.
3 There were frequent referenda by which rank and file members could express their opinions.
4 There was a high degree of participation of rank and file members in the day-to-day running of the union.
5 There was a strong sense of 'community' existing between members: they shared leisure pursuits etc.
7 The union had a long history of democratic procedures which members were keen to retain.

8   Union representatives did not have special benefits which would make them want to cling to power at any cost.

However, the authors accept that this may be a special and unusual case and that most large organisations do not share the qualities which encouraged democracy in the union they studied.

Studies which oppose some of the predictions in Weber's ideal type that bureaucracies are always the most efficient types of organisation because they are rule bound, provide discipline and precise procedures for action, include the following:

1   Gouldner (*Patterns of Industrial Bureaucracy*)

He studied the organisation of a plant in the USA which was mining gypsum and making wall boards for which the gypsum was an ingredient.

He found the following features:

(*a*)   There was less bureaucratisation in the mine than in the factory. In the mine the miners often made their own decisions as to procedures. Not all duties were clearly defined.

(*b*)   In the plant on the surface there were strict rules of procedure; there was division of labour and a hierarchy of power.

He noted how attempts to impose greater bureaucratisation on the miners by management was rejected because of the strong norms of solidarity which developed among them.

2   Burns and Stalker (*The Management of Innovation*)

They suggest that it is useful to clarify Weber's ideal type of distinguishing two types of bureaucratic organistion.

Type of bureaucracy	Characteristics	Features of bureaucratic organisation
Mechanistic	Stable market. Standardised product. Steady demand. Example: the car industry.	Hierarchy of power. Chain of command for supervision and discipline. All staff have clearly defined roles. Little initiative or responsibility.
Organic	Unstable market. Changing product. Fluctuating demand. Example: the electronics industry.	No hierarchy of power. No chain of command for supervision and discipline. Staff do not have clearly defined roles. All contribute to problem solving.

3   Blau: (*The Dynamics of Bureaucracy*) studied a Federal Law Enforcement Agency and an Employment Agency in the USA. He found

(*a*)   There were many unofficial practices used by employees which actually increased their efficiency. For example, having private discussions with colleagues about problems rather than consulting with supervisors which was the approved procedure.

(*b*)   There was more success in the employment agency in finding clients jobs where the employees adopted informal and cooperative methods.

(c)   In order to develop greater efficiency in the allocation of scarce jobs interviewers were assessed according to the number of people they placed. As a result, competition developed among interviewers, but many applicants were not placed in the most appropriate jobs. Where interviewers were encouraged to cooperate rather than compete there was greater and more effective productivity.

Blau showed that official procedures do not always maximise efficiency. His work shows the importance of examining informal bureaucratic structures.

Goffman's analysis of 'total institutions' differs from previous approaches to organisations because of its emphasis on the understanding of action in terms of meaning. Outline Goffman's concept of 'total institutions'. Examine his distinctive approach and show how it can be used in the study of such organisations as asylums, prisons or boarding schools.

Using a range of case studies illustrate the concepts and ideas which interactionist sociologists have used to study organisations. Point out the distinctiveness of the interactionist approach.

To answer questions such as these you must be familiar with
(a)   the interactionist perspective
(b)   the methods of the interactionists
(c)   some relevant studies, especially Goffman
(d)   organisation theory.

▶ *Some relevant studies*:

1 J. A. Roth ('The treatment of TB as a Bargaining Process'). In this paper he explains how he used an interactionist perspective to illustrate how members of the same organisation could have different goals and how they set out to achieve them with varying levels of success: also how aims were changed and modified over time.

His data was obtained from his own observations as a patient, an attendant and later as a sociological observer. He explains how in his last role he spent much time 'hanging about' the hospital wards and offices, attending therapy conferences, making rounds with doctors and listening to staff discuss their problems and patients discuss theirs.

(a)   The goals of the professionals in the hospitals and those of the patients were never entirely the same. Often they were in conflict. For example, the patients generally wanted more privileges and greater freedom; the staff wished the opposite.

(b)   Conflicts were usually resolved by 'bargaining'.

(c)   He illustrates how patients, through their own observations and pooling of information, learned which nurses were likely to give certain drugs and nursing services. They learn how to manipulate the restrictive system to maximise freedom and choices.

(d)   The process of anticipation and modification of behaviour and goals continues so long as the process of interaction is maintained.

(*e*)   He concludes that the bargaining process is not a matter of open threats and the development of power positions, it is much more subtle.

2 Goffman (*Asylums*)

He also uses an interactionist perspective to show how behaviour of people in the organisation results from their perception of events and the meanings they derive from processes of interaction.

TOTAL INSTITUTIONS

These are organisations which place barriers between themselves and the outside world. These barriers may include 'locked doors, high walls, barbed wire, cliffs, water, forests or moors'.

The types of institutions and settings that he has studied include: mental hospitals, prisons, monasteries and army barracks.

Central features

1 All aspects of life are conducted in the same place or under some authority.
2 Each phase of the life of each member is conducted in the company of others.
3 There is a tight schedule in daily activities.
4 The activities are justified as part of a rational plan to fulfil the aims of the institution.
5 There is a clear distinction between 'staff' and 'inmates'.
6 Inmates are excluded from decision making.

Significance in society

1 They are controlling organisations. They control and supervise large numbers of people as 'blocks'.
2 Their goals are often determined by ideological considerations and the aim may be to prevent inmates from being contaminated by unacceptable beliefs in the outside world (e.g. religious organisations).
3 Some total institutions may serve useful social functions, in caring for those with special needs.
4 Others, such as mental hospitals, may, in Goffman's words, 'serve as storage dumps for inmates . . .'

In his paper 'The Moral Career of a Mental Patient' he describes how, through a series of humiliating interactions with staff and other patients, the inmate comes to establish a new role and a new self-image which explains his predicament. He learns how to become a mental patient.

Points of criticism: 1 As always, observational studies rely on the skills of the observer and his ability to interpret evidence. Goffman, interestingly, draws his from a wide range of sources including novels (Kerkhoff, *How Thin the Veil*), autobiography (T.E. Lawrence) and his own observations.

2   The question arises, can the observer be sure that the interpretation of events offered is the 'true' explanation?

3   The studies are invariably on a small scale from which it may be difficult to make wider generalisations.

4   They are sometimes accused of ignoring events outside the organisation studied which may affect behaviour inside.

SUMMARY

1   A distinction can be made between formal organisations (bureaucracies) and informal organisations (which arise for example, among groups sharing similar norms and cultural values).

2   Organisations can be studied from a functional/positivist perspective or from an interactionist/phenomenological perspective.

3   Weber presented an ideal type model which is a useful measuring rod. It helps to generate research and theory building.

4   He saw an increasing trend towards bureaucratisation in modern industrial societies, although he saw some possible dangers in the process.

5   Some writers have subsequently produced some support for his concern that bureaucracies were likely to reduce people's freedom and choices (Michels).

6   Others have argued that all large organisations tend to become undemocratic structures. Their main goal always is survival at the expense of all others (Selznick).

7   Some researchers have found evidence that this may not always be the case (Lipset *et al.*).

8   In their debate with Weber, some writers suggest that bureaucracies may not always be efficient and rational in their pursuit of goals (Gouldner).

9   To clarify this point further some researchers have distinguished between types of organisation: mechanistic and organic. The suggestion is that the structure of the organisation varies with its type. In the organic type the goals of workers and management may diverge yet the organisation does not collapse (Blau).

10 Another school of sociology (related to the organic perspective) focuses more on the organisation in terms of the processes of human action within them, rather than on the goals (Goffman). This view holds that organisations are made up of people and they change and alter methods, goals etc. according to people's actions and reactions.

RACE RELATIONS

CONTENTS

The areas on which questions are asked:
1 Definition of terms.
2 Trends in immigration and emigration and the factors which affect them.
3 The problems of prejudice and discrimination facing ethnic minorities in specific areas of social life:
(a)   employment   (b)   housing   (c)   education.
4 Legislation and its effectiveness.
5 Theories to explain racial tensions and the class and status positions of ethnic minorities.
6 Comparative data: social and cultural differences between minority groups in Britain.

To prepare adequately for this section of the exam you must decide whether you will cover all the areas or some specific ones. Whichever issues you decide to cover you will need to know:
(a)   Some basic statistics (from surveys, census returns).
(b)   Definitions of key terms (such as 'race', 'immigrant').
(c)   Details from at least one study.
(d)   Some knowledge of recent legislation.
(e)   Some knowledge of competing theories.

DEFINITIONS OF TERMS

Some questions will specifically test your knowledge of the meaning of terms:

Distinguish between racial *discrimination* and racial *prejudice*. Which do you believe to be more significant in *race* relations in contemporary Britain?   (Ox)

Others may make use in a question of terms which you should not take for granted:

Outline the position of *immigrants* in Britain in the housing market. Base your answer on relevant research.   (Wel)

How have sociologists helped us understand the experiences of *ethnic minorities* in either employment or housing?   (AEB)

Some questions you may feel are ambiguous in their use of terms:

The *coloured population* is extremely small. In no area or occupation do they form concentrations of political or economic power. . .

Outline the educational disadvantage facing *blacks* in Britain. . .

It is best to make the meaning that you are adopting for the purpose of your answer clear early in your essay.

Race There is no universally accepted meaning of the word 'race'. Attempts have been made to identify distinct groups on the basis of biological and physiological characteristics which are then frequently related to skin colour. It is often used in negative and confusing ways.

Sociologists argue that beliefs about the world are socially constructed. Beliefs about 'races' are closely related to contemporary attitudes existing in society, and often serve as a label to identify differences.

Race relations One means of establishing the relative status of different social groups is by reference to their race. Those with least status tend to be the groups who it is assumed are the most recently arrived. They are identifiable as 'strangers', by virtue of skin colour or cultural differences. These can then be used to justify differential treatment and can give rise to hostility between groups.

Ethnic groups Many writers prefer this term and it tends to be used to describe groups on the basis of cultural characteristics (e.g. food, language, dress, religion etc.).

Prejudice A person is prejudiced who holds pre-conceived beliefs about others and pre-judges them on this basis. It is normally used in its negative sense.

Discrimination This is the act of prejudice. Since 1965 it has been unlawful to treat a person less favourably on the grounds of colour, race, ethnic or national origin.

Immigrant This means anyone who has recently arrived from another society in which they have habitually lived. It may be criticised because it is widely used to refer to non-whites rather than to EEC citizens or people of British descent who have lived abroad most of their lives. Of black people in Britain 40% are British born.

Racism This is the dogmatic belief that one race (however defined) is superior to another and that there are identifiable racial characteristics which influence behaviour (e.g. the idea that white people have higher IQ).

Racialism This means putting the beliefs of racism into practice so that some people become subject to discrimination, hold lowest status and are deemed to have fewer rights.

TRENDS IN IMMIGRATION AND EMIGRATION

Describe the major trends in immigration into and emigration from Great Britain since 1971 and discuss their implications.

What have been the factors influencing the rate and composition of immigration into Britain in recent years?

To answer such questions you must:
(*a*)   present relevant statistics
(*b*)   draw conclusions from them.

Table 1: Migrants by country of last origin (1000s).

Year	Old Commonwealth (Australia, Canada, New Zealand	New Commonwealth Indian sub Continent	West Indies	EEC	USA	Total
1971	52	24	5	21	22	200
1976	40	27	4	25	16	191
1979	31	33	5	23	13	195
1981	20	27	3	23	17	153

Table 2: Age structure of migrants (1000s) 1981.

Under 16	4	8	–	5	4	33
16–24	7	8	1	9	4	45
25–44	7	8	1	8	7	60
45–59	1	3	–	1	2	11
60+	2	–	–	–	–	4

Table 3: Emigrants by country of destination (1000s).

1971	99	8	8	31	17	240
1976	63	6	3	31	21	210
1979	50	6	3	29	26	189
1981	79	3	3	29	25	233

Table 4: Age Structure of emigrants in 1981 (1000s).

Year	Old Commonwealth (Australia, Canada, New Zealand	New Commonwealth Indian sub Continent	West Indies	EEC	USA	Total
Under 16	19	1	–	5	5	51
16–24	14	1	1	8	6	49
25–44	37	1	1	14	11	108
45–60	5	1	–	2	2	17
60+	5	–	–	1	1	8

Table 5: Migration into and out of Britain 1964–84 (1000s).

Mid year to mid year	Total inflow	Total outflow	Net figure
1964–5	223	281	−58
1966–7	232	326	−94
1969–70	224	306	−82
1971–2	196	240	−44
1973–4	183	255	−72
1977–8	162	198	−36
1983–4			

Source: *OPCS*

Some conclusions:

The definition of a migrant (which is open to criticism from a sociological point of view) means someone who having lived abroad for at least twelve months declares an interest to reside in the UK for at least twelve months. The definition of an emigrant is the converse.

Table 1
1 This shows that the number of immigrants to the UK fell between 1971 and 1981 from 200,000 to 153,000.
2 Within the total 153,000 approximately 20% came from the New Commonwealth, 15% from EEC countries, 14% from the Old Commonwealth, 10% from the USA and the remainder from other parts of the world.

Table 2
1 This shows that in 1981 of all migrants to Britain 40% were in the 25–44 age group and 53% were under 25.
2 In 1981 of those migrants from the New Commonwealth 33% were in the 25–44 age group and 56% were under 25.

Table 3:
1 This shows how it is unusual for there to be more people entering the country than leaving. 1979 is an exception.
2 The majority of those leaving go to the Old Commonwealth.

Table 4
This shows that in 1981 the majority of all those emigrating from Britain were aged 25–44 and a slightly smaller proportion (40%) were under 24.

Table 5
This clearly shows that the trend since 1964 has been for a net outflow of population from Britain.

Table 6: The total estimated coloured population of UK 1966–1986.

Year	Number (millions)	% of the population
1966	1.1	2.2
1971	1.3	2.4
1976	1.8	3.3
1986	2.0	4.0

FACTORS AFFECTING IMMIGRATION

1   *The economy of Britain:* In the 1950s and 60s the British economy was buoyant and immigrants came seeking work. Many were recruited by large companies (such as London Transport) seeking labour. As the economy became depressed numbers entering Britain declined.

2   *The economy of the country of departure:* Most of the migrants from the New Commonwealth are seeking better prospects than they can find at home.

3   *The political and religious factors:* Many migrants have come to Britain to seek escape from political or religious persecution: For example, Jews in the 1930s; Hungarians in 1956; Ugandan Asians in 1971.

4   *Educational opportunities:* Some migrants may wish to take the opportunity to provide their children with a good education in Britain.

5   Legislation: numbers tend to increase just before the introduction of legislation which limits numbers who can be accepted for entry. In the 1950s legislation in the USA limiting number of West Indians allowed to settle caused them to divert to Britain.

6   Many simply exercise their rights as either British passport-holders or member of the EEC to enter and seek work.

7   Although female migration always lags behind that of males, in 1982 about 70% of people accepted for entry on arrival were the wives and children of those already settled.

PROBLEMS FACING ETHNIC MINORITIES IN BRITAIN

EMPLOYMENT

What is the pattern of employment of Asians and West Indians in Britain? How would you account, sociologically, for this?   (Cam)

In the 1960s the major problems facing immigrant groups were associated with housing, whereas now they are associated with employment. Discuss.

To answer such questions you must be familiar with the details from a range of studies. The following are some typical examples. Remember to use your illustrations to argue a case. In the first question (above) are you going to argue that the pattern ·has developed and changed over time or that it has remained fairly static and unchanging? In order to account for your answer it is useful to be able to relate your facts to a theory which accounts for the position of ethnic minorities in Britain. In the second question above you must decide whether you think it is true that the *major* problem facing immigrant groups has changed from that of housing to employment. You may wish to argue that both problems are so closely interrelated that it is not easy to say which is the major one, or again, that the problem of employment has always been the most serious one facing immigrants to Britain. You must know which line of argument you intend to follow for the purpose of your essay before you start to write. You should therefore note points from research to help you reach your conclusion. Never list details in note form (as they appear below) but link issues together in clear sentences to try to prove your argument. The mark you receive will be based on how well you answer the question set and not on the amount of unrelated authorities and their research that you can list. The following examples are therefore provided to remind you of the kind of detail you should be looking for from your reading or from your notes.

1 *Colour and Citizenship* E. Rose 1966
(*a*)   The occupational distribution of male immigrant groups in London showed a fairly widespread range over a number of occupations with no overwhelming concentration of any in a specific job. However, there was evidence of quite large numbers of West Indian men in woodworking, transport and engineering work.
(*b*)   In the West Midlands the pattern for male migrants showed greater concentration and less difference between each group.
(*c*)   There was some similarity between male and female patterns. Indian-born women were well represented in clerical and professional jobs in London. The most important occupations for West Indian women are in service jobs (especially engineering and nursing).
(*d*)   In the West Midlands all male immigrant groups were badly under-represented in white-collar jobs. Those from India were the best represented in these occupations. The West Indians and Pakistanis were hardly represented at all.
(*e*)   He concluded that all immigrants were less well represented than the total population in those occupations usually considered to be the most desirable and over-represented in those least liked.

2 *Racial Discrimination in England* W. Daniel 1966
His team used three actors, a Hungarian, an Englishman and a West Indian to apply for the same jobs, houses, mortgages and insurance policies. They were all given the same appropriate qualifications. It was found that the West Indian had least chance of success. This was still the case if he was given better qualifications than the others.

3 *The Extent of Racial Discrimination*, MacIntosh and Smith 1975
They used 13 actors to apply for the same jobs. They conducted 821 tests in 6 towns. They found that the coloured applicant suffered discrimination as follows:

White-collar work	30% occasions
Skilled manual	20% occasions
Unskilled work	46% occasions

4   CRE Report 1980

This found that unemployment rates among ethnic minorities was at least four times greater than for whites. It said that insufficient time was spent by the government in promoting better race relations whilst great expenditure was provided to limit immigration. At least 40% of black people are British born and deserve more help.

5   *Ethnic Minorities in Britain* (Home Office Report 1983)

This report confirms the high level of discrimination against coloured people in contemporary Britain, especially in employment. It indicates higher levels of unemployment and lower wages among West Indians and Asians. When unemployment is rising then the number of unemployed among ethnic minorities increases more rapidly than among the rest of the population. Of the coloured labour force, 73% is concentrated in the South East and West Midlands. They suffer a disproportionate number of unemployed. The report also shows that those in work undertake longer hours and more shifts to bring their pay into line with white workers. They are increasingly concentrated in less secure jobs in older industries. As a result of their low earnings, a high proportion of dependants and higher housing costs, they experience a greater degree of poverty than white households.

6   *Black and White Britain* (Policy Studies Institute Report: 1984)

This presents a pessimistic picture of the social and economic position of black people in contemporary Britain. Their opportunities have scarcely changed since the 1950s. Black Britons are still largely confined to the worst jobs and housing. The increase in national unemployment has limited their chances of mobility and black unemployment is nearly twice the rate for whites. Enormous efforts need to be made to help black people move out of the low-status and low-paid jobs that most are in.

HOUSING

Outline the position of immigrants in the housing market. Base your answer on research studies.   (Wel)

This is a fairly straightforward question for which you will need detailed references to relevant studies, such as those listed below. However, you may encounter a more general question in which you must balance material to show a wide knowledge of several areas of difficulty facing black people; the problem of housing is then just one important aspect of the answer. For example:

How have sociologists helped us to understand the experiences of ethnic minorities in any one society?   (AEB)

1   *Racial Discrimination in England*, W. Daniel (1966)
A West Indian, a white immigrant from Hungary and a white English tester were all given identical qualifications and asked to apply for accommodation in each of six areas. The applications to landlords showed that the West Indian was discriminated against two thirds of the time when flats which did not exclude him in advance were tested in practice. The Hungarian experienced little discrimination. There was a strong similarity between the pattern of results in all six areas. There was no less discrimination against the West Indian when he was applying for the accommodation in a 'professional role' as a hospital registrar, than when he was applying as a bus conductor.

2   *The Experience of Race Law in Housing* E. Burney (1972)
She makes the point that under the 1968 Race Relations Act it became illegal to discriminate against someone on the grounds of their colour. Landlords or their agents were no longer allowed to operate a colour bar. Building societies had to remove from their application forms questions which implied less favourable treatment of people of overseas origin.

3   Government White Paper 1975
This stated that people should not be confined to an estate or an area nor be compelled to leave simply on the grounds of colour. It accepted that like many coloured immigrants to Britain over the last twenty years many were forced into the cheapest and poorest accommodation. But it concluded that it would be neither appropriate nor practicable to single out immigrants for special help since comprehensive housing action programmes are necessary for all citizens.

4   *Ethnic Minorities in Britain* (Home Office Report 1983)
This found that in housing, many West Indians and Asians are subject to a 'coloured tax' by landlords and forced to pay more for run-down accommodation. They found some evidence to suggest that there is much overcrowding, especially among Asian families. Discrimination in the private sector is still thought to be substantial. There has been some movement of West Indian families from privately rented accommodation to council house property. This may relate to the problems they have in obtaining mortgates and finance to purchase their own homes.

5   *Black and White Britain* (PSI Report 1984)
This stated that 'the separation of the jobs and residential location of British people of Asian and West Indian origin is so firmly established that it generates among both whites and blacks assumptions, expectations and behaviour that perpetuates it . . . discrimination is still a fact of life. . .'
A more complex question is one that takes you into a discussion involving a theoretical analysis as well as a presentation of facts. For example:

Racial tension is the result of competition in the housing market. Discuss.

One useful way of approaching this type of question is to present a Weberian analysis followed by an example in which the method was adopted. Remember, too, that it is always useful to be able to add concluding points which offer some criticism or confirmation of the arguments presented. Consider the following structure:

1   Weber's view starts from the assumption that there is always a plurality of competing groups in a society. They compete for scarce resources.

2   Race relations can be viewed as a form of power relationship which arises when people of different ethnic membership are in competition.

3   Each group has its own access to power by joining relevant power groups and each shares particular life chances.

4   Any group may suffer disadvantage at one level (for example in housing) but hold power in another (membership of a union may give power in work).

5   Immigrants may well suffer disadvantage in the housing market because they tend to have low social status in the eyes of the local white residents with whom they are competing. (Although this view would suggest that they are not necessarily powerless in all other spheres of social life.)

▶   An example of a study in which the view is tested:
     Race, Community and Conflict, J. Rex and Moore (1963) (see also page 242)
     They conducted their study in an area of Sparkbrook, Birmingham, to examine the conditions of housing faced by various ethnic groups. They included about: 44% English; 23% Irish; 16% West Indian; 8% Pakistani; 1% Indian and 5% others. They identified three housing zones. The one which contained the majority of immigrants was that with the poorest and most dilapidated property. The middle classes who once lived in the area had long since moved out to more desirable areas further from the city centre.

     Rex and Moore identify a hierarchy of housing classes; the immigrants fill the lowest of these since they are of lowest status and have fewest resources to rise into higher groups consisting of outright owners of property.

     The authors conclude that the immigrants come to be seen as the creators of the decaying areas; these 'perceived' meanings about the behaviour of ethnic minorities are translated into real facts about their lifestyles and life chances. They create their own communities, cinemas, restaurants etc. 'Being a member of a housing class is of first importance in determining a man's associations, his interests, his lifestyle and his position in the urban social structure. . .'

Points of criticism: 1   Davies and Taylor conducted a study between 1966 and 1968
                           (*Race Community and No Conflict*) in a poor area of Newcastle-Upon-

Tyne which showed that Asians had a very strong drive towards property ownership. This was not just the result of a desire to avoid exploitation of landlords, but more because they have an ethic of hard work and ambition. They conclude that an explanation of the behaviour of the Asians in this area couched solely in terms of 'colour discrimination' and of 'passive victims', makes little sense.

2   Rex and Moore imply that the housing structure is independent of the wider economic class structure, where Marxists would argue that such factors must be seen as the fundamental source of social conflicts. It is seen as a mistake, therefore, to try to distinguish many housing classes and status groups. There are either owners or non-owners; the latter are subject to dangers of exploitation.

EDUCATION

The problems encountered by racial minorities in the educational system are no different from those faced by white working-class children. Discuss.

In all societies there are both similarities and differences in the experiences of various ethnic minorities compared with the rest of the population. Examine these similarities and differences in the sphere of education.

1   *Children of West Indian Immigrants* (Rutter *et al.*)
The researchers compared the educational achievements of a group of non-immigrant children from a London borough with a similarly non-immigrant group on the Isle of Wight. They found that those from London had more problems and lower educational attainments.

They also compared children whose parents were born in the West Indies with those of indigenous families. They found:

(*a*)   Children of West Indian background had even more problems. They also had lower levels of attainment.

(*b*)   The children of West Indian parents born in Britain had a reading age on average ten months above their counterparts born in the West Indies.

(*c*)   West Indian parents fell mainly into Classes 4 and 5. Their housing conditions were often poor and overcrowding was more frequent. Family size tended to be larger.

(*d*)   However, they found a very warm and caring relationship between West Indian parents and their children. They conclude that much of the concern about high rates of 'problem' behaviour in West Indian parents and children is unjustified.

2   Research by G. Driver 1981
His work challenges the accepted belief that West Indian pupils do less well in school than English children.

(*a*)   He sampled 2,300 school leavers and found that the academic results of West Indian girls and boys were, for the most part, better than those obtained by English children.

(b)   English boys did better than English girls in their level of qualifications, but West Indian girls were ahead of West Indian boys.

(c)   His evidence suggests that West Indian children may do less well than their English counterparts at primary or even at the start of secondary school, but they begin to catch up and improve later.

3 *Racial Equality in Training Schemes (CRE Report 1985)*

This found that black pupils are four times more likely to be suspended than whites. The CRE blames insensitive teachers who do not appreciate cultural differences as a cause of the behaviour about which they complain. Rastafarian culture was a common source of friction.

4 *The Swann Report 1985*

The aim to change behaviour and attitudes in such a way as to promote a genuinely multi-racial educational system.

To suggest policies to combat racism in education.

The committee was concerned that the children of some ethnic minorities were not doing as well as they should in the present educational system.

Table 1: In all CSE and GCE O level exams percentage of children gaining 5 or more high grades.

West Indian	6%
Asian	17%
Others	19%

Table 2: In CSE and O level percentage gaining higher grades.

	English	Maths	In A Level 1+ pass	University entrance
West Indian	15%	8%	5%	1%
Asian	21%	21%	13%	4%
Others	29%	21%	13%	4%

Findings

1 Racial discrimination and social deprivation are more important factors in West Indian underachievement than IQ.

2 Single-sex schools may be important in multi-racial areas to encourage Muslims to keep their children in education.

3 Asians seem to do as well as white children despite deprivation (see tables above).

4 None of the minority groups was found to be looking for assimilation in the majority community other than in terms of being fully accepted and equal members of society.

5 Ethnic minority children tended to come from homes suffering greater economic and social deprivation than the white children.

6 Racial prejudice does not have identical effects on every minority group and white attitudes varied towards the different groups.

Reasons for the different levels of performance between children from different ethnic groups seems likely to lie deep in their respective cultures. For example, the Asians may do better because they prefer to keep a low profile and accept an ethic of hard work which is transmitted through their close family ties. Teachers may assume that their only difficulty is that of language; whereas they may perceive West Indian children as potentially 'less able'. They are treated differently, attract fewer resources and respond less well.

Recommendations
1 Opposes the idea that ethnic minorities should set up their own schools.
2 Rejects the idea of bilingual teaching. This should be left to the local community.
3 Schools should adopt clear policies on racism.
4 Priority should be the learning of English.
5 There should be a non-denominational approach to religious education.
6 The government should fund teacher exchanges between all white and multi-racial schools.
7 Britain must be accepted as a multi-racial and multi-cultural society and all pupils must be enabled to understand what this means.
8 It is necessary to combat racism, to attack inherited myth and stereotypes and the ways they are embodied in institutional practice.

Theoretical intepretations to explain the situation of immigrant children in the educational system.

Functionalist view	Marxist view	Interactionist view
The assimilation of all children into 'the British way of life' is possible. It is a matter of time before values are assimilated and appropriate norms of behaviour absorbed. The function of education is to promote value consensus. The process is slow because it will take many generations to complete socialisation.	The underachievement of children from some ethnic minority groups can be understood in terms of the serious deprivations they face, both social and economic. Parental aspirations are low, the culture of the school is unfamiliar to them and the teachers are often hostile. It is fundamentally a class problem.	To understand why the children of ethnic minorities do not do well it is necessary to focus on the processes of interaction which occur in the classroom. If teachers perceive a West Indian child to be 'less able' and treat the person accordingly, this discrimination may force the child into negative forms of behaviour.

LEGISLATION AND ITS EFFECTIVENESS

How effective have recent legislation changes been in reducing racial discrimination in Britain? (Ox)

To answer a question on this topic you need to establish the nature and extent of the problems faced by ethnic minorities between 1948 and 1981.

You also need to know the dates and details of various pieces of legislation that were passed and enforced in those years.

Finally, you must decide (on the basis of research findings) the exent to which they have been successful in achieving:

(*a*) Limitation in numbers entering the country.
(*b*) More harmonious race relations.

The major pieces of legislation and some brief points from each are listed. For a balanced essay you should try to relate the legislation and its aims to the specific problems with which it endeavoured to deal.

Legislation to control entry

1948 (Labour) British Nationality Act. This replaced 1914 legislation. It established the right of all citizens of Commonwealth countries to enter Britain to work and settle.

1962 (Conservative) Commonwealth Immigration Act. The first Act which limited entry to those holding work permits and to their close relatives.

1968 (Labour) Commonwealth Immigrants Act. This denied entry to British subjects of Asian descent who were threatened with explusion from Kenya.

1969 (Labour) Immigration Appeals Act. This gave right of appeal to special tribunals and limited number of dependents who could enter.

1971 (Conservative) Immigration Act. Patrials (anyone with at least one British grandparent, or who had been naturalised, or lived five years in Britain) might enter freely. Also anyone closely related to them or who had been resident in Britain before 1973. Irish and EEC citizens had right of entry. All others needed permits.

1981 (Conservative) British Nationality Act. This further tightened the definition of those who can claim British citizenship:

a. Those already settled here.

b. Those with one British parent who have been registered abroad at birth.

Those with British passports who have lived abroad and have no recent connection of residence in Britain will not be allowed to enter and settle.

Legislation to protect minorities

1965 (Labour) Race Relations Act. This made it a criminal offence to discriminate on the grounds of colour, race or ethnic origin, in providing goods, facilities or services. It also established the Race Relations Board, to monitor the Act and advise complainants.

1968 (Labour) Race Relations Act. This gave more powers to the Board and it established the Community Relations Commission. This was to advise the government and to try to foster better race relations in the community.

1976 (Labour) Race Relations Act. The Race Relations Board and the CRC were merged into the Commission for Racial Equality (CRE). This was given powers to make formal investigations and to prosecute offenders. Employers became responsible for the unlawful acts of their employees. The Act bans positive discrimination in favour of ethnic minorities. All services are to be offered equally to all whatever their colour. (In 1985 a GLC-funded women's group was fined £125 for deliberately hiring a black woman at the expense of a white applicant.) In the same week three national daily papers and a London evening paper were criticised by the Press Council for mentioning the colour of a 17-year-old black youth who was convicted of murder.

THEORIES TO EXPLAIN RACIAL TENSION

Outline two competing theories which sociologists have presented to explain racial tension in contemporary Britain.

This type of question is inviting you to display knowledge of the theoretical issues which are associated with the views of either functionalists, Marxists or Weberians to the question of race relations. In the same way other questions may appear in which you can utilise the same information although the word 'theory' may not appear. For example:

Where do ethnic groups fit into the British class structure?   (Ox)

FUNCTIONALISM

There are two related areas:

Functional segmental theory	Functional pluralism
All societies consist of various segments with their own subcultures. Different groups live in separate areas of cities; race has become an additional feature of segmentation. Conflict between groups is based largely on these cultural differences. People are naturally suspicious of newcomers, especially 'dark strangers'. They are perceived as a threat. Differences are experienced in terms of colour, religion, lifestyle etc.	This view adds that races do not fit neatly into the categories described by Marx and Weber based on class and status differences. a. Ethnic groups cut across classes. b. In every society there are a variety of groups based on religious, economic, cultural and ethnic differences. Pluralists dispute the idea that immigrant groups are necessarily subject to the domination of particular classes. They prefer to describe a process in which both conflict and consensus exist, regulated by government policies. If ethnic groups suffer discrimination it may be the result of their failure to adopt mainstream British values.

Summary points:

From a functionalist perspective it may be functional to have ethnic minorities in a society since they may meet specific demands for labour in certain occupations and they may provide specific skills or services. It may also help integrate the members of the host society more into the mainstream of their own society by being able to identify 'strangers' of lower social status and class. Their presence may also help explain social disorders and conflicts: they may become a convenient scapegoat for such problems.

Patterson (*Dark Strangers*) argues that such conflict and misunderstanding may only be a temporary state. Such problems can be overcome in due course as the ethnic minorities come to accept the dominant values of the host society.

Points of criticism:

1　There is not much evidence yet to show that second- and third-generation members of ethnic minorities have become more accepted and integrated in British society.

2　The view underplays major social inequalities based on class factors.

3　Major social conflicts (riots etc.) tend to be minimised.

Marxist interpretations	Weberian interpretations
1. Racial inequality is directly linked to social inequality. 2. Racialism is a consequence of capitalist economic structure. 3. Racial hostility reveals levels of alienation and class division. 4. Racism is a means of ruling-class control. 5. The hostility of working-class people towards ethnic minorities is evidence of false class consciousness. 6. Ethnic minorities become part of a pool of surplus labour, open to exploitation and easily dispensible. As a result they are forced to live in the poorest areas, work in specifically migrant occupations, face high levels of unemployment at times of economic depression. 7. They are faced with constant denigration in the media where the negative image of the 'immigrant' is deeply embedded in the culture of the host society. This derives from the time when they were subject to colonialisation.	1. Racial inequality is related to people's perceptions which arise out of processes of interaction in everyday life. People behave in accordance with the meanings they derive from events. 2. Racial hostility is part of the construction of daily reality by which some people make sense of complex events going on around them; e.g. if they are competing for scarce resources (jobs, homes) then the presence of ethnic minorities may be seen as a threat, especially in times of economic crisis. 3. It is largely irrelevant as to whether or not real racial differences exist; the fact that they are perceived to exist is enough to explain the hostility that results. 4. Those with greater access to the scarce resources have higher class and status positions than those who don't. Status and class positions are constantly changing as people achieve and lose access to power. 5. An immigrant is not necessarily destined to remain in a low-status or class group. These are flexible groupings and subject to change.

Points of criticism
a. Not all members of ethnic minorities are in the lowest social classes and they do not all live in the poorest areas.
b. Weberians argue power is available to all.
c. It presents a very pessimistic picture of race relations.

Points of criticism
a. It may present an overoptimistic view of contemporary race relations.
b. It presents a picture of a very fluid society. In reality there may be limited chances of mobility for members of ethnic groups.
c. Marxists argue that it is a mistake to place more emphasis on status differences rather than class factors.

Following the riots in Brixton in 1981 Lord Scarman produced a report. Its main recommendations were:

1 The early introduction of an independent element into police complaints procedures.
2 The doubling of police training.
3 A statutory framework for police-community consultations.
4 Racist marches to be banned.
5 The recruitment of police from ethnic minorities.
6 The elimination of racially biased policemen by careful recruitment.
7 Better management training for inspectors and sergeants.
8 Racial prejudice in policemen to be an offence punishable by dismissal.
9 Improved patterns of police patrol in inner-city areas.
10 The use of plastic bullets, etc. only in grave emergencies.
11 A better coordinated attack on inner-city problems.
12 Local authorities to check housing policies for discrimination.

In 1985 riots again occurred. Writing of those in Birmingham, Cashmore (*New Society*, September 1985) said that the government in trying to rein back local authority spending sidestepped some of the aims of Scarman. 'It has drip fed black youth with pointless YTS schemes . . . it is out of touch with the forces in modern society. . .' He argues that the economic insecurity, deprivation and enforced idleness of young blacks is at the core of the problem.

Harris, writing of the riots in Tottenham in 1985 (*New Society*, 4 October 1985), says 'it was not a race riot; half of those who appeared before the magistrates were white'; although as Murji points out the incident which sparked the events was the shooting by police of a black mother of six children.

Gaskell and Smith (*How Young Blacks See the Police*) conducted a study following troubles in Toxteth in 1985 to examine the hostility felt by young blacks towards the police. (Of their sample 41% said they thought the police were 'bad' or 'very bad'. They concluded that blacks feel police hostility as a kind of group experience. A folk history of unpleasant, frightening experiences with the police has 'worked its way into the shared beliefs of black youngsters'.

Reiner (*New Society*, 25 October 1985) says that inequalities in housing and employment mean that blacks figure disproportionately in the young street population. They have a group consciousness. The common experience of discrimination means that respectable adult blacks will have common cause with them. 'All this could turn an underclass into a dangerous class.'

COMPARATIVE DATA

Compare the social situation of any two ethnic groups in Britain. (Ox)

A question of this type could be answered by reference to the similarities and differences of their experiences in obtaining housing, work etc.

Another approach would be to include details about the cultural variations between two groups and relate these to their social experiences in contemporary Britain. It would be useful to be able to make reference, therefore, to such details as countries of origin, religious traditions, family structures etc. The same material could be used in a question such as:

Discuss reasons for immigration from New Commonwealth countries into Britain since 1950. What light has research thrown on the experiences of any two groups?

	Sikhs	Pakistanis	West Indians
Place of origin	The Punjab (India)	Pakistan (founded in 1947, formerly part of India) and Bangladesh: until 1971 part of Pakistan.	The Caribbean Islands
Numbers in Britain	460,000 (1981); 70% of all Indian migrants are Sikh.	355,000 (1981)	940,000 (1981)
Religion	Sikh	Muslim	Christian/Rastafarian
Historical background	The British went to India in the 18th and 19th centuries as colonial administrators. They justified their presence as the 'discoverers' or by military conquest.		The Spanish conquered the islands in the 16th century. They imported slaves to work the plantations. Later British colonists maintained slavery.
Reasons for migrating to Britain	1. Wartime service 2. To improve living standards.	1. Originally part of Commonwealth and holders of British passports. 2. To improve living standards.	1. Wartime service. 2. Recruitment: (London Transport; Nursing, etc. 1950s). 3. As British passport-holders.
Cultural characteristics.	Wear turbans; beards. Strong religious values; ethic of hard work and equality.	Strong extended family ties. Wives do not always have good English.	Share many values of western society music, sport etc. Rastafarians seek African roots.
Main problems faced	1. Discrimination in work, housing. 2. Frequent attacks. 3. They are clearly identifiable.	First generation developed a guest complex. Second generation more aware of problems.	1. Discrimination. 2. Subject to negative stereotypes. 3. Concentrated in manual jobs.

All members of ethnic minority groups are subject to the effects of an economy in decline. They are easily scapegoated and find it difficult to obtain jobs, housing etc. Pakistanis may be seen by white working class as the greatest economic threat, but West Indians may be the most disappointed of the minority groups.

CHAPTER TWENTY-TWO

WORK

CONTENTS

The following topics are widely covered on all the examination boards:

1 The impact of industrialisation.
2 The significance of work on people's lives:
   (a)   Work as a source of identity.
   (b)   The functions of work.
   (c)   Prior orientations and expectations about work.
3 Factors affecting attitudes towards work:
   (a)   The organisation of work.
   (b)   Alienation.
   (c)   The impact of new technologies.

THE IMPACT OF INDUSTRIALISATION

The origins of sociology lie in the attempts of early writers like Comte and Durkheim to explain the causes and consequences of social change. They were concerned in particular with the transition from one type of society to another (from rural to urban, pre-industrial to industrial) as well as changes in social institutions. These are the special province of sociology, hence the interest in their change, especially in relation to the processes of industrialisation.

Consider the following questions:

To what extent is technological innovation the cause of social change?	(Cam)
Examine the impact of industrialisation on the structure of the family.	(Wel)

INDUSTRIALISATION

The introduction of power invention and power-using machines made from metals. The source of wealth in the society is transferred from the farm or small cottage industries to large-scale complex economic organisations. These include factories, banks, shops etc. The inventions of improved forms of transport, electricity and other technologies all help to modernise methods of production.

The functionalist view of change

1 Social change is an evolutionary process which occurs as a result of the changing specialisation in structure and function of institutions.
2 There is a constant adaptation of the impact of external factors (climate trends, military threat etc.) and internal factors (e.g. demographic changes, cultural values, religious teachings, new leadership, as well as new inventions and technologies).
3 New technologies are necessary to help produce the goods and other items required to meet the needs of the society and its members.

The Marxist view of social change

1 Change arises from the inherent conflict in the structure of society. In every society the forces of production correspond with a particular set of social relationships of production. These give rise to disruption.
2 The methods of production, the technology and the social relations generated by them, are the basic feature of the society. The economic infrastructure helps to shape the social superstructure.
3 The exploitation of one group by another is the source of social change.
4 The weaknesses of the infrastructure lead to the breakdown of institutions and social organisation and the creating of a new social structure.

Weber's view of social change

1 He accepted the Marxist theory that the emerging middle classes took every opportunity to accumulate wealth and other resources and that conflict arose between groups in competition for scarce economic resources, causing some change.
2 He looked for unique factors as sources of change. He argued that one such feature was the appearance of a particular form of religious teaching, namely Protestantism, in the sixteenth century.
3 He suggests that at certain times and places change can occur from religious beliefs since these can affect economic behaviour. Protestantism preceded western capitalism making the accumulation of wealth both a religious and a business ethic.
4 He concludes that the major change from a feudal to a capitalist system could have occurred, with all its subsequent effects, without the appearance of Calvinism.

Conclusion: It is generally agreed that there is no single theory of social change which is seen as a normal feature of every society.

Industrialisation and the family

The Functionalist view	The Marxist view
1. Families become more socially and geographically mobile in their search for work and new homes.	1. Families become the prime source of labour for the capitalist economy.
2. They become smaller in size with the introduction of new methods of family planning.	2. Family members, especially women, are exploited in a capitalist economy. They provide a source of cheap labour and they are essential for the maintenance of the home.
3. They become more independent of wider kin. The nuclear family becomes the functional pre-requisite for an industrial society.	3. As an agency of socialisation the family becomes an important means of ensuring the transmission of the ruling-class ideology.
4. They become more democratic in structure with more wives going out to work.	4. Cooper (*The Death of the Family*) says that 'an emploitive family produces an exploitive society', as the family prepares its members for their roles in society.
5. There are improved living standards.	5. Instability and conflict are inevitable.
6. They may become less stable and more prone to divorce, separation.	

Is there a logic of industrialism which explains social change?   (Ox)

▶ *Main points*:

1   Historically, industries developed from small groups of workers who brought different skills together to form larger units. The factory system was the basis of the division of labour.

2   The division of labour means that many people contribute to the production of a complex item by undertaking at least one, often simple, task. It is a term associated specifically with industrialisation. The opposite is 'craft production' in which one worker is responsible for the completion of the entire product.

3   Subsequent changes in technology have had profound effects on workers and their attitudes to work. All industrial societies have problems of organising appropriate and efficient working structures.

4   Sociologists endeavour to understand the effects and impact of these productive systems. They wish to know whether there is a logic of industrialism.

▶ *Discussion of the concept*:

1   Eldridge (*Sociology and Industrial Life*) says that those who want to argue that there is a logic of industrialism want to point to the similarities of structure and process which accompany industrialisation in different societies.

2   Inkles (*Industrial Man*) says that 'insofar as industrialisation, urbanisation and development of large-scale bureaucratic structures create a standard environment . . . to that degree they should produce relatively standard patterns of experience, attitudes and values.' He suggests that from an analysis of cross-cultural studies there are certain similarities common to all industrial societies. In all, the highest levels of job satisfaction are among white-collar and skilled manual workers. The implication is that if conditions of work become increasingly alike in societies subject to industrialisation, then

attitudes and values will become similar, so producing a 'homogenised culture'. He suggests that this process is already advanced in the USA and may follow elsewhere, so that in the future there may be a fairly uniform world culture.

3   Miller (*The Dockworker*) also contends that there are widely shared conditions associated with dockwork which seem to produce a universal dockwork subculture. The conditions include the casual notion of employment; the arduousness of the work; the danger; the lack of career structure; the necessity of living near the docks and the self-perception of being a member of a low-status working-class group. The subculture includes such values as: solidarity with fellow workers; militant unionism; liberal/radical politics but conservative views about work practices.

However, Miller does not deduce that all industrialisng societies must necessarily produce a dockwork subculture at some stage in their industrial history. This is because:

(*a*)   Dockwork is derived from the international commercial system which is always changing.

(*b*)   Every society is subject to its cultural norms and values.

(*c*)   Feldman and Moore (*Comparative Perspectives*) argue that whilst there are some common core structures in industrial societies they see the ultimate influences as political activity.

(*d*)   Kerr (*Industrialism and Industrial Man*) believes the logic of industrialism will lead to a stage in which class warfare will be forgotten and in its place will be a contest between interest groups.

THE SIGNIFICANCE OF WORK FOR THE INDIVIDUAL

Questions on this topic area are asking you to discuss:

Why do people work?

What is the influence of work on people's lives?

On what basis is work chosen: for the satisfaction it provides, for enjoyment and self-fulfilment or the opportunities it offers to enjoy life outside work?

SOURCE OF IDENTITY

What evidence is there to suggest that occupation is a major source of personal identity in industrial society?   (Cam)

Daniel ('What Interests the Worker?' *New Society*, March 1972) discusses some of the views put forward by writers who have tried to explain what people may want from their work..

1   Maslow (*Motivation and Personality*) said that everyone has basic needs. As one is satisfied then the next in the hierarchy becomes important. The ultimate need is to develop one's abilities, to be

creative and to express oneself. In adulthood, this is sought and achieved in work. Hence Maslow would be critical of any working structures that denied the individual these opportunities.

2 Hertzberg (*The Motivation to Work*) suggests that people seek five main goals in work which when satisfied can produce a strong sense of satisfaction. These include obtaining:

(*a*) A sense of personal achievement.
(*b*) Praise and compliments in work.
(*c*) A degree of trust or responsibility.
(*d*) Promotion and fresh challenges.
(*e*) High levels of intrinsic satisfaction.

INSTRUMENTAL ATTITUDES

Lockwood and Goldthorpe in their study of the car workers in Luton found that the majority had a strongly instrumental attitude towards their work. They tended to see their work as an instrument for achieving a particular end, which was to obtain as high an income as possible to increase their living standards and have plenty of leisure time. They grew up expecting that work would be tedious and unpleasant. They expected to be rewarded for doing it by obtaining high pay. Work was therefore seen as a way of making money and not as a place for developing friendships, social skills, personality development or new challenges. The attitude would normally be associated with:

(*a*) those from a class which has come to accept such values and transmits them from one generation to the next

(*b*) those with low educational qualifications who have little job choice, and who have had unhappy work experiences.

INTRINSIC SATISFACTION

This means that workers gain a sense of value and enjoyment from the work itself. It is important not for extrinsic reasons, but because it provides opportunities for self-development and personality growth.

The attitude would normally be associated with those who:

(*a*) have come from a social class which promotes such values and transmits them from one generation to the next

(*b*) have remained in the educational system and obtained high qualifications. They can exercise some choice in their work

(*c*) have specific skills which they wish to use in their work.

Drawing on relevant sociological evidence assess the view that both manual and non-manual workers are now characterised only by instrumental attitudes.

To answer this question, or its converse:

In modern society, work is performed mainly for intrinsic reward. How valid is this claim for both manual and non-manual workers?

you must consider a range of relevant studies. For example:

(a)   Lockwood and Goldthorpe (*The Affluent Worker*) suggest that the answer to the question what do workers want from their work is a complex one. Certainly different groups of workers seem to want different things. The shop-floor workers had often deliberately chosen tedious and repetitive work because it was highly paid. They placed more emphasis on the instrumental rewards the work offered. 'Their social experiences and social circumstances were such that they had an instrumental orientation to work . . .'

(b)   Wedderburn and Crompton (*Workers' Attitudes and Technology*) also found evidence that there were only a small proportion of manual workers who considered job satisfaction an important consideration. Most were concerned about pay and security.

(c)   Blauner (*Alienation and Freedom*) found that where workers gained little opportunity for meaning and purpose in their work because the product was standardised and their contribution to the manufacturing process was limited, then they gained little or no intrinsic satisfaction.

▶ Examples of studies which describe workers who gain intrinsic reward:

(a)   Mumford (*Job Satisfaction: A Study of Computer Specialists*) found high levels of intrinsic satisfaction among the workers he interviewed. He comments that there can be very few jobs in industry which evoked the level of enthusiasim he found. It seems that data processing provides a continuously challenging work state (see Table 1).

Table 1: Degree of satisfaction with work choice (%)

Have you ever regretted your decision to become programmers?

	Yes	No	No answer
Users	13	87	–
Manufacturers	4	91	5
Consultants	3	93	4

Mumford concludes that an analysis of the variety of skills required by the programmers showed they required a multitude of skills which were an important factor in job satisfaction.

(b)   Sykes (*Work Attitudes of Navvies*) describes a participant observation study of navvies on a construction site in the north of Scotland. He describes the hard and dangerous work, the long hours and limited chances of relaxation. The navvies displayed hostility towards the employers and the management. Few were members of a union. But he noted how norms of hard work and individual skills were important among them. Although they were motivated by instrumental attitudes (they wanted high wages), at the same time they drew some intrinsic satisfaction from feats of hard work, and from their ability to do the work quickly, efficiently and without much supervision.

(c)   McGuire (*Threshold to Nursing*) suggests that research shows the principal attraction of nursing is the opportunity it offers for service to others. Linked with this is the intrinsic interest of the work and the opportunity to advance the education of the entrant.

Conclusions:

1   To some extent whether or not people find intrinsic or extrinsic satisfaction in their work relates to their prior expectations. The affluent workers expected work to be tedious but well paid.

2   Generally, there seem to be higher levels of intrinsic satisfaction among white-collar workers, although this may vary between jobs. The modern office may not be unlike a factory for some workers.

3   Some low-skilled workers may gain some levels of intrinsic satisfaction but their prime motive is likely to be monetary reward.

4   Work attitudes are also related to the way the work is organised, the influence of the technology of production being significant in this respect.

What can we learn from research of the influence of work on people's lives? Illustrate your answer with reference to specific studies in the sociology of occupations.

The significance of work

Worsley (*Introducing Sociology*) says that work is crucial as a source of income. But it has other significant aspects. It 'gives the worker identity and status . . . When we ask the question "what is he?" the kind of answer we normally expect is a statement about the work a person does: "he's an engineer" or "he's a dentist". Such words are not merely labels which inform us about the kind of technical functions a person fulfils in society but they are also a major key to social placement and evaluation . . .'

Examples of research:

1   Lockwood and Goldthorpe (*The Affluent Worker*) showed that the work experience affected the assembly-line workers' attitudes towards several aspects of their lives:

(a)   Their family life: They became more home centred (privatised). Tightly knit work groups were rarely found. Workplace friends and friends outside work were separate social categories.

(b)   Their leisure activities: They spent more time in family activities and less in communal associations with workmates.

(c)   Their political values: They retained support for the Labour

Party which was seen to represent their interests. These values were reinforced in the workplace.

2   Parker (*The Future of Work and Leisure*) argues that a range of social behaviours are influenced by a person's occupation. As society becomes more industrialised work often becomes less intrinsically satisfying for larger numbers of people. They may begin to seek more from their non-work leisure time. As work becomes less of a central life interest, so work and leisure become separate worlds.

3   Carter (*Into Work*) says that work is particularly important for the school leavers. It provides them with the money and independence which enables them to identify with a 'teenage culture' in which the excitement of motorbikes, girl and boy friends, music and dancing predominates.

Theoretical perspectives

The Functionalist view of work

1. Work enables people to obtain a sense of achievement and fulfilment.
2. It enables people to become more socially mobile by means of a promotional ladder. This is a source of status.
3. It provides a sense of identity and personal worth.
4. It provides opportunity to develop personality and skills.
5. It provides an opportunity to enjoy leisure.
6. Durkheim (*The Division of Labour*) said that work helped to integrate people more closely into their community as they came to rely on each other more and more.
7. The interdependence of skills and the exchange of goods, together with the learning of moral values which guides good behaviour, all help to provide a structure for cooperation.

The Marxist view of work

1. Mills (*White Collar*) says that the work that most working-class people do enables them to forget the problems of life without being able to solve them.
2. Bowles and Gintis (*Schooling in Capitalist America*) argue that for the working-class, work enables the ruling elite to control their income, opportunities and skills.
3. It is seen as a source of alienation and class division.
4. Sennet and Cobb (*The Hidden Injuries of Social Class*) point out how dull repetitive work helps reinforce in the workers the view that they lack skills and ability. It also makes it more difficult for them to use their leisure in constructive ways.
5. The hierarchy of the division of labour helps reinforce the beliefs that workers have about the inevitability of a hierarchy in society.

ATTITUDES TO WORK

A report by the Office of Health Economics said 'perhaps the most significant factor associated with sickness absence is job satisfaction.' Studies show that more days are lost through sickness than strikes. Sociologists have been variously interested in understanding the factors that affect people's attitudes to work; how and why they are motivated in work and how to find ways of analysing the relationship between work and the individual.

What are the causes of alienation? Can it be overcome by restructuring work? Discuss with reference to empirical studies.

ALIENATION

Blauner (*Alienation and Freedom*) describes alienation as a general syndrome made up of objective and subjective conditions. It emerges from relationships between workers and the socio-technical conditions of employment. He defines it in terms of the following conditions:

(*a*)   Powerlessness of the worker to exert control over the work.
(*b*)   Meaninglessness of the work.
(*c*)   Isolation of the worker from colleagues by noise, distance etc.
(*d*)   Self-estrangement of the worker who lacks a sense of involvement.

He conducted investigations of workers in various industries to see the extent to which they could be described as being alienated.

Printers: Their technology required skill, judgement and initiative. They were free from much external supervision. They saw the finished product. They were not socially isolated but well integrated into their local community. They were involved in their work. He concludes that they were not alienated workers.

Textile workers: They were largely machine minders. They did experience powerlessness and were subject to strict supervision. Their product was standardised and required little skill in it. However, he concludes they were not alienated workers because they were involved in a small closely knit community united by ties of kinship and religion. This accounted for the low levels of self-estrangement. Subjectively, they were not dissatisfied.

Automobile workers: The assembly line gave them little or no control over their work. The work was routine and fragmented; the product was standardised and they had no identification with it. They were socially isolated and there were high levels of self-estrangement. He concludes that they did not form occupational communities. They were dissatisfied both objectively and subjectively. As a result he sees them as highly alienated workers. Blauner is led to the conclusion that mass production is an important source of alienation (although it is not inevitable). He sees automation as a way of ending this trend. It may help increase levels of consensus and work satisfaction. It would lead to a decline in class consciousness and worker militancy.

Some criticisms of the two views:

Criticisms of Marxist view

1. Marxists assume that all workers who sell their labour to the owners of the means of production must be alienated, especially those doing tedious work.
2. Marx does not provide a clear way of measuring alienation.
3. Workers who enjoy apparently tedious work may object to the view that they are 'de-humanised' by such experiences and are deluded in failing to realise it.
4. Automation is seen as a source of increased alienation, although some research suggests it adds enjoyment for some workers (especially the low skilled).

Criticism of Blauner's view

1. Mallet (a Marxist) says that automation is another way by which capitalist owners increase profits and deny control to workers.
2. Automation may heighten alienation for some workers by reducing skills.
3. Workers who enjoy tedious work may never have had the opportunity to take a responsible and demanding job.
4. Such workers would seem to be alienated from an objective perspective. Why should not this be more significant than their subjective attitudes?
5. Daniel's research suggests that not all workers enjoy automation. The highly skilled workers show levels of dissatisfaction and hostility.

Attempts to increase levels of job satisfaction

1 Re-designing and re-structuring the work:
   (a)   Increasing the workers' responsibility and control.
   (b)   Increasing the variety of work experience (job rotation schemes).
   (c)   Increasing chances of promotion, achievement etc.
2 Improving the working environment:
   (a)   Better opportunities to rest and relax.
   (b)   Provision of meals etc.
   (c)   Improved factory/office design.
3 Improving the industrial relations:
   (a)   Better worker/management relations.
   (b)   Better union/management relations.
4 Provision of new technologies:
   (a)   Micro-electric systems.
   (b)   Automation.
5 Increased worker participation:
   (a)   Indirect (a representative is sent to board meetings from the shop floor).
   (b)   Direct: worker cooperatives and full shop-floor decision-making opportunities.

Comment:

Marxist critics might argue that most of these attempts to improve job satisfaction are not far removed from the ideas of Elton Mayo in that they are concerned to find ways of making the workers more productive and disguise the levels of exploitation which operate. They would argue that tedious jobs are always tedious.

However, the ideas of worker participation might find more favour. An efficient and apparently effective cooperative system has been established in Mondragon in Northern Spain since 1956. It is based on the principles of Robert Owen (1771–1858) and the Rochdale Pioneers in 1884. The principle is that profits should be returned to the workers who have shares in the enterprise.

However, in Britain such cooperatives have been largely unsuccessful in recent years since they lack any government support in times of crisis and it has been found difficult to establish the same rights for new members as are held by the long-standing workers.

ORGANISATION OF WORK

Sociological theories of the workplace include both 'scientific management' and 'human relations' theories. Give a brief outline of both these approaches and examine the major criticisms of them.   (AEB)

1   *Taylor's Scientific Management.* He was the first advocate of the use of scientific methods for the organisation of work, at the end of the nineteenth century. He was the father of 'time and motion' studies. He devised incentive schemes to motivate workers, based on three main principles:

(*a*)   Select the best men for the job.
(*b*)   Instruct them in efficient methods of work.
(*c*)   Cash incentives.

The efficiency of manual labourers was greatly increased as a result.

Points of criticism:
1   He made no allowance for differences in industrial organisations.
2   He did not recognise the need for flexibility.
3   He aroused great hostility among workers.
4   He discarded workers who would not meet the requirements of the scheme.
5   He did not allow for fatigue in stressing output.
6   He did not allow for the social attitudes of the workers.

2   *Mayo's Human Relations School.* His work was conducted in the 1920s and 30s in the Hawthorne Plant experiments in the USA. His work took into account the social values and attitudes of the workers. His team studied the psychological aspects of small groups of workers making telephone components. He noted that the worker is not an isolated automaton whose output is solely associated with his own health, physical environment or cash incentives. He is a member of a team of workers whose emotional and subjective perceptions must be taken into account. He found that the norms that develop in a work group help to shape the approach to the work task of the members.

It had not been previously realised that to disrupt group structures in factories could lead to increased dissatisfaction. Although working conditions were improved by reorganising work groups, production declined.

Points of criticism:
1   Mayo focused entirely on the internal factors of the factory, organisation, the social relationships between workers.
2   Life outside was ignored. There is no consideration of class factors which may lead to inequalities and which shape the attitudes of workers towards their work.

3   His analysis is concerned only with social integration inside the factory and with managerially induced forms of cooperation.
4   To increase production he advocated the use of skilled personnel to help solve any problems facing workers in their relationships.
5   Where conflicts and disputes arise in the factory, Mayo treats them as pathological, rather than normal and inevitable. If management was doing its job properly all conflicts would disappear and there would be no need for unions, since there would be harmony, high levels of production and little turnover for labour.

Assess the relative importance of various factors which shape workers' attitudes towards their work.   (JMB)

A useful approach to this question would be to structure it around a discussion of a socio-technical systems analysis.

This suggests that workers' attitudes can be best analysed in terms of influences outside the place of work, and inside in terms of the methods of production. It usefully combines a structural functional view with that of social action theory.

The external factors	The internal factors
1. The market situation (its size and stability). 2. Relations with competitors. 3. The loction of the industry. 4. Type of product and demand for it. 5. Trade union organisation.	1. The technology and method of production. 2. The methods of payment. 3. The social structure of the shop floor (norms etc.). 4. Worker-management relations.

▶   *The value of the approach*:
1   By combining the two perspectives it is possible to understand the effects on the worker of objective facts (such as the demand for the product, wage rates, the methods of production) together with the impact of subjective perceptions.
2   The social action perspective takes account of the actor as a defining agent in making sense of the world.

Weber said action is social in that the subjective meanings take account of the behaviour of others.

Goldthorpe has said that wants and expectations are culturally determined variables. He says it is necessary to study these expectations and to see how they have developed from the family, school and community.

Among the factors external to the work from which people will derive meanings about themselves and what to expect in work are:
(*a*)   Class membership and home background. This may be the source of a person's horizon of expectations and sense of worth and potential.
(*b*)   Education. Also a source of self-perception deriving from levels of success, treatment, cultural values.

Among the internal factors from which meanings will be drawn is the shop-floor culture.

The work of Willis (*Working-Class Culture* ed. Clarke *et al.*) and Benyon (*Working for Fords*) indicates the following factors:

(*a*)   There is an emphasis on the mental and physical will to survive in the face of a difficult and often dangerous or tedious environment.

(*b*)   There is an emphasis on masculinity and toughness. This helps perpetuate sexist attitudes as well as the chance of falling into deviant patterns of behaviour.

(*c*)   There is a sense of shared difficulty with fellow workers. Also a clear distinction between 'us' (the workers) and 'them' (the management).

(*d*)   There is little sense of loyalty to the company since being laid off, put on short time or being made redundant is always a possibility.

(*e*)   Instrumental attitudes tend to be constantly reinforced.

IMPACT OF TECHNOLOGY

Examine the role of technology in shaping the attitudes of workers.   (Ox)

The socio-technical systems approach remains useful for this type of question.

Woodward (*Management and Technology*) classified industrial technology into three categories and indicates how these can be related to work attitudes.

Unit production involves traditional craft work. Workers spend much time on all aspects of the job. They often work in small teams. As a result tightly knit cohesive work groups tend to evolve.

Mass production involves continuous production of large numbers of identical objects, usually by assembling smaller parts. Workers perform short, repeated assembly operations. Parts are usually moved by conveyor belt. This helps prevent the workers feeling that they are involved on the total production of the object. There are high levels of noise and it is difficult for cohesive work groups to form.

Process production involves an automated system in which the plant processes goods with little human intervention. There are two views:

(*a*)   The worker gains more control over his working environment; increases status and sense of involvement.

(*b*)   There is a reduced level of interest. The worker is further 'dehumanised' since there is so little involvement in the production.

Research shows that the constraints on the workers vary according to the type of technology used:

1 Clack (*Strikes and Disaffection with Assembly-Line Work*) suggests a link between mass production methods and strike-prone industries. 'The propensity to strike may be greatest for industries which segregate together large numbers of persons who have practically heavy and unpleasant jobs and least for industries where individuals are isolated or doing relatively light, pleasant work . . .'

2 Sayles (*Behaviour of Industrial Work Groups*) identifies types of behaviour associated with different technologies.
(*a*)   Apathetic: Those who seldom make use of strike activity. There is little homogeneity among the workers (e.g. drill press operators).
(*b*)   Erratic: Those who become militant from time to time (e.g. welders).
(*c*)   Strategic: Those who often take action because they hold key positions in the industry (e.g. wire drawers).
(*d*)   Conservatives: High status, generally professional workers who seldom or never take strike action.
He concludes that 'the internal structuring of the work operations . . . affects significantly the behaviour characteristics of a group . . .'

3 Lupton (*On the Shop Floor*) reminds us that not all behaviour can be explained in terms of the technology of production. For example, the external environment of the car industry is comparatively unstable, the demand for the product varies. Workers can earn relatively high wages at some times of the year, but when there is a market change they may suddenly be laid off. He suggests that this is one reason why there is a high degree of militancy and aggressive bargaining in the industry.

4 Cooper and Cox (*Manchester University Study* 1985) compared the mental comfort of those working with visual display terminals on word processors with secretaries and copy typists who did not work with such machines. They found higher levels of job satisfaction among the secretaries and typists. The machine operators reported more anxiety and depression. They lacked a clear definition of their work roles, the equipment was often shared by others, and they were largely tied to the machine. The other workers who were not affected by the new technology felt they had better career prospects and enjoyed the contact they had with other workers in the company. There are other questions on the topic of technology which arise and for which you should prepare:

---

*Does technological change inevitably lead to the de-skilling of occupations? Illustrate your answer with specific examples.   (Ox)

What are the major consequences of automation for workers?

What are the major consequences of the introduction of computers into manual and clerical work?

---

1   The main types of new technology
    (*a*)   Micro-electronics is a name that applies to all electrical components made to very small dimensions. The silicon integrated circuit consists of a layer of silicon etched with chemicals. They are formed into tiny chips. They have a capacity to handle and store information and are produced at low cost.
    (*b*)   Automation is a type of industrial production in which the input of raw materials and the output of completed goods is controlled by robots and computers with the minimum of human intervention. (Automation is also prominent in the home with automated washing machines, central heating systems etc.) It is different from mechanisation in that this describes the techniques of mass production in a factory based on the division of labour around conveyor belts and the assembly line.
2   What is meant by 'skilled work'?
    It would include work done by those with high levels of qualifications and training (Classes 1,2,3a and 3b). These would include about 65% of the population. In answering question* (above) you must consider which occupational groups are most likely to be de-skilled by the introduction of new technology.
3   In which areas of work do the new technologies have most effect? There is much unresolved debate about this, but many commentators suggest that office work is most open to the effects of the micro chip. It is estimated that in Germany office employment could fall by 40% by 1990. In Britain there has been a decline in the numbers employed in telecommunications, the production of cash registers etc. since 1971. On the other hand there has been a growth in the numbers employed in the production of office machinery, TV games etc.
    Automation and the use of robots is likely to have most effect in large manufacturing industries (car manufacturers account for 50–60% of all robot users.)
4   Among which skilled workers will the new technologies have least effect?
    Although micro-processors may be introduced into the offices of professional workers it is less likely that they will be adversely affected by them. Lawyers, doctors, nurses, teachers etc. are examples of professions in which a personal approach is necessary to provide information, advice, comfort and the personal interpretation of information. Also less likely to be de-skilled are those craftsmen who operate in small units providing a special service.

AUTOMATION

Daniel (*Automation and the Quality of Work*) examined the attitudes of workers towards the introduction of automation in the petrochemical industry. He contrasted the optimistic view (that it helped re-humanise tedious work by integrating the operators into a management team) with a pessimistic interpretation. This suggests that automation increases alienation so that the operator becomes 'a dial watching, button pushing robot . . .' His findings indicate some support for the optimistic view. He noted that with few exceptions the men found the work more interesting and satisfying when it was automated.

But workers with qualifications who found themselves de-skilled by the effects of automation were more dissatisfied. They had less chance to realise their abilities and they were working alongside people with no skills or qualifications.

Advantages of automation	Disadvantages of automation
1. Worker is not tied to the machine or its pace of work.	1. There may be higher levels of unemployment in automated industries.
2. Worker has to take responsibility in emergencies.	2. Many workers are de-skilled since they are only required to check controls.
3. Worker may become part of the management team.	3. Less concentration is required for previously skilled workers.
4. Worker may have more time for training, education etc.	4. The quality of output is dependent on the computer which controls the machine. The workers lose responsibility.
5. There may be a shorter working week.	5. Trade unions may begin to lose members as the manual work force contracts.
6. There are fewer repetitive and tedious jobs for workers to do.	6. Costs of large manufacturing companies are reduced, smaller businesses cannot compete.
7. Preferred by the unskilled.	

MICRO-ELECTRONICS

Research findings indicate the following disadvantages:

1   The Cambridge Economic Policy Group Report predicted that there will be 3–5 million people unemployed as a result of the impact of micro-electronics by 1999.

2   Barron describes four main effects:

(a)   It will limit competition. Some companies will go out of business because they fail to match their rival's use of the new technologies.

(b)   There will be skill displacement.

(c)   There will be major job losses as micro-electronic processes produce goods cheaper and quicker.

(d)   Effects will vary between industries. The more an industrial sector uses micro-electronics the more it will be hit.

3   'The Impact of the Chip Technology': a survey by Metra International. This was described as the most extensive analysis so far of jobs and skills that will be affected by the new technologies in EEC, North America, Japan and Scandinavia. It identifies sectors of office work and other industries where it says that more than 50% of jobs will disappear in the next ten years. The report concludes that 'it is easier to point to skills for which there is a diminishing demand than to those where people should be trained.'

The areas of work most likely to be adversely affected include: semi-skilled work, machine tool operators, clerical workers and assembly line workers, especially where the work is accompanied by the application of computer aided design. This will help to de-skill the workers.

4   'New Technology and Women's Employment': this report predicts that among women workers there will be a range of 10–40% job losses because a high proportion of women are in part-time factory work and in offices. In 1985 the white-collar union ASTMS said that 'one chip can replace 800 white-collar workers'.

5   1985 Report by Warshaw (a clinical psychologist) said that research was indicating that VDU operators are increasingly vulnerable to stress-related disorders, the root of which was job dissatisfaction.

Some advantages:

1   Johnstone (*Who's Afraid of the Micro Chip*) says that the public has been badly informed and often misinformed about the potential of computers. They may create more work.
    Opposing the view of the ASTMS he says 'a chip can increase a worker's productivity by 100%'.

2   Handy (*The Future of Work*) says that the new technologies can increase people's skills. 'The secretary becomes an information manager and a ticket clerk a personal travel agent . . .'

3   Engelberger says that companies must introduce more robots if they are to become more competitive and produce more wealth for the country. At the present Britain is bottom of the robot league: In 1978 Japan had 42,000, Sweden 1000 and Britain 200.

4   Some occupations will be subject to growth as a result of micro-electronics: writers, computer programmers, insurance offices, small businesses. Also small towns will benefit as they become attractive to particular occupational groups who use the new technologies. Also, where a company makes use of staff resources, the technologies may not increase redundancies but encourage people to develop new skills in their use.

5   A 1985 Government White Paper denied that there was any relationship between increasing levels of unemployment and new technologies. A further £120 million is to be spent to encourage their development by the government until 1990.

Some unresolved points

1   Kneale 1985 says that 'the once unthinkable is becoming irrefutable. The computer boom is over . . .' In 1987 the Federation of Recruitment and Employment surveyed 300 big companies and concluded that the day of the computer specialist had passed. They now wanted workers with a range of skills.

2   Freeman and Mclean (Sussex University researchers) argue that the effects of the new technologies are still largely unpredictable. They say that no one has a decent model of technical change. There is need for much more research. We do not know the extent to which technologies de-skill, nor under what conditions they create jobs.

3   1985 Department of Trade and Industry Report says 'Office automation is not so far a great economic success'; benefits are 'somewhat unconvincing . . .'

4   1986 'Micro-electronics in Industry' Report stated that more than 80,000 jobs have been lost in the last two years because microchips have been used in products and production processes. It was also reported that the lack of skills and the poor level of training in industry prevents those who lost their jobs from finding new employment. Women were found to have lost fewer jobs than men.

5   A study published in 1988 (Create or Abdicate) suggests that the growth in jobs by 1992 will be greatest in banking, insurance, credit granting institutions, accountancy and software services.

INDUSTRIAL RELATIONS

CONTENTS

Questions on this topic tend to fall into the following areas:

1 Industrial conflict:
   (a)   The extent of strike activity.
   (b)   Statistical detail and interpretations.
   (c)   Variations in levels of strike activity.
   (d)   The significance of research and case studies.
   (e)   Theoretical perspectives in analysing strikes and disputes.
2 Trade Unions.
3 Professions.

INDUSTRIAL CONFLICT

How widespread is industrial conflict in Britain?

This is difficult to measure because it can take various forms:
(a) Strikes
(b) Overtime ban
(c) Go-slow and work to rule
(d) Absenteeism
(e) High turnover of labour
(f) Sabotage
(g) Pilfering
(h) Inefficiency

STRIKES

Hyman (*Strikes*) says that there are five elements in a strike:
1 There is a stopping of work.
2 It is temporary.
3 It is a collective act.
4 It involves employees.
5 It is calculated to achieve a particular goal.
A strike is a power struggle which reflects some level of discontent felt by the employees and for which they require some negotiating in order to achieve a conclusion. It refers to a stoppage which lasts a full working day or involves ten workers.

However, strikes are more complex than may appear on the surface. This is illustrated by the study by Lane and Roberts (*Strike at Pilkingtons*).

1   It started over a dispute about wage calculations.
2   Unusually, it spread rapidly to other departments.
3   It took the union, which originally opposed the strike, by surprise.
4   The authors suggest that the origins of the strike may have been related to changing attitudes to work.
5   Different groups of workers had different views as to what the strike was about so that a small wage miscalculation escalated into a serious seven-week stoppage.

Table 1: Industrial stoppages.

Years	Stoppages (to nearest 50)	Days lost as a result
	(in 1000s)	(in millions)
1911	850	10.1
1921	750	85.8
1931	400	6.9
1941	1250	0
1951	1700	1.6
1961	2700	3.0
1971	2200	13.5
1981	1350	4.2
1982	1550	5.2

The points to note from the statistics are:

1   The Donovan Commission (1968) said that in terms of working days lost the UK's record had been about average compared with other countries. In 1983 data compiled by the International Labour Organisation which makes international comparisons indicated similar facts (see Table 2).
2   There have been frequent occasions in the past when the number of working days lost was greater than in recent years.
3   The number of days lost does not relate directly to the number of disputes. It is more a reflection of the length of the stoppage; e.g.: In 1978 there were more stoppages than in 1979 but only a third of the number of days lost.
4   It is interesting to note that more days are lost through sickness and absenteeism than through strikes; e.g.

> 1977   Number of days lost through   strikes: 10.4 million.
>   sickness: 310 million.

Explain why the level of industrial conflict appears to vary between different industries and different societies.

Jackson (*Industrial Relations*) says that strikes are the most visible and spectacular manifestation of industrial conflict. As a result much attention has been focussed on the strike figures which are regularly published by the government. It is these details which allow researchers to make historical and international comparisons.

Table 2: Industrial stoppages: working days lost per 1000 workers in all industries 1972–81. International comparison.

Italy	1,217
Spain	949
Canada	944
Irish Republic	699
Australia	674
UK	531
USA	428
France	191
Sweden	138
Japan	99
West Germany	23
Holland	19

Points to note from the statistics are:

1 Britain's industrial performance is not much worse than many others.
2 There may be some difficulty in making direct comparisons since there are differences between countries in their definition of a strike and their thoroughness in recording.
3 Strike rates may be lower in some societies as a result of specific cultural factors. In Japan, for example, there is a norm of deference to superiors.

In Britain the government publishes official statistics which indicate:

(*a*) The number of official stoppages (those supported by the union and for which strike pay may be provided).

(*b*) Those which are unofficial (where the workers take action without the support of the union).

(*c*) The numbers of workers involved and the number of working days lost. (If five men strike for ten days then 50 working days are lost.)

UNOFFICIAL STRIKES

Records have been kept since 1961. They indicate that the proportion of strikes known to be unofficial has remained within the range of 93–98%.

Whittingham and Towers (*Strikes and the Economy*) point out:

(*a*) The typical British strike is brief (on average lasting less than three days) and unofficial.

(*b*) Britain suffers from unofficial strikes to a greater extent than any other western democracy.

Table 3: The % of all strikes which were unofficial
1962–80.

1961	96.8
1964	97.2
1966	96.9
1968	96.2
1970	95.9
1972	93.6
1974	95.7
1975	96.6
1978	96.4
1980	95.0

Points to note:

1 Some strikes are unofficial because they are opposed by the union executive.
2 Some remain unofficial until a ballot is taken of members' attitudes. This may be time consuming and a strike may be settled before it can be made official.
3 Unofficial strikes may be harmful because they are difficult to resolve.
4 Also, the public seldom distinguishes between 'official' and 'unofficial'. The unions are then blamed.

Account for the variations in strike rates.

Table 4

Industrial stoppages   **The number of workers directly involved**

	1972	1974	1976	1978	1980	1982
Mining and quarrying	342	307	39	104	87	225
Engineering and ships	680	733	415	519	367	686
Textiles	18	31	9	14	6	7
Clothing	7	6	6	8	1	4
Construction	210	22	51	40	30	10
Transport	218	135	43	97	112	481
All other	251	388	107	221	239	690

In presenting an answer to this type of question you should consider:

1 The division of labour.
2 The significance of the technology in creating less interesting work or in de-skilling work.
3 The concept of alienation.
4 Major causes of disputes.

Table 5

Major causes of disputes

	1911–47	1966–74	1980–85
Basic issues: wages, hours of work	61%	57%	'Wage disputes were the main
Frictional: discipline, working arrangements	30%	29%	reason for strikes'.
Political: trade union principles	9%	14%	

5 Kerr and Seigal (*The Interindustry Propensity to Strike*) conducted a comparative study. They noted that some industries (especially mining and docks) were more strike prone in all societies studied. There were others (especially agriculture and railways) which tended to be much lower. Their theory was that the most strike-prone industries were those in which:

(*a*)   The worker was part of a close-knit community where strike activity was a norm and there was solidarity in values.

(*b*)   The workers were cut off from frequent contact with other occupational groups.

(*c*)   The workers were employed in industries which were likely to fall into decline in importance in the economy.

The most strike-free occupations were found to be:

(*a*)   Those where the workers were all integrated into the wider society.

(*b*)   They were members of occupational groups where striking was not a norm.

Points of criticism: 1 They relied on statistics about which they had no guarantee of accuracy.

2 They tended to ignore some industries (e.g. steel).

3 Their study was conducted in the 1950s. With the development of mass media there are fewer occupational groups who are isolated from the views and values of others. With increasing unemployment there is less cohesiveness among working groups. Hill (*The Dockers*) found little evidence of community integration among the dockers he studied.

What light does research throw on industrial relations in contemporary Britain?

---

1 Department of Employment Report based on research into the distribution and concentration of industrial stoppages in manufacturing industry in Britain for the years 1971–3 showed the following:

(*a*)   The popular impression of the British worker constantly on strike is a myth. On average 97.8% of manufacturing establishments were generally free of stoppages and 81.1% of employees were in strike-free industries.

(*b*)   Over the three-year period 95% of factories were free of strikes.

(*c*)   Of the 5% of factories where strikes occurred two thirds had only one strike.

(*d*)   Of 60,000 factories surveyed, strikes occurred in 150. They concluded that in manufacturing, Britain does not suffer from a problem of widespread industrial stoppages but from a concentration in a relatively few number of factories.

2 McCarthy *et al.* (*Strikes in Post War Britain*) also argue that Britain is

not strike prone, rather there are particular industries which are. They describe how strikes fall into four categories:

(*a*)   Macro-stoppages: large, official disputes.

(*b*)   Small, localised strikes, usually short.

(*c*)   Hybrid, a combination of the two.

(*d*)   Political, resulting from opposition to new legislation.

They say that strikes develop when union members and officials believe they cannot secure their desired ends in any other way. Although stoppages cause dislocation they are an unfortunate necessity in a democratic society.

3   Daniel and Millward (*Industrial Relations in Britain*) showed that:

(*a*)   The traditional strength of the unions has been in manual work. This area is now in decline and as a result there is a loss in membership. This may result in fewer strikes in the future.

(*b*)   Many unions were making more use of non-strike action as a means of expressing discontent (e.g. overtime bans; work to rule.) They say that the incidence of strikes is no longer an adequate measure of levels of overt industrial action.

(*c*)   The existence of dispute procedures was not found to prevent strikes and multi-unions were not a cause of strikes.

(*d*)   Many managements had come to accept the closed shop as an advantage. It assisted in administrative efficiency.

Workers and employers engage in disputes for a variety of reasons, many of which are specific to their own work situation. Use case studies to illustrate this proposition. To what extent are sociological perspectives useful in analysing specific disputes?

The miners' strike 1984–5

The strike started in March 1984 because the Coal Board wished to close uneconomic pits. There ensued a debate as to the meaning of 'uneconomic' which was never resolved. The NUM decided to call out its members until the Board changed its policy. It did not do so and the NUM was ultimately forced to concede defeat in March 1985 as the union began to split and men drifted back to work.

▶   *The NUM's argument*:

In 1972 there were 289 collieries employing 281,000 men.

In 1984 there were 174 collieries employing 180,000 men.

They wished to protect the jobs of those remaining in the industry.

▶   *The Glyn Report 1984 stated*:

(*a*)   Some pits described by the Board as uneconomic were in fact profitable.

(*b*)   The social cost of closing the pits was not taken into account.

(*c*)   It would have been cheaper to subsidise pits to be closed rather than pay out unemployment benefits.

▶   The Lloyd Report (*Understanding the Miners' Strike: 1985*) suggested that the strike failed because:

(*a*)   It was started in spring when demand for coal falls.

(*b*)   Public sympathy was lost through alleged acts of violence by miners on picket lines and the death of a taxi driver taking a working miner to the pit.

(c)   There was strong media opposition to the miners' leaders who were portrayed as leaders of a revolutionary vanguard.

For the second case-study example see reference to *The Strike at Pilkingtons*.

SUMMARY

1   A strike can be viewed as a normal feature of industrial life.

2   Although unions are frequently blamed for having too much power, it must be remembered that only 5% of strikes are officially backed and organised. More often the union fails to control its membership.

3   It is difficult to identify the actual causes of a strike. The real cause may be connected to the social and economic changes in the society, affecting the workers' expectations and perceptions of events.

4   Not all strikes successfully achieve their aims.

5   In contemporary Britain it does appear from Table 4 that strikes are more frequent in occupations which have certain characteristics. They tend to be those which are dangerous, tedious, noisy, repetitive and lack most of the features associated with intrinsic satisfaction.

6   Strikers often suffer hardship as a result of their action: they may not get strike pay and they may not receive any social security benefits unless there is extreme hardship.

7   Researchers tend to agree that in terms of working days lost as a proportion of total working days, strikes are insignificant. They may, however, help develop a 'bad reputation' for British manufacturers.

8   Turner (*Is Britain Really Strike Prone?*) has pointed out that whatever inconvenience is caused by a strike the extent of economic damage is frequently exaggerated by the media reports. Losses are presented in terms of the selling price of the product. The savings are not taken into account (e.g. wages, fuel, power and material costs).

9   Research findings suggest that if there is a strike problem in Britain it is sectoral (located in certain industries) rather than national.

How can industrial conflict be explained sociologically? Compare two theories of such conflict.

The Marxist perspective

1. Strikes are symptoms of the conflict which arises when the owners of the means of production exploit the workers.
2. These conflicts are based on class interests.
3. In a capitalist economic system such conflict is inevitable since the interests of employers and employees are irreconcilable.
4. Employers are concerned to maximise their profits. The employees will strike when they become aware of the level of exploitation. No amount of social engineering in which tedious jobs are made to appear more interesting will prevent the conflict which is endemic to industrial organisations.
5. In times of economic depression management may manufacture strikes to save costs and reorganise.
6. For the Marxist strikes are completely understandable in terms of class exploitation.

The Weberian perspective

1. This perspective stresses the subjective perceptions of the actors in social situations. The focus is on how these perceptions affect their pursuit of particular goals.
2. Workers have a particular perception of their work environment which will be based on a variety of influences. These include the external and internal factors (see page 323). The decision to strike will be based on how they translate their experiences into meaning.
3. Lane and Roberts (*Strike at Pilkingtons*) note that 'workers can be drawn into a strike without being conscious of a wide range of grievances . . . it can gather momentum under normal working conditions . . .'
4. From this perspective 'a strike is a social phenomena of enormous complexity . . . which is never susceptible to complete description or explanation' (Gouldner.)

The Functionalist perspective

1. This perspective starts from the view that it must be possible to achieve a strike-free economy by locating and removing areas of possible conflict and discontent.
2. If workers and management shared the same values and goals, and ways of achieving them were introduced, then industrial disputes would disappear.
3. This would entail careful industrial reform rather than any radical change in the structure of society as a whole.
4. Strikes are themselves functional in that they are indications of levels of dissatisfaction among workers which need to be dealt with by management. Also an occasional strike may act as a useful safety valve for letting off steam when discontent reaches high levels.
5. From this perspective strikes are understandable in terms of lack of value consensus and adequate socialisation.

TRADE UNIONS

Why do workers join trade unions?   (Ox)

A trade union is an organisation of employees who combine together to improve their return from and conditions at work.

Chief aims:
(*a*)   To improve the working conditions of their members.
(*b*)   To improve wage rates.
(*c*)   To present the case of their members to management in matters of policy.
(*d*)   To provide members with legal advice.
(*e*)   To provide educational and welfare provisions for members.
(*f*)   To provide funds for the Labour Party from the political levy.

Types of industrial action:
(*a*)   Official strikes.
(*b*)   Unofficial strikes.
(*c*)   Token strikes.
(*d*)   Overtime ban.
(*e*)   Go-slow or work-to-rule.
(*f*)   Sympathetic action.
(*g*)   Blacking of goods from companies who have helped to break a strike.

Possible reasons for joining a union:

(*a*)   In some occupations people are obliged to join. This is known as a closed shop.

(*b*)   Where there is choice they may join because it is the social norm among the work force to do so.

(*c*)   Some may believe it is 'moral' to join since any benefits may be obtained by the union for all workers regardless of whether or not they are members.

(*d*)   Some may join for the protection offered.

(*e*)   Some may join because they are Labour Party supporters.

Types of union:

The type of union that people join has traditionally depended on their type of occupation:

Craft unions: members are generally skilled, having acquired a trade or craft through a period of apprenticeship; e.g. ASLEF.

Industrial unions: usually found within one particular industry; e.g. NUR.

General union: members are often semi- or unskilled. The largest is the TGWU.

Occupational and often white-collar unions: usually attract members of a single occupation or profession. However, these are increasingly becoming general categories. There are fewer unions which fit the categories precisely. This is particularly true as unions amalgamate. For example, TASS was originally an entirely white-collar union. But in recent years it has begun to merge with non white-collar unions. The result has been to increase its membership to over 300,000 but to dilute its original purpose to act for a particular category of white-collar workers.

Describe and account for the major changes in the size, number and distribution of trade-union membership since 1945.

Table 1: The size and number of trade unions

Year	Men	Women	Total
1940	5.6	1.0	6.6
1951	7.7	1.8	9.5
1961	7.9	2.0	9.9
1971	8.4	2.8	11.1
1976	8.8	3.6	12.4
1978	9.2	3.9	13.1
1979	9.4	3.9	13.3
1981	8.4	3.8	12.2
1985			

Source: *Social Trends*

Table 2: The number of trade unions

1940	1951	1961	1971	1981	1985
1004	732	664	532	430	400

Comment:

(*a*) Membership of unions grew rapidly in the 1970s. The number of unions declined as a result of mergers.

(*b*) Membership fell by about 8% between 1979 and 1981 and has fallen more severely since as a result of high levels of unemployment. There has been a further decline of 17% between 1981 and 1988.

(*c*) In 1973 eleven had a membership of more than 250,000. This accounted for more than 60% of the total of all trade-union membership.

(*d*) The largest falls in membership have been in unions operating in industrial sectors. Statistics indicate that from 1979 to 1981 textiles lost 47.3%, clothing lost 27.9% and construction lost 20.6%.

(*e*) Some unions have increased in membership. In the years 1979–81 the greatest increases were in professional and scientific 5.7%, services 3.1% and banking and insurance 0.3%.

(*f*) Nevertheless the largest unions remain:

Table 3	Membership in millions
Transport and General Workers Union	1.5
Amalgamated Union of Engineering Workers	1.0
National Union of General and Municipal Workers	0.6

(*g*) The number of trade unionists in the TUC in 1988 was 8.8 million (following the expulsion of the EETPU) of whom 2.8 million were women.

What problems does trade-union involvement in politics create in contemporary Britain?

Some points to consider:

1 It would be useful to consider the concept of 'a problem'. Who defines an issue as 'a problem'?

  (*a*) Opposition groups?

  (*b*) The mass media?

2 Can it be argued that involvement in politics creates problems for the union membership? If so in what sense?

  (*a*) It may divide the membership; e.g. the NUM is divided following the strike 1984–5. A new mineworkers' union has emerged: Colliery Trade and Allied Workers.

(*b*)   It may divide the union leadership, some of whom wish to pursue policies which accept Conservative legislation.

3   What is the nature of the political involvement of unions?

(*a*)   There is a traditional association with the Labour Party. It was formed in the 1900s as the Labour Representation Committee, being renamed the Labour Party in 1906. Its origins lie in the demands of the trade unions to have some party representation in Parliament. The unions provide over three quarters of its funds from the political levy paid by members unless they contract out.

(*b*)   As a result of the connection unions are perceived to be a powerful pressure group helping determine Labour Party policies.

(*c*)   A small proportion of Labour MPs are sponsored by unions which means they defend them in Parliament.

(*d*)   Bell (*Labour into the Eighties*) suggests that the relationship has its weaknesses for the Labour Party too. It may be discomforting to rely so heavily on a particular sectional interest, especially when the unions are not the most popular of vested interests in Britain today.

(*e*)   From the point of view of the Conservative Party the involvement of the unions in politics is seen as a potential danger. As a result legislation has been introduced to curb union activities. The miners' strike of 1973 helped to defeat the government of Mr Heath in the 1974 election.

(i) The Employment Act 1980 limits the number of persons allowed to take part in a picket at any one place of work.

(ii) Trade Union Act 1984 stated that unions must obtain a majority of those participating in a ballot in favour of strike action to secure immunity for damages resulting from losses. Union members may request a postal ballot, the costs of which will be refunded by the government. (The usual turn-out in a postal vote is about 20% and in the workplace 30–40%). It also allows members to vote by ballot every ten years on whether they wish the union to spend money supporting political parties or causes.

(iii) Further legislation is proposed which may force the election of all union leaders.

(*f*)   From the point of view of the unions there is a tendency towards the election of union leaders who are less militant in their attitudes. In 1985 Ray Buckton, the leader of the train drivers' union, was described as 'the last of the old guard left-wing on the TUC's general council . . .' Several unions are defying TUC policy by accepting government funds for postal balloting and some are showing greater cooperation with the government. (In 1985 Mr Tebbit, architect of recent labour laws, officially opened an extension of the Electrician Union's training school.)

Are trade unions democratic organisations?

---

1   The structure of unions in Britain has been described as among the most complex in the world, whereas no other European country has a trade-union movement with a structure as simple as that of Germany and the Netherlands.
    (*a*)   The national executive provides the leadership.
    (*b*)   The area committee controls the local organisation.
    (*c*)   Local branches allow members to meet to discuss problems.
2   All unions have sets of rules and regulations which determine the way in which they run their affairs. All important decisions are discussed at the annual conference.
3   Most unions have representative democracy, in that members elect, approve and appoint leaders. However, some leaders have life appointments.
4   Michels said that oligarchy is inevitable in large organisations. All such groups need to develop bureaucratic structures to attain their ends. The price of bureaucracy is the concentration of power at the top of the hierarchy.
5   If unions are not democratic then it could be argued that the fault is with the membership who fail to attend meetings and cast votes in elections. Alternatively, it could be argued that once leaders have obtained their positions of power then it is not in their interests to encourage greater democracy or changes which would jeopardise their positions.
6   It is likely that union leaders would argue that their organisations are democratic in that they favour the growth of democracy in the work-place. One of their aims is to encourage the extension of the control and power of the worker in his working environment.
7   Shop stewards are elected by workers on the shop floor to act as a link with the full-time officials in the union branch office, to act as their spokesman and to deal with relevant issues on their behalf.
8   For an organisation to be democratic either members must be able to vote directly on every issue that affects them (direct democracy); or they must elect representatives to conduct affairs in their interests (indirect).
    For elections to be democratic they must be held regularly in secret and provide a choice of candidates.

Account for the growth of white-collar unionism since 1945.

Definition Jenkins and Sherman (*White-Collar Unionism*) say they have a 'detestation for the semantic game of defining white-collar workers . . . the term is overtly male chauvinistic . . . women rarely wear white collars . . .'

Lumly (*White-Collar Unionism in Britain*) suggests that the term refers to such occupations as administrators, managers, professional workers, scientists, technologists, draughtsmen, creative occup-ations, clerical and office workers, shop assistants, salesmen and commercial travellers.

These categories include those normally described in Classes 1,2 and 3a.

Clerks, office workers	34
Shop assistants	16
Lower professionals	17
Managers and administrative	16
Higher professionals	9
Others	8

▶ *Important points*:

(*a*)   Women provide the majority of clerical and teaching staff and approximately 45% of all white-collar workers.

(*b*)   The Women's Movement and the Equality package of 1975 may have helped to encourage more women to take collective action, although women in professional occupations more frequently join staff associations, which are less militant.

Table 5: White-collar membership of trade unions (in millions).

1948	1964	1970	1980	1985
1.9	2.6	3.5	5.1	5.5

(*c*)   In 1910 there were 3.3 million white-collar workers.

In 1971 there were 10.0 million.

In 1985 approximately 50% of the work force was performing non-manual labour.

Table 6: The five largest white-collar unions (1977).

1. National Local Government Officers' Association	709,000
2. Association of Scientific, Technical and Managerial Staffs	441,000
3. National Union of Teachers	296,000
4. Civil and Public Services Association	226,000
5. Technical, Administrative and Supervisory Section (of Amalgamated Union of Engineering Workers' Union)	178,000

1   The increase in membership in the 1970s was associated with increased chances of social mobility as more workers moved into white-collar occupations from manual groups. They may have been more trade-union-minded.

2   In times of economic decline white-collar workers became more concerned to protect their economic position so that strikes among teachers and other professionals may become more frequent.

3   Also at times of economic depression those in the most secure white-collar jobs may become more trade-union-minded to ensure their protection.

4   Unionisation of white-collar jobs has occurred in many occupations

which involve the use of machines and technology which makes offices not unlike factories. It may be that such workers hold working-class attitudes towards trade-union membership, which emphasises the importance of collective action.

5   The decline in the status of white-collar workers may also have helped in the development of union membership among this occupational group.

6   White-collar unions have begun to recruit in the new 'high tech' industries which have developed with the growth of the micro-electronics technology. Some have also encouraged mergers with smaller unions which might otherwise cease to function.

Has the changing status of white-collar workers affected the growth of white-collar unions?

▶   *The argument that it has not:*
1   Social status is based on subjective opinion as to someone's prestige and standing in society.
2   Traditionally, white-collar workers have always had higher social status than manual workers in British society.
3   This has remained the case even though their incomes have fallen behind those of many sectors of manual workers.
4   The result is that they tend not to join trade unions in large numbers (even though there are a high proportion of white-collar workers in the occupational structure) because they do not share the same value system as manual workers. They wish to distinguish themselves from them.
5   If they do join unions it is for reasons other than concern about status.
6   It is more likely that they will join an organisation which accepts the existing social structure and which does not have an ideology of opposition; i.e. a professional association.

▶   *The argument that it has:*
1   Behaviour can be understood in terms of class membership. As those in white-collar jobs (especially in Classes 2 and 3a) come to suffer similar economic problems to those in the lower working classes, so they will begin to behave in similar ways.
2   The membership of a trade union provides the opportunity for collective action.
3   The more that people come to perceive and accept that conflict in society is inevitable and that unions provide the individual with a range of benefits, so even formerly high-status employees become more inclined to join an appropriate union.
4   More and more white-collar workers are employed in environments which are not unlike those of manual workers.
5   Promotion opportunities for lower level white-collar workers are diminishing and their jobs are less secure.
6   As these employees' perceptions of their social status alters so do

their attitudes towards unionism; the result is that traditionally non-striking groups, like teachers, become more militant.

Has industrial conflict been institutionalised?	(Cam)

Discuss the functions of trade unions in Britain.	(Wel)

The Marxist perspective

1. Trade unions are compelled to act in aggressive ways because the capitalist economic system gives rise to conflict.
2. Allen (*The Sociology of Industrial Relations*) says that trade unions result from a society which has as its main precepts the sale of labour, and divisions between buyers and sellers.
3. Miliband (*The State in a Capitalist Society*) says that compared to employers trade unions have little power. They are a countervailing elite seeking to balance the power of the owners of the means of production.
4. Hyman (*Strikes*) says that the view expressed in the media that unions attack the 'national interest' is a smoke-screen disguising the true interests of capitalists.
5. Trade unions should be the source of class consciousness.

The Functionalist perspective

1. In capitalist society power is dispersed among a variety of groups.
2. Trade unions help to provide those with least power some chance of expressing discontent.
3. In this way they help to institutionalise conflict by helping to ensure that it is dealt with through recognised methods.
4. Since conflicts in society are inevitable these must be controlled by legitimate means. Employers and employees are two sides of a balanced struggle.
5. Trade-union membership helps provide workers with a necessary sense of unity. They become more integrated into the capitalist society.
6. Trade unions are also an essential feature of a democratic society since they provide the opportunity to express discontent.
7. They help create social order in industry embodied in a code of rights.

The Weberian perspective

1. This perspective teds to be a more non-committed one. Actors are said to have goals which they seek to achieve by specific means. These goals will include some which trade unions claim to be able to achieve for workers.
2. Therefore, a worker's reaction to trade-union membership is a reflection of the strength of his belief that such action will help achieve desired goals.
3. There is a continuous conflict of interest in industrial relations but these are not necessarily class interests. They may be conflicts between status groups. Union membership may be perceived as a way of achieving or protecting status.
4. The growth and decline in union membership can be accounted for in terms of changing images, attitudes, motives and perceptions held by people in relation to specific goals.

PROFESSIONS AND PROFESSIONAL ASSOCIATIONS

What are the primary characteristics of a profession? In what sense is teaching a profession?

Greenwood's typology of a profession (in *Man, Work and Society*, edited by Noscow and Form) suggests that members have:

1 High social status because the occupation is difficult to enter (e.g. medicine; law).
2 Social power and prestige (there are a high proportion of lawyers in Parliament; most top professionals are among the highest paid).
3 High academic qualifications.
4 Specialised knowledge of which the lay person is ignorant and often legally prevented from obtaining.
5 Special code of ethics which control behaviour. This includes confidentiality between client and practitioner. Breach of the code can cause the professional to be disciplined or prevented from practising.

6   A special culture. Members share specific norms, values and sometimes a special form of clothing (e.g. wigs and gowns).

7   A controlling body or association which supervises their activities and helps ensure their immunity from critical comment by lay people (e.g. Law Society).

One way of judging the extent to which an occupational group has succeeded in becoming professionalised is to see how many of the characteristics it has which are described by Greenwood. Some which claim professional status lack many of the attributes of the highly professionalised occupation, such as doctors. They were organised into a professional group in 1858 and were given a monopoly on the practice of medicine. This gave them strong control over their market worth. Teachers, on the other hand, failed to achieve the same level of professionalism before state intervention in education in the nineteenth century. The teachers never gained control over their methods of training, standards of entry etc. They do, however, have some of the qualities of a profession; but lacking a controlling organisation they are more likely to join trade unions than professional associations to improve their market situation.

NB: In answering such a question notice how important it would be to go through points 1–7 and indicate which apply to teaching and which do not.

What are the major characteristics of professional associations?

Professional association are independent bodies which seek to advance the economic and status interests of their members who are drawn from specific salaried occupations in various organisations. Legally, professional associations are different from trade unions in that they are normally incorporated under the Companies Act or they have been granted a Royal Charter.

Some examples:

British Medical Association (BMA)
Royal Institute of British Architecture (RIBA)
British Association of Chemists (BAC)
Institution of Professional Civil Servants (IPCS)
Chartered Institute of Public Finance and Accountancy (CIPFA)

Members of well-established professions are obliged to join their professional association (e.g. doctors are subject to the BMA and lawyers to the Law Society). The association or controlling body may have the right to:

(*a*)   Discipline members or prevent them from practising.

(*b*)   Determine the educational standards necessary to enter the profession and set up the educational establishments to train new members.

(*c*)   Prevent the lay person from gaining access to specific knowledge which is the province of the professional.

(d)   Promote the image of the profession as being committed to public service.

(e)   To negotiate with the government on behalf of members. (In some cases the professional association may sponsor new trade unions to carry out their protective function).

Professional associations tend to remain isolated from each other and from trade unions (even though they may have overlapping membership). They see themselves as independent and non-political bodies existing to protect their professional standing while giving public assurance that high standards and competence are being maintained.

Consider the view that 'professionals are the servants of power'.

Consider the view that professionals serve society as a whole.

In answering such questions it is useful to adopt theoretical perspectives:

The Functionalist view

1. Integration: Durkheim discussed the possibility of establishing a moral order in society in which concern for others was crucial for maintaining stability. Membership of a profession helps to integrate people into occupational groups. The association controls training and education and establishes proof of competence and a code of ethics.

2. Service to the community: Professionals serve society as a whole, not sectional interests. They are trained to provide care, advice and assistance to those who require specialist advice on complex issues. This helps promote an orderly and caring society.

3. Rewards: Professionals are rewarded according to their functional importance for society as a whole. Those with access to more valuable knowledge are more highly rewarded. Work performed by professionals involves 'central values' (health, justice etc.). It is functional for work related to these areas to command high standards.

4. Expertise: Professionals serve important functions for society in that they have access to important knowledge which is too complex for most lay people to master.

5. Professional authority: It is always necessary to have a hierarchy of power in any society. The professional is the most able and best qualified in the occupational structure. However, it is also necessary to have methods of controlling and disciplining those who fail in their social duties. If errors are made blame can be located.

6. Professional associations: Their function is to ensure that the professionals are of the right educational standard; that they behave according to the rules of their profession. In this way clients are protected and confidence maintained.

Points of criticism

1. The integration of professionals is into a value system which promotes power and elitism. They are not really concerned about public service, since professionalism is a strategy employed by particular occupational groups to improve their market situation.

2. Professionals serve only the ruling elite, e.g. accountants and lawyers are in the service of the rich and powerful. Mills (White-Collar) says 'they are employed teaching the financiers how to do what they want within the law . . . and how best to cover themselves . . .'

3. Once groups have the power to define their services as more valuable than others then they can further their own interest. The image of public service is an ideology used by them to justify their high status and rewards. These are also high because they fulfil the needs of the rich who make up most of their numbers.

4. Their expertise is mythical. Lawyers deliberately make the law inaccessible. Illich (Medical Nemesis) says that most serious illnesses were in decline before the development of the medical profession. It is the ills of capitalist society that bring bodily illnesses. By treating them as medical problems their real causes are obscured.

5. The concept of professional authority is part of ruling-class ideology to damp down opposition to exploitations by justifying differentials in reward and status between different types of occupation. Professionals are the servants of power in that they serve the interests of power elites. Their authority is misused.

6. The power that the controlling body has to determine entry ensures that the profession can eliminate competition and ensure that the demand for their services remains high. Illich has referred to the monopoly which professions have in specific areas of social life as 'occupational imperialism'. In controlling conduct the association promotes the view that professional conduct is above reproach and that professionals are committed to public service. In fact the occupation is controlled in the interests of its members.

INDEX